Advance Praise

"This exquisitely crafted text, written by master clinicians, initiates readers into a narrative approach that insists upon mystery and wonder as indispensable tools in the therapeutic process. Through a series of beautifully narrated vignettes from clinical practice, it showcases imagination as an 'ideal traveling companion for young people.' It is not only pitch-perfect in balancing theory, compelling exemplar, and succinct advice for therapists and parents, but is also compulsively readable, a compliment generally reserved for popular novels rather than professional texts."
—**Cheryl Mattingly**, author of *The Paradox of Hope: Journeys through a Clinical Borderland*

"This book is a treasure trove for therapists. As you turn its pages you will find bright baubles, sparkling jewels, and finely crafted gold leaf. What else would you expect in Wonderland? You will also encounter problem monsters, and children with strange powers. You must learn to counter the pathological, the dull, and the unfair, but don't worry! This book of dramatic surprises will help you immensely. Put it down at your own risk."
—**John Winslade**, PhD, professor of counseling at California State University, San Bernardino

"From the get-go, engaging prose makes this book fun—yes, fun!—to read. Vivid transcripts reveal the powers children have when their imagination, ingenuity, and sense of humor are engaged. Creativity is central to narrative therapy, as is moving past one-size-fits-all solutions. It is refreshing to learn how the creative capacities of each child and family can be channeled towards elegant and often unique resolutions of the challenges they face, and to see the 'wonderfulness' of the individual child so centrally featured. This book affirms the effectiveness of collaboration between adults and children in the realm of imaginary know-how."
—**Jennifer Freeman**, MFT, REAT, coauthor of *Playful Approaches to Serious Problems*

"More than a must-read for clinical professionals, and more than a supportive guide to parenting, *Narrative Therapy in Wonderland* is a book for anyone who faces Problems and seeks strategies for overcoming them. The authors' simple yet far-reaching message is that our Problems are not in ourselves. Our Problems are out there, external and tenacious. But Problems can be outwitted, and this book shows how. *Wonderland* elevates narrative therapy from a professional clinical practice to a way of life."

—**Arthur W. Frank, PhD,** author of *The Wounded Storyteller* and *Letting Stories Breathe*

Narrative Therapy in Wonderland

NARRATIVE THERAPY IN WONDERLAND

Connecting With Children's Imaginative Know-How

DAVID MARSTEN
DAVID EPSTON
LAURIE MARKHAM

Norton Professional Books

An Imprint of W. W. Norton & Company
Independent Publishers Since 1923

Note to Readers: Standards of clinical practice and protocol change over time, and no technique or recommendation is guaranteed to be safe or effective in all circumstances. This volume is intended as a general information resource for professionals practicing in the field of psychotherapy and mental health; it is not a substitute for appropriate training, peer review, and/or clinical supervision. Neither the publisher nor the author(s) can guarantee the complete accuracy, efficacy, or appropriateness of any particular recommendation in every respect.

Copyright © 2016 by David Marsten,
David Epston, and Laurie Markham

All rights reserved
Printed in the United States of America
First published as a Norton paperback 2024

For information about permission to reproduce selections
from this book, write to Permissions, W. W. Norton & Company, Inc.,
500 Fifth Avenue, New York, NY 10110

For information about special discounts for bulk purchases,
please contact W. W. Norton Special Sales at
specialsales@wwnorton.com or 800-233-4830

Manufacturing by Sterling Pierce
Production manager: Christine Critelli

ISBN: 978-1-324-08210-1 pbk.

W. W. Norton & Company, Inc.,
500 Fifth Avenue, New York, N.Y. 10110
www.wwnorton.com
W. W. Norton & Company Ltd.,
15 Carlisle Street, London W1D 3BS

1 2 3 4 5 6 7 8 9 0

"And these *petits textes* with the sloping brow, the crooked legs, and the veering eye, that one commonly despises, will enter in the dance where they will execute movements neither more nor less honorable than the others."
—Michel Foucault
Polemic: Monstrosities in Criticism

"We can't know. Sometimes we just have to accept there are things we can't know. Why is your sister ill? Why did my father die?" She held my hand. "Sometimes we think we should be able to know everything. But we can't. We have to allow ourselves to see what there is to see, and we have to imagine."
—David Almond
Skellig

CONTENTS

ACKNOWLEDGMENTS		ix
INTRODUCTION	Kindling Our Imaginations: Down the Rabbit Hole We Go!	xiii
CHAPTER 1	Elements of Narrative: The Plot Thickens	1
CHAPTER 2	In Pursuit of Children's Virtues: The Wonderfulness Interview	27
CHAPTER 3	Meeting Problems in Wonderland	49
CHAPTER 4	Where's the Fun in It?	73
CHAPTER 5	The Therapist's Imagination Lends Inspiration	95
CHAPTER 6	The Relational Composition of Identity: Letters, Testimony, and Ritual	129
CHAPTER 7	Weird Science: Imagination Lost	157
CHAPTER 8	It's All Mom's Fault! A Figment of the Imagination	175
CHAPTER 9	Grow Me Up—Grow Me Down: Travails With Sneaky Poo and Sneaky Wee	199

CHAPTER 10	"Somebody Needs to Pay!" A Young Man's Coming of Age in a Culture of Male Domination and Entitlement	219
CHAPTER 11	Making Progress Toward Progress	245
EPILOGUE	Imagination Revived	263
NOTES		267
REFERENCES		271
INDEX		285

ACKNOWLEDGMENTS

We want to thank all of the people who lent support to the writing of this book. To begin with, we wish to acknowledge Deborah Malmud for believing in the project and helping to shape our book proposal. We are similarly grateful to Benjamin Yarling for overseeing our work from beginning to end and for his kindness and guidance along the way. We want to thank Christine Dahlin for her prudent feedback as the book's conceptual editor. Equal thanks are due to our copyeditor, Karen Fisher, for her assistance with fine-tuning our writing. We also appreciate Sheryl Rowe's direction through the last stages of editing, typesetting, and proofing.

We are indebted to Joshua Egan-Reid for the generous donation of his artwork, *"Cousin," Acrylic on board,* for the book's jacket. The book can be enjoyed for its cover alone. Many thanks to Lisa Johnson for her invaluable contributions to David Marsten's story in chapter 5. We also want to recognize Ali Borden, Peggy Sax, and Larry Zucker who read early versions of chapters and offered wise and considered opinions.

We are grateful to Stephen Madigan, Peggy Sax, and Kathie Adams for providing venues where our ideas were met with interest and enthusiasm. Thanks to all those who participated in our workshops at *Therapeutic Conversations 13* and *14, Re-authoring Teaching, Inc.,* and the *LA PoMo* gatherings. And thank you to Lorraine Hedtke and John Winslade, who gave us opportunities to teach in their school counseling program at California State University, San Bernardino as we were developing our lines of thought.

We want to acknowledge our families for their patience and support these last few years. In addition to the love they have always shown, their extra care during the writing of this book was enormously sustaining. Last, but certainly not least, we will be forever obliged to the families who permitted us to share their stories. Their generosity of spirit made this book possible.

Special acknowledgment is due Jennifer Freeman and Dean Lobovits, coauthors, along with David Epston, of *Playful Approaches to Serious Problems: Narrative Therapy with Children and their Families* (1997), W.W. Norton, publisher. This wonderful book has been a source of inspiration and learning for a generation of narrative practitioners and continues to be as important today as it was the day it was first published. We owe them a debt of gratitude.

I (DM) would like to express my appreciation for the team at Miracle Mile Community Practice (MMCP). While I was busy with the book, they kept an eye on "the shop," upheld the rigor of the training program, and brought MMCP into the 21st century by seeing to its online presence. Their dedication at a time when I was pulled in many directions is deeply valued. I also want to acknowledge John DePaola at Pepperdine University (Irvine, California) for his friendship and prayers during trying times, first when my sister, Susan, died after a long bout with cancer, and later, after the loss of my mother, Esther, to Alzheimer's disease. And many thanks to my dear friend and colleague, Duncan Wigg, who I have worked alongside every Wednesday these past 10 years in the narrative training program he built at Pepperdine University's Irvine campus. Through the "thick and thin" of the book project, Duncan was a constant source of comfort. Finally, my deep gratitude to David Epston for suggesting we write a book and for his unstinting encouragement.

I (DE) want to thank David Marsten who agreed to join me in 2009 to "try out" a new venture in working with young people and

ACKNOWLEDGMENTS

their families. I turned to David, a respected colleague whom I had known roughly since the time he established one of the earliest narrative therapy training programs in Los Angeles in 1992; and a colleague, Lisa Johnson (Narrative Practices, Adelaide), and we set out together. This led to a number of coauthored papers and a book chapter. By and by, it was clear to us that we had by no means run out of steam which led us to think about a book project to "corral" what was happening in our respective practices. Lisa was called to other duties and had to exit. Happily, Laurie Markham, who was working as a field-based family therapist, agreed to join us. Having already published and taught narrative courses at the graduate level, she hit the ground running. Believe it or not, this writing project was a very unusual honeymoon for Laurie and David. Coauthoring a book is the best test I can think of for an enduring love.

I wish to express my own personal and abiding affection for Jenny Freeman and Dean Lobovits, whose friendship, my wife Ann and I, have cherished and renewed several times a year, dating back long before we set about writing *Playful Approaches*. Jenny and Dean were like-minded and like-spirited, and we began to collaborate as early as 1988, at first to turn this like-mindedness and like-spiritedness into workshop trainings, agency supervision, and the design of postgraduate training in the Family Therapy Program at John F. Kennedy University. Through the years, we have turned to each other again and again to refresh our creative spirits, and in many ways, I consider this book a part of their legacy.

I (LM) want to express my sincere thanks to David Epston for inviting me on board. It has been an extremely rewarding collaboration. For their mentorship in field-based work, I wish to thank the intensive services team at the Occupational Therapy Training Program, a public mental health agency in Los Angeles County. And thank you to Marc Lynn, a friend and former colleague at UCLA Behavioral Health Associates. Our daily conversations about the particularities of narrative work with families in a medical setting were incredibly nourishing. And much is due to my current colleagues at the University of Southern California, including Kristan Venegas and

Mary Andres, for allowing me the time needed to help bring the book to its final form.

Chapter 5 includes an edited version of Marsten, D., Epston, D., & Johnson, L. (2012). The corner: One good story deserves another. *Journal of Systemic Therapies, 30*(2), 71–88.

Chapter 6 includes an edited version of Epston, D. (2012). Mother appreciation parties. *Journal of Systemic Therapies, 31*(3), 78–86.

The Epilogue includes an excerpt from Marsten, D., Epston, D., & Johnson, L. (2011). Consulting your consultants, revisited. *The International Journal of Narrative Therapy and Community Work, 3*, 57–71.

INTRODUCTION

Kindling Our Imaginations
Down the Rabbit Hole We Go!

A boy about 4 years old and his father walked into a gelato and coffee bar, where the authors typed at their computers in fits and starts. Sitting at a corner table, their cursors blinking expectantly, the authors envied the boy with his heaping scoop of Rocky Road (with marshmallows) and apparent disregard for such adult concerns as calorie count. Upon finishing the last bite, he stood and wandered over to a small water sculpture nearby. His father guessed what he had in mind, reached into his pocket, and pulled out an assortment of coins. He fished out a penny and handed it over. Making his way back to the fountain, coin in hand, the boy whispered something inaudible and reluctantly dropped it in. Back at the table, when asked what he wished for, the boy declared, "To be a Ninja Turtle." His father smiled and gave him a second penny, and the ritual was repeated.

"What did you wish for this time?" his father asked.

"A princess," the boy replied. Laurie turned to her comrades and quipped in a low voice, "He's already been co-opted by patriarchy!"

"Or maybe he wished to *be* a princess?" David M. posited weakly. With his next penny, the boy returned and made a third and final wish for "an animal."

"What kind?" his father prompted.

"A hippopotamus," the boy announced. He then made one last trip to the fountain before they departed, kissing the ceramic stones on its outer edges, perhaps for good luck, or as an expression of appreciation for its charmed properties. Father and son appeared equally satisfied, each having fulfilled a vital role in the theater that unfolded.

It is no surprise that the things the boy wished for are undoubtedly different from those any adult would have dared dream up. For those of a more mature disposition, wishes are often of a calculable variety, such as a debt-free existence, a bigger house, a winning lottery ticket, weight loss, or perhaps love—all things potentially of this world, though some may pose longer odds than others. But for a child[1] with wonder in his eyes, it is the impossible that is made plausible. The novelist Carlos Fuentes writes of young people's potential to transcend everyday experience through flights of imagination:

> Though subject to school and especially the family, at that time of life we have more freedom with regard to what binds us than at any other period. It seems to me this is because in childhood, freedom is identical to imagination, and since here everything is possible, the freedom to be something more than the family and something more than school flies higher and allows us to live more separately than at the age when we must conform in order to survive, adjust to the rhythms of professional life, submit to rules inherited and accepted by a kind of general conformity. We were, as children, singular magicians. (2011, p. 58)

As therapists, we may marvel at children's imaginative triumphs, but given our advanced age, it is unlikely we would recognize their fantasies as vital to the therapy hour or find ourselves inclined to invest wholeheartedly in their designs. If imagination were given room, it would likely be for reasons other than its direct mobilization. The therapist might have more familiar notions in mind such as building rapport, establishing safety, indulging a young person, or observing and interpreting projective play. And what need for imagination when protocols are already in place? (I can name that problem in three notes! Bipolar disorder. Next patient! Reactive attachment disorder. Next! ADHD. Next! OCD. Next!) Matters can be quickly settled and what remains is to undertake prescriptive measures with the promise of serving up happy, secure, and focused children.

But in making the world thoroughly readable, have we sacrificed its mysteries in the name of what is supposedly proven? Have we succeeded in locking away our own imaginations as professionals? Have we reserved a space for make-believe only on those occasions when nothing is at stake? Or is it precisely those moments when something truly matters that imagination is most urgently needed?

Over the course of this book, we attempt to illustrate the potential in turning to imagination again and again, even under dire circumstances. Problems, including those that are most impressive, can be tricked by Ninja Turtles, outwitted by (feminist) princesses, and even swallowed whole by hungry hippos. Any encounter with a real problem would not likely draw such inspiration from the mind of an adult, but for a young person, it can be a no-brainer.

Why Wonderland?

Rabbits and the holes they burrow in otherwise tidy yards are commonly thought to be a nuisance. Each spring, homeowners can be spotted making pilgrimages to their local hardware stores and nurseries, hoping to divine the secrets of pest management (e.g., repellents, poisons, traps). No level-headed person would ever dream of traveling down a rabbit hole in hot pursuit of a furry offender as Alice does in Lewis Carroll's *Alice's Adventures in Wonderland*. When problems such as pests and pestilence invade our otherwise orderly worlds, it can be a most serious matter, seemingly leaving no place for imagination or fancy. But Alice's encounter with a downy trespasser is far from typical. For one thing, the white rabbit wears a waistcoat and checks the pocket watch he holds in his tiny paw. And then there is the matter of his capacity for speech—"Oh dear! Oh dear! I shall be too late!" he frets (Carroll, 2000, p. 2). Alice does not disappoint when she sees him dart below ground. Like any child worth her imaginative weight, she dives precipitously into the unknown.

In our meetings with young people, entering counterworlds is not so much a physical departure. It is a migration from the expected to the unexpected, from what might be considered the normal state of affairs to one decidedly at variance with it. The space is reconfigured as one in which we depend on young people to take us to new domains without ever leaving the room. We avail ourselves of the kind of fresh engagement that brings us to a breach or what the anthropologist Victor Turner (1969) calls the "limen" or threshold. It is a point of entry that promises something novel by way of the "subjunctive" and what might be possible, rather than the "indicative" and what is plainly before us. This is where we are likely to encounter an impulse that "transgresses or dissolves the norms that govern structured and institutionalized relationships and is accompanied by experiences of unprecedented potency" (Turner, 1969, p. 128). Young people can move along the margins of conventional daily life looking for passage, and like the characters in their favorite storybooks or movies, discover that so much more is possible once they find it. Deborah O'Keefe explains how fantasy literature can help show the way:

> Fictional characters who find marvelous places are like participants in a religious ritual going through "threshold" activities. The most memorable scenes in fantasy stories are often the moments of transition: like C. S. Lewis's children crawling into the old wardrobe and coming out in Narnia, Alice falling down the rabbit hole, or Dorothy flying through the cyclone in her house. (2003, p. 79)

It is this sort of transition that interests us. It offers a perspective from which more is conceivable and young people are anything but helpless. We are far more inclined to attempt to join them rather than clip their imaginative wings and draw them down to a grounded understanding. O'Keefe suggests it may do us all some good as we attempt to pass through to parts unknown: "People do not outgrow this need to illuminate ordinary life by visiting extraordinary universes" (2003, p. 21). We may need to offer young people support and encouragement as they negotiate the space from the real to the imaginary, but they return the favor along the way as we become reacquainted with worlds of possibility we may have left behind and almost forgotten.

Imaginative Know-How

This is a book about imagination—the imagination we can arouse in young people and their families, and the imagination they can awaken in us as practitioners. We define imagination as "the ability to deal resourcefully with unexpected or unusual problems" (Imagination, 1992, p. 645). Alice is not far into her enterprise, having gamely followed the white rabbit into the abyss, when she realizes that logic will hardly do. She tries, at first, to deal in adult conventions, considering whether she might find her bearings by estimating her latitude and longitude, even as she plummets, or the possible distance she has traveled during her long descent—maybe "four thousand miles down" (Carroll, 2000, p. 4). But these sorts of calculations add up to very little. Thereafter, she realizes that measuring her new surroundings will require something beyond the rational approach so readily relied on "up above." Take, for example, the problem Alice confronts in trying to get around. After eating a cake with magical properties and growing 9 feet tall, she realizes that her feet, now far down below her, may willfully rebel. She is so disturbed by the absurd (though entirely plausible) prospect of suddenly being carried off that she decides to send her feet a Christmas card. She hopes this solicitous gesture will win them over and keep them "in line"—at least through the holiday season.

It is this sort of imaginative know-how we wish to reserve a space for in therapy with young people. Too often, adults, under the tutelage of professionals, adopt sincere proposals that are nonetheless timeworn and, in the end, leave little to the imagination. Sometimes it seems fewer and fewer ideas (e.g., structure, limit setting, positive reinforcement, modeling, boundaries, consistency) are recommended to wider and wider audiences with little regard for the diversity of family and community life. The effects of such one-size-fits-all solutions can be dulling for families and practitioners alike.

Drawing inspiration from Alice, we rely on young people, who, with our assistance and the backing of loved ones, might show us something unforeseen. We attempt to cultivate a sense of possibility and address problems creatively by the following methods:

- Connecting with young people's wonderfulnesses[2] and imaginative know-how
- Replacing psychiatric nomenclature with local and whimsical descriptions
- Enlisting young people's imaginations in service of their values and preferred visions for their lives
- Determining how best to meet and address problems in accordance with young people's skills and knowledges[3]
- Counting on practitioners to recognize imaginative know-how as the very kind of knowledge most suitable to the occasion
- Calling on community to witness young people's imaginative feats

Narrative Therapy's Underpinnings

All of the practices described in these pages are shaped by particular commitments. Keeping with the tradition of narrative therapy, we draw from a broad range of scholarship, including feminist theory, sociology, anthropology, post-structuralism, and narrative theory in fashioning a unique approach to direct practice. At first glance, you might be wondering, what do these disciplines have to do with young people, their imaginations, and the problems that enter their lives? How much do I actually need to understand about them in order to start doing narrative therapy with young clients? Can I just skip over theory and get right to practice (Chapter 2)? The answer is both yes and no. One could certainly adopt elements of narrative therapy as techniques to add to a proverbial bag of tricks (e.g., "I love externalizing problems!") without ever delving into the philosophical and political bases for such a departure from the more familiar linguistic practice of internalizing and privatizing problems (Epston, 1998; Tomm, 1989; White, 1988–1989). While it is not necessary to run to your nearest college admissions office to apply for an additional degree in French post-structuralist theory, it might do some good to consider narrative's underpinnings, given that we locate this practice within a set of principles. We will, however, make every effort to keep things lively by coupling exposition with vignettes of practice. In the end, we hope we will have struck the right balance, providing a view of narrative therapy that will support your own imagination rather than leave you only with ours, which may impress (you will decide for yourself) but certainly has its limits.

Let us now offer a few words of introduction to each of these disciplines and suggest how they influence our approach to therapy with young people and their families:

- Feminist theory reminds us to strive for equal footing. Domination of one group (e.g., adults, professionals) over another (e.g., children, families) suppresses imagination and gives prominence to one set of biases and practices, even granting them the appearance of truth. With this in mind, we attempt to flatten hierarchies of professional status and generation.
- Sociology has shown us the seams and tears in the fabric of the social order and how invention most frequently makes its way in from small openings at the edges of convention. We look to the margins in our direct practice, where imagination is likely waiting and young people are found to be instrumental.
- Anthropology reminds us of the diversity in the world and the importance of learning about cultures. It encourages us to "exoticize" our own Western cultural practices (Bourdieu, 1988), rather than claim the center position as if we are the sun lighting the way. It brings humility within reach and guards against a deadening view of other populations as

"inferior civilizations." We may be mightier than young people, and we may know things they do not yet know, but if we follow their bread crumbs, we just might arrive at wondrous and rewarding destinations.
- Post-structuralism tells us there is always more than one reading of the self. It offers a reprieve from science's mandate to get to the bottom of things or the core of our natures. When we encounter young people who have been monogrammed, not unlike sport coats or bath towels (e.g., OCD, ODD, CD, ADHD, PTSD, DMDD, BP), we are less inclined to consolidate around a seemingly stable medical view and instead ready ourselves to look for contradiction and variety. It is only when we replace our certainty with curiosity and our scientific mind "with the sense of wonder that might be evoked by the Shaman" (Bracken & Thomas, 2005, p. 193) that our imaginations are unlocked and multiple expressions of identity become available for engagement.
- Narrative theory tells us that we are storied selves. We come into focus in the stories we tell about ourselves and in those that others tell about us. When pursuing an understanding of young people's plights, we resist detached and studied rationales because "there is a heartlessness to logic" (Bruner, 1986, p. 13). Young protagonists' struggles and triumphs can fit dynamically into story lines and drive plots forward. In this way, we breathe life into new tellings of the self "as an art form" (Bruner, 1986, p. 13). Once a narrative achieves momentum, it can circulate and enjoy a certain vitality and verisimilitude. We have much more to say about narrative form in Chapter 1.

Our Aim

We endeavor to demonstrate over the course of this text the potential for children to assume intentional stances and bring about dramatic changes by the most imaginative means. The resulting experience can be invigorating rather than burdensome as they engage as partners in family life rather than as passengers, or worse, as empty vessels waiting to be filled up. We take our cue from Alice, who is anything but docile as she makes her way through a perilous world. Similarly, we depend on young people's capacities to arrive at well-considered positions as they come face-to-face with stubborn and startling problems. Assisted by our questions, they establish sound platforms from which decisive action is made possible. By this means, they become compelling figures in unfolding dramas.

Narrative Therapy in Wonderland

CHAPTER ONE

Elements of Narrative
The Plot Thickens

What makes for a good story is worthy of consideration. A narrative is made memorable because something happened and is ripe for the telling. It is especially after something unexpected has occurred, or a normative value has been transgressed, that we turn to narrative to make sense of events. A narrative "begins with an explicit or implicit indication of a stable canonical state of the world, then goes on to an account of how it was disrupted, elaborates on the nature and consequences of the disruption and climaxes with an account of efforts to restore the original canonical state, or to redress its violation" (Bruner, 1996, p. 166). Stories are most enthralling when there is an arc—something has gone wrong. The outcome is in question and how it all turns out will carry real consequences.

Stories, whether we realize it or not, shape how we think about and live our lives. We are always engaged in readings of the world that tell us who we are, and if we are lucky, provide a sense of affirmation (Frank, 2010; Mattingly, 2010). Consider the mere mention of an A student, a Girl Scout, or a spelling bee contestant. Each of these characterizations is instantly recognizable and, at least in the broadest sense, conveys a favorable image. Though they offer no more than glimpses, they signal promising stories yet to be told. By the same token, narratives can set us adrift, casting us out of the mainstream, revoking our membership, and denying us a sense of place. Imagine the impact of being known as a slow reader, a benchwarmer, or someone who is picked on. Each of these figurations heralds a fuller telling of a potentially problematic identity. In our work, it is the ways in which young people are portrayed within the context of story lines that can inhibit or subsidize a sense of possibility and hope (Denborough, 2014). Allow us to take you down this theoretical road as we consider the power of narrative.

As we begin, keep in mind that this chapter is not meant to offer a complete record of narrative theory. There are tall, teetering stacks of books and many professional journals devoted to such an endeavor. It is a field unto itself, relied on by historians, filmmakers, novelists, playwrights, anthropologists, sociologists, feminist scholars, and philosophers, in addition to those of us who are engaged in therapeutic practice. While we aim to explore key elements of the theory, this book is meant for therapists and their practical (though still creative) purposes.

Language and Culture

We are undoubtedly affected by experience, but it is not until we turn to language that we are able to make meaning of what has transpired. The days have passed since we thought of language as strictly representational. Rather, language is understood to go a long way toward coloring our experience. We are not simply using words as tools, enlisting them to convey something that was already there and merely awaiting description. Instead, words are intentional and can determine what is possible to know. Michael White reminds us, "We have to be very sensitive to the issue of language. Words are so important. In so many ways, words are the world" (1995, p. 30). We are enlisted by language and the metaphors currently in circulation, and as a result, events are made meaningful and memorable as we speak (Bruner, 2004; Winslade & Monk, 2000).

As we engage in conversation, it is important to remember that all words are not equal. Some have been imbued with greater force. They have become more than words. They have been put on reserve for official use, funded, placed in texts, and widely distributed. They have been professionalized and authorized by science. They have been joined into vast collections, made canonical, elevated, and arranged to inspire awe. When they come into dialogue they are not to be trifled with. A simple phrase can establish the speaker's credibility (e.g., "Children need structure"; "It is only natural that children test limits").

Language is loaded up with cultural bias and history. Though certain terms currently enjoy the kind of favor that would seem to deliver immutable truth, their suspect lineage is not beyond detection. Mikita Hoy draws on the work of Mikhail Bakhtin to make the point: "Within every single word, within every single utterance, Bakhtin identifies a large and ancient collection of ideas, motives, and intentions utilized by centuries of speakers and writers. All language ... is prestratified into social dialects, characteristic group behavior, [and] professional jargons" (Hoy, 1992, p. 767). The everyday terms with which we convey meaning and the metaphors close at hand can limit what is possible to say and thus to know (Madigan, 2011). As we collect our thoughts and prepare to speak, language operates with gravitational force, pulling us in toward predominant ideas that we mistake as inviolate. Bakhtin points to how a "unitary language gives expression to forces working toward concrete verbal and ideological unification and centralization" (1981, p. 271). When we refer to the "terrible twos," "childlike innocence," seeing the world "through the eyes of a child," and "childish things," we may be more engaged by these frequented phrases than we are utilizing them of our own volition. It is as if these sayings were placed on the tips of our tongues by the storytellers who came before us, poised to roll off the moment we open our mouths. These truisms contribute to story lines and popularized images of young people as if they were incontrovertible (e.g., "The middle child feels neglected"; "It is a teenager's job to rebel").

The language we employ to make young people fathomable,

depending on its prominence on the cultural-linguistic landscape, is made more or less evocative. Arthur Frank explains that "people's stories, however personal they are, depend on shared narrative resources" (2010, p. 14). We are all familiar with the phrase "the purity of a child" and the resulting view of children in possession of a kind of original wisdom (e.g., "from the mouths of babes"). This image is instantly suggestive and would seem to place them outside of language and the grand narratives warehoused by our culture, untouched by society and its corrupting elements. But as the inexorable encroaches, and they are ineluctably drawn into the social world, who they were before the hourglass ran out—its last grains of innocence having fallen—is forever lost—or so the story goes. Paul Cloke and Owain Jones point to industrialization as the abrasive social–economic moment that gave rise to this wistful view of children:

> Rurality, and in particular wild countryside, was thus elevated in opposition to the growing spaces of the industrial cities. . . . At the same time, the child became a key figure in romantic thinking because the child was associated with this newly desired nature. . . . Both were seen as pure and innocent, even edenic states . . . untainted by the development of adulthood and the development of "society," respectively. (2005, p. 323)

Once acquainted with the world of steel and soot, children must begin their apprenticeship in a society that eagerly awaits them and by which they will be forever altered. Ironically, we still depend on language, metaphor, and a familiar cultural narrative to conceive of such an instinctive image. But this does not make it any less convincing. Parents can feel confronted by an impossible challenge—to protect their children from a culture that would rob them of their natural gifts in order to remake them in its soiled image.

Today's parents often find themselves battling two fronts. They must scan the *outside* world for possible dangers, while also paying close attention to what could be going wrong *inside* their daughters

Elements of Narrative

and sons. It is the language of defenselessness (e.g., vulnerability) and dysfunction (e.g., abnormality) that lends itself to the occasion of therapy. Consider an initial telephone call David M. (DM)[1] received from Beverly, the mother of 9-year-old Maureen, in which she introduced him to her daughter in diagnostic terms:

> **Beverly**: (Gravely) I'm afraid she might have an anxiety disorder.
> **DM**: What are you noticing that has you concerned?
> **Beverly**: Well, she's always had separation issues. (DM is reminded that parents no less than professionals have been enlisted by clinical language.)
> **DM**: I may have an idea of what you mean, but can you say a little more?
> **Beverly**: Well, she's always resisted going on playdates, unless I go with her. I never thought much of it until now.
> **DM**: What has you thinking about it now?
> **Beverly**: When Maureen's grandfather passed away, I noticed a change in her. He died recently of a heart attack. Since then, she's been preoccupied with the idea that her papa might still be alive if only she had watched him more closely during his final visit. Yesterday, she asked me about the warning signs of a heart attack. She's too young to be burdened by such things. She should be enjoying her childhood.

Beverly went on to explain how Maureen had become increasingly concerned with the health and well-being of family members. In recent weeks she took to calling her mother at work to make sure she was all right, unable to wait for her safe return home. She also began "collecting mementos" (e.g., movie ticket stubs, receipts) "so if something bad happens to one of us, she'll have a keepsake."

Given this initial description of Maureen, DM could have easily entertained a psychiatric explanation. Upon meeting her, his search for evidence of an anxiety disorder would have proven fruitful given the power of diagnostic language to shape perception (Madsen,

2007). At some point during the first interview he would have turned his evaluative gaze on Beverly in pursuit of a causal agent. (Did she contribute to Maureen's anxious attachment?) In no time, DM would have secured the role of lead agent. It would have been his talent for assessment that garnered attention, making it unlikely that Maureen (or Beverly) would come to be known apart from their dysfunctional identities.

But what if there were such culturally vetted phrases as "the tenacious twos," "the intellect of a child," "the ethics of a child," or "the hardiness of a child"? How might we be impacted? If these terms were widely circulated in our social world, would they orient us differently as we prepared for a first encounter with Maureen? Would we be better positioned to consider her virtues as well as her "vices?" Might we readily detect signs of her spirit and will? Beyond concern for her protection, would we also take note of her potential to grapple with the existential realities of life—and even death?

Characterization

In literature and film we find young protagonists who are made estimable both by their virtuous deeds and by the precarious circumstances in which they are found. When they come into view in story lines, they are often discovered in close proximity to some form of peril. In Marc Caro and Jean-Pierre Jeunet's film, *The City of Lost Children* (*La Cité des Enfants Perdus*, 1995), 5-year-old Denree is kidnapped, and it is up to his much older brother, One, and a 9-year-old orphan, Miette, to rescue him. The story is set in a surreal world in which children are abducted for the purposes of siphoning their dreams. Miette appears to have drowned. One is inconsolable. In the nick of time Miette is saved from an otherwise certain death. She reunites with One to restart their desperate search for Denree. It is the hazards characters face and their unsecured futures that make them all the more creditable and worthy of our rapt attention.

Similarly, in the magically-real film *Pan's Labyrinth* (*El Laberinto del Fauno*, 2006), young Ofelia is given three death-defying tasks in order to achieve immortality, including the retrieval of a key from the underground den of a vile king-size toad and the procurement of a dagger from the sterile dining room of a ghastly child-eating monster. In the course of events, her mother dies while giving birth, and her sadistic stepfather, Captain Vidal, takes charge, placing her under constant watch. Despite her tragic loss and subsequent confinement, Ofelia valiantly carries out her assignments. The sociologist, Arthur Frank tells us, "Many stories, if not most and possibly *all*, involve some test of character: a decisive moment at which a character's response declares what sort of person she or he is" (2010, p. 29). In the penultimate scene, Ofelia is left with the choice of sacrificing her own life or that of her newborn brother. She chooses the former, underscoring her virtue in stark contrast to the Captain's brutality.

At first glance, the sort of heroism exemplified by Miette and Ofelia would seem reserved for the silver screen or the pages of prized fiction and far beyond the outer limits of everyday life. The tales we hear in our practice may seem of a milder complexion, and the characters featured in them as eminently recognizable. But upon closer inspection, the young people we meet and the plotlines in which they appear demonstrate a capacity for equal parts trial and exploit. It is a matter of availing ourselves of the remarkable elements of each that would distinguish young champions. We unlock our imaginations in anticipation of an intrepid child and attend to characterization more as coauthors than clinicians. We believe in the power of a well-conceived central figure, knowing that a thinly drawn protagonist will struggle to face challenges, win others over, or drive a plot forward. The problems children encounter can be recognized for the threats they pose and the proving grounds they provide, upon which young people can establish themselves as meritorious. We search out the extraordinary within the ordinary and come face-to-face with awe-inspiring children. Before anxiety wrested authorship rights, vying for the greater share of Maureen's reputation, she was more abundantly represented in family life. Consider a story that might have been given only passing attention and made perishable if not for the interest it was shown:

> Beverly: We're a little late because I had to speak with my youngest daughter's teacher. Ann is having trouble adjusting to school this year, even with her big sister there. (Beverly looks at Maureen with appreciation.)
>
> Maureen: (Reassuringly) But it's getting better.
>
> Beverly: That's true. That's what her teacher told us.
>
> DM: (To Maureen) How do you know it's getting better? Were you at the meeting today?
>
> Maureen: Yeah, but that's not how I know.
>
> Beverly: Maureen has been a real help, (turning to Maureen) haven't you, sweetie?
>
> DM: In what ways has Maureen been a real help? (There might be something to learn about Maureen apart from her struggles with anxiety.)
>
> Beverly: She talked with Ann before the new year started. And Maureen walks her to class. They head off together absorbed in conversation. I'm sure she's reassuring Ann.
>
> DM: Is that right, Maureen? Do you talk with Ann on the way to class?
>
> Maureen: I told her that she has a nice teacher, because Mrs. Ward was my teacher when I was in second grade. And that I'll come and get her when school's over.

Hearing about her response to Ann's struggles, DM gave thought to what it might suggest about Maureen as a noble figure, rather than assessing her for further possible deficits, or worse, making a mental note that separation anxiety seems to run in the family. Instead, he was taken with the seeming fact that Maureen might know a thing or two about anxiety and how to deal with it, if not yet on her own behalf, certainly on her sister's.

Already, there was the promise of a riveting drama featuring 9-year-old Maureen, who, at the same stage of life as Miette and Ofeila, suffered a grave loss. And as if that was not torment enough, anxiety imperiled the rest of her family. It elevated every sniffle to a possible case of pneumonia and each parting with her mother to the prospect of a tragic end. How would Maureen come to meet the anxiety that plagued her? Might she prove as memorable a leading figure as the two young protagonists immortalized in film? Given her gifts as a big sister, what might we expect in the way of her potential to subdue the anxiety that would seem intent on consuming her?[2]

Linking Events in Sequence

To understand narrative form, we look through a causal lens and see that "one thing happens in consequence of another" (Frank, 2010, p. 25). Two or more events are linked together in a meaningful way. And it is the manner in which they are arranged that provides both speaker and audience a way of making sense of what has occurred. When Maureen walked into DM's office some weeks later and reported with pride, "I didn't worry today!," this certainly constituted a significant event, but without embellishment, we do not have a story—not yet. DM provided the platform for elaboration in the form of questions:

> **DM**: How did you do it, Maureen? How did you have a day without Worry? Did you tell it to get lost? (Here we are deliberately capitalizing the first letter of the problem's name, as if it were a proper noun. In narrative therapy, problems are personified and treated as having separate motives. This is further illustrated in Chapter 3.)
>
> **Maureen**: (Assertively) I decided I was going to be happy today.
>
> **Beverly**: That's right, sweetie. You told me the minute you woke up, didn't you? (Maureen nods in agreement, seeming satisfied with her achievement.)

Only now do we have the makings of a story. We follow a chain of events in which a 9-year-old girl opened her eyes one morning and, before Worry could take hold, told her mother she intended to be happy. Over the course of the day, she did just that, and as a result, Worry did not dare bother her. But any story worth telling requires attention to detail. DM's questions helped to warm her imagination: "So did I hear right, Maureen? Did you decide this morning to be happy? And is that the reason Worry couldn't get to you first?" Once Maureen answers in the affirmative, there are many more questions to come, such as, "Maureen, once you make a decision, can you get things going your way rather than Worry's way?" and "Can I learn more about what you are able to do when you make up your mind about things?" and "Is what you did for your sister, Ann, to help her when she was worried about school, similar in any way to what you did today?" This last question introduces the possibility of a talent that has been in Maureen's portfolio for some time.

As you might imagine, Maureen savored the kinds of questions that placed her ahead of the problem and provided an opportunity to treat herself as the main character rather than languishing in the role of novice—being directed by adults and misdirected by problems, but having no sense of direction herself. But we are getting ahead of ourselves. For any story to achieve prominence, more leavening is needed. Otherwise, though a story may show initial lift, it can suffer the same fate as a soufflé when met by the slightest breeze or change in atmosphere. Unable to withstand the force of the problem, any conclusion initially reached will be reconsidered little more than hot air.

Temporality

No sooner had Maureen risen to the occasion than Worry proved it could still get a rise out of her. One way of accounting for the durability of problems is the extent to which they have been richly storied. A key element in achieving this richness is the establishment of their presence across time. Any problem with staying power lays claim to an eminent past or, more pointedly, to an infamous past. Just listen to Beverly's concern as she is carried back in time: "Maureen was vulnerable from day one. She always had difficulty with change and worried a lot. When I went back to work she had a harder time than her sister, even though she is the older one. The week I started my job, she had a lot of trouble falling asleep and staying asleep through the night." We can think of the problem as having cast a spell, drawing Beverly (and us if we are not careful) into a trance in which past events take on a troubling hue as Maureen's current plight is made evident throughout her history. The problem's incantation, having fixated on specific plot points from the past, next summons a foreboding future. Dark speculation about what awaits her unsuspecting child takes hold: "What if she never outgrows it? It's manageable now while I'm here, but as she gets older, what will she do if she doesn't learn how to deal with things?" With the story having been woven across time, the problem sits back and admires its handiwork, not unlike the beloved spider from the cherished children's story *Charlotte's Web* (White, 1980).

You may remember how Charlotte knitted messages into her impressive web so that her curl-tailed young protégé, Wilbur, would, upon reappraisal, be considered too valuable to ever suffer the ignominious fate of being roasted and served up whole. In Maureen's case, instead of gazing up to behold such glistening commendations as "Some [Girl]," "Terrific," and "Radiant" (p. 114), we are more likely to be confronted by the labels "Overly Sensitive," "Ill-Equipped," and "Anxious." Both venerable and infamous stories utilize time, selectively weaving loose ends into an elaborate fabric, or in the case of problems, into a darker-threaded fabrication. All it takes is the right collection of carefully chosen events (some spider's silk) and a storyteller's impulse of the most lackluster kind.

Stories make time travelers of us all. We are on expeditions as narrative practitioners, not for the purposes of digging up priceless relics from the past (e.g., "Tell me about your childhood"), or for spying on predestined futures with the priestly powers of an oracle, but rather for entering into contested spaces. In a contested space, a wide range of plot points may be selected from. Numerous contrasting strands are there for the weaving. It is only when we reduce the array of possibilities to a single pattern, as if there is no variation or alternative design, that life is constricted and both past and future, once open and abounding with possibility, are foreclosed (Morson, 1994). Having heard accounts of both Maureen's trials with Worry and her triumphs over it, on her sister's behalf and her own, the outlook is expanded for multiple and competing images of a 9-year-old activist and her worthy foe. We can now begin to distinguish the problem's aims from the young person's with questions that invite:

- Two accounts of history:
  ◊ What are some of Worry's favorite stories from your past?
  ◊ What are some things about you from the past that are important to remember that Worry would love you to forget?
- Two possible futures:
  ◊ If Worry had its way, what kind of a future would it design for you?
  ◊ If the future that awaits you is based on your dreams rather than Worry's nightmares, what might it look like?

Though some may recommend that we live in the moment as a possible remedy for hauntings from both past and future, narrative form has us lingering in the current hour for only so long before carrying us backward and then forward. Stories depend on time, generous amounts of it. As the developmental psychologists Eleanor Ochs and Linda Capps remind us, "The structure that is the best candidate for distinguishing narrative is chronology" (2001, p. 18). Stories "thicken" (Geertz, 1973; White, 1997) as we look back over our shoulders, picking up memories of a certain variety along the way. It is the particular collection of memories that can shed light on a seemingly decided future with the promise of an optimal harvest—or a failed crop (Freedman & Combs, 1996).

Hilde Lindemann Nelson offers a first-person account of time and its implications for our sense of identity: "They are the backward-looking stories that constitute my understanding of who I have been in relation to them, but at the same time, these backward-looking narratives create the field of action in which I can construct the forward-looking stories that guide my future relations with them" (2001, p. 77). There can be a sense of destiny as we look forward as a result of what was encountered looking backward. Rather than attempting to avoid traveling altogether, turning in our passports and remaining in one time zone (as if that were even possible), we are only too happy to prepare for departure. We would simply challenge any right the problem would claim to be our historian or booking agent and tour guide.

Persuasive Narratives

Narratives take hold and live through us. They function as frameworks for our identities. They tell us who we are and what is possible for our lives. As Lindemann explains, "We treat ourselves and others according to our narrative understanding of who we and they are" (2014, p. 49). When Maureen became known to her mother and teacher, and perhaps to herself, as an anxious child, unable to manage Worry, she settled into an impoverished identity position made conceivable by the problem. Any commendable experiences that might have contributed to rich story development dematerialized and seemed more phantom than substance. As concerned parents reach out for help, and teachers, school counselors, therapists, and psychiatrists join the conversation, the problem can demand all of our attention. But we refuse to accord it exclusive rights. Notice instead, how the problem can be treated as an interloper, as we catch sight of a preferred story line, with its own potential powers of persuasion.

>   **Beverly**: Everything seems to stress her out lately. If I'm in the back of the line picking her up from school and she can't see me, she worries I'm not there or that something happened to

me. The other day she overheard me talking to my mom, who, as you can imagine is not feeling well at the moment—

DM: Do you mean since losing your father?

Beverly: He was my stepfather. I always thought of him more as my mom's husband, although I grew to love him over time. My father died when I was 25, so when Papa Jim came into our lives, I was already on the West Coast. But he is the only grandfather the girls ever knew.

DM: So your mother's been through this twice.

Beverly: Yes, it's been difficult for her—first my father, and now Moe's grandfather, although there were many years in between. It's just the ladies now, right, sweetie? (She turns to Maureen and puts her arm around her.) But we're all going to be around for a long time. (Turning back to DM) Before she went to bed last night, she asked me if Nana was going to die.

DM: (To Maureen) Is Worry pretty strong right now?

Maureen: Yeah.

Beverly: She's our sensitive one. I told her Nana is just going through a lot right now. (Turns to Maureen) But your Nana's a survivor. (Turning back to DM) She and her Nana are very close in spite of the fact that my mother lives in Chicago. They e-mail and Skype, and we're going back this spring to visit. Moe is the most excited. (Although there may be more to learn about what Worry can stir in Maureen, little is yet known about what excites her—perhaps something to do with her connection to her Nana. There is no telling whether excitement might figure into a preferred story line. This is the mystery and pleasure of our practice.)

DM: Maureen, is it true you are more excited than your sister and mom about seeing your Nana?

Maureen: Yeah.

DM: Can you tell me why, or can you guess why you're the most excited in the whole family to go on this trip to Chicago?

Maureen: I don't know.

DM: Is it because you love flying on airplanes, or is it because you love traveling? Is Chicago your favorite city, or is it because you miss your Nana? (Offering various possibilities in an effort to spark Maureen's thinking.)

Maureen: I miss my Nana.

DM: Beverly, is Maureen's deep feeling for her Nana part of her sensitivity? (DM is wondering if Worry has left little room for Maureen's sensitivity to be interpreted as anything other than vulnerability.)

Beverly: Oh, there's no question!

DM: I wondered if that was the case. Can you tell me more about Maureen's sensitivity? Before Worry came into the picture, what was her sensitivity like?

Beverly: Gosh . . . the first thing that comes to mind is how much she's always cared about everybody, especially her sister.

DM: Can you say something more about the quality of her caring for Ann.

Beverly: Ann's younger than Moe, but not by much. There's a total of 19 months between them. We wanted to have them close together. You hear stories about older sisters being jealous when a newborn arrives, especially so soon, but that didn't happen. She loved her from day one. (We are on the trail of something special that might further provide a contrasting account of Maureen.)

Beverly goes on to tell stories that illustrate the tender feelings Maureen has always had for her younger sister.

Beverly: From day one she would dote on her. When I sang to the little one, Moe would sing with me, even before she knew the words. She'd do her best. And we'd watch over her together, wouldn't we?

Maureen: Uh-huh.

DM: Is it possible that Worry has been taking advantage of Maureen's sensitivity lately? Before Worry showed up, did you think of her sensitivity differently? (Looking into the past for elements of a preferred narrative.)

Beverly: Yeah, I thought of it as a gift. (She appears meditative.)

DM: A gift? If it is a gift and not meant for Worry's purposes, then for what purpose might it be intended? (Distinguishing Worry from sensitivity has made room for an emerging story.)

Beverly: For loving! (She tears up.)

DM: What brings tears to your eyes as you're giving voice to Maureen's capacity for love? (This question is intended to assist Beverly in stepping further into a rich telling and for Maureen to be acknowledged for her gift.)

Beverly: It's just that—her capacity for love. She's my special girl. (Beverly looks lovingly at her daughter.)

DM: Maureen, are you gifted at loving? (This question is intended not only to honor Maureen, but also to give her the chance to consider whether this description fits.)

Maureen: Yeah. (Though she answers modestly, as would most people in response to such praise, she appears proud.)

DM: How good are you at loving your Nana and your sister?

Maureen: Really good!

DM: And how do you explain it? How did you get so good at loving?

Maureen: Because of when I was born.

DM: What do you mean? (DM is taken by surprise.)

Maureen: I was born close to Valentine's Day, right (Looking at her mother)?

Beverly: (Smiling) That's right. February 10th. She was our Valentine's week baby.

DM: Were you touched by love from the very beginning?

Maureen: I already knew how to love before I was born. (The story thread now reaches further back in time. DM guesses that it might be traced to Beverly and other loved ones and may be part of a family practice. But that remains to be seen.)

With the aid of DM's questions and Beverly's testimony, what might otherwise have been overshadowed was now brought back into the light.

Similarly, but with an economy of words, Wilbur's (spindly) eight-legged defender, Charlotte, managed to give rise to a story about a pig who was anything but ordinary, capturing the imaginations of all who met him (White, 1980). People came from far and wide to study the celebrated swine and stood in awe, staring down at him and then up at the web and then back again at Wilbur. Charlotte's words carried visitors to a different realm—one of astonishment. As Wilbur sat in plain view below Charlotte's web and the terms she had sewn into it, he too was emboldened by an emerging story and saw new possibilities for just what kind of a pig he might become. The people who traveled to the farm, and even those who lived there and tended to it daily, were, if not transported, at the very least inclined to entertain "a sense of the mysterious within the ordinary" (Faris, 2004, p. 46). Such is the potential of stories.

It bears repeating that we have a strong interest in getting to know problems. We are well aware that if ignored and left to their own devices, problems would be only too happy to skulk about wreaking havoc in the lives of young people and their families. Problems must be given attention, though not undivided attention. But that is not to deny them their due or overlook their penchant for mayhem, as Chapter 3 illustrates.

Constraint

Narratives draw on lived experience, no matter how imperfectly recollected. Our accounting of the past relies inescapably on memory, and memory is always partial and subjective (Bruner, 2004). We may feel the irresistible temptation, especially when rehashing contested events and our prominent role in them, to claim to know what actually transpired (e.g., "No, that is not what I said, and that is not the way I said it!"), but our fellow interlocutor will likely object, no matter how vehement we may be. As tempting as it is to cast oneself in the role of objective observer, none of us to date has attained such divining powers.

Narratives are not just highly subjective, but highly selective as well. They do not cover a complete record of lived experience. This would be unwieldy and would involve such minutiae that a single day's chronicle could easily fill hundreds of pages, as was demonstrated in the narration of a day in the life of Leopold Bloom, the antihero in James Joyce's *Ulysses* (1986). In actual practice, one arrives at the end of a day with only the smallest sum of surviving details in one form or another "for the record." This serves the needs of the narratives we live by, be they in support of preferred descriptions, or conversely, for the purposes of a problem story. In either case, narratives are made sturdy, not by their exhaustive detail, but by means of careful selection. David Carr explains how giving shape selectively to an emergent narrative, while limiting its range, ultimately supplies it with the concentration any story needs to achieve coherence: "All extraneous noise and static is cut out. A selection is made of all the events and actions the character may engage in, and only a small minority finds its way into the story. In life, by contrast, everything is left in; all the static is there" (1986, p. 123).

Narratives home in. At their most effective, they organize according to a particular theme (e.g., incorrigibility, incompetence, villainy, goodness, heroism, courage, pathology). They collect plot points that coincide with one another. Once the premise of Maureen's gift of sensitivity was brought back into view through the recollection of sentiments and actions (e.g., her love for her grandmother; her lifelong care for Ann), it stood as a potentially sustainable narrative alongside the more recent report put forward by the problem. It is in this way that we preserve a young person's sense of dignity and worth by denying the problem sole story-telling rights.

We draw a distinction between constraints in service of the problem that would usher young people into foreclosed spaces, their stories written in stone and their authorship rights usurped, and those that would provide a framework for rich, though still concentrated story development. We aim to invigorate those narratives that reserve a place of prominence for young people. Situated in a story line whose thesis was her capacity for love, Maureen was positioned to experience her life more abundantly, even on those occasions when Worry visited. Rather than being restricted to a single account of a young girl with an anxiety disorder, she now had access to a competing narrative about a girl whose sensitivity, though sometimes costly, was principled and praiseworthy. From this new literary vantage point, Maureen would still be subject to Worry—after all, life can be trying—but rather than being unmoored, she cut a striking profile in a cogent narrative.

Suspense

We are careful to differentiate narrative therapy's interest in story development from a time-honored therapeutic practice—that of reframing (Watzlawick, Weakland, & Fisch, 1974). We are not lone storytellers. If we were, we would shape the story and only contend with the challenge of how to pitch it to families. We would singlehandedly construct narratives that illustrate the practitioner's talents. This would make us more than essential. It would make us central to the process.

Instead, we are drawn to a practice in which we are "de-centered but influential" (White & Morgan, 2006). Our influence, though undoubtedly necessary to the creative process, reserves the leading role for young people in alliance with family members. We stretch our imaginations and invigorate the space for innovation but never fill it by deciding, however tactfully, the best direction for young people's lives. As a result, we do not know and do not want to know ahead of time what is likely to happen next. Imagine a story in which both character and plot become largely recognizable from the outset and the events, though they have not yet unfolded, are easily predicted with the final outcome hardly in doubt (e.g., think of animated Disney films or action-adventure blockbusters). In practice, this would make the therapist part psychic. The practitioner would tell the story to the family, who had been made distraught by the problem, in this way: "Here is what you can expect going forward," draining it of suspense and making anything in the way of a creative process largely unnecessary.

Some may treat reason as a more fitting companion than suspense in the realm of direct practice, but we reserve the space for theater, believing that there is more vitality to life as an unfolding drama than to life that is thought to be plainly visible. The plot only shows itself as it advances. There is a sense that events could take us in this direction or that. Gary Saul Morson explains how "the creative process typically traces not a straight line to a goal but a series of false leads, missed opportunities, new possibilities, improvisations, visions, and revisions" (1994, p. 24). In this way the story is alive. There would have been no way to anticipate that Maureen's sensitivity could be appropriated by Worry, and no way to predict that her capacity for love would inspire her to carry on. As we shall soon see, Maureen decided the terms by which she would live and love, according to her own moral code.

Stories are at their best when what happens matters and can alter the course of events in ways that defy prediction, though they are not beyond what is possible to imagine. We still depend on constraint to the degree that it offers the necessary borders to render stories coherent as they take shape. Otherwise, we would find ourselves telling not a story with increasing distinction, but fragments of stories, none of them ever realized as anything beyond unbraided strands. Instead, we trace one strand and then another in anticipation of an emerging pattern the young person might find most pleasing. Even still, we cannot predict its ultimate design. And therein lies suspense.

Resonance

We invite young people into reflection. It is not enough to resist Temper, for example, because it is commonly thought to be the more prudent response. We want to learn something about a possible motive supporting such an action. We are careful not to ask only how she or he did it, as if it is enough that all principles supporting proper behavior are assumed or already settled in the minds of others. Normalizing interests would have us knowing ahead of young people that they ought to be even-tempered (rather than oddly tempered), productive, forgiving, cooperative, considerate, and respectful. Lev Vygotsky cautioned us long ago that "direct teaching of concepts is impossible and fruitless. A teacher who tries to do this usually accomplishes nothing but empty verbalism, a parrotlike repetition of words by the child, simulating a knowledge of the corresponding concepts but actually covering up a vacuum" (1986, p. 150). Of much greater value is the engaged child who considers her or his location in the world, what she or he has come to know, and the experience of knowing that is just out of reach but almost felt. We ask questions that are meant to elicit rather than deliver values. We might be heard asking:

- If Temper would lead you to get even, why not just follow its instructions?
- If the adults in your life have told you to think before you act, and Temper has told you to act before you think, what would you tell yourself if you were doing the thinking and acting? Why?

Given that young people are not regularly consulted on such matters, it is likely they will be caught off guard at first, but with persistence on our part, they may soon realize they are being accorded certain rights (e.g., to think) and take pleasure in their inclusion and in drawing their own conclusions. The interview is intended as genuine inquiry founded on young people's moral commitments with the possibility that there is something they might have in mind (and at heart). The unfolding story becomes a matter of personal interest. Cheryl Mattingly tells us, "A therapeutic plot occurs in a kind of gap, a space of desire created by the distance between where the protagonist is and where she wants to be" (1998, p. 70). Questions, such as the following, are intended to support young people in coming to their own verdicts:

- If Meanness were to tell you what matters most, would this match up or differ from what matters most to you?
- Would life be better in some way if you made room for Meanness rather than doing what others are suggesting and leaving it behind?

Young people can be challenged to puzzle through things, or they can be blunted by the effects of compliance-based training. Issues at hand need not lead to foregone conclusions. In narratives of consequence, main characters are challenged to ponder the implications of their actions and are pressed to make choices for reasons that are vital to them. In our conversations with young people, they can be found at the center of deliberations.

Allow us to illustrate briefly what is made possible when the therapeutic conversation is organized around the young person's interests and storytelling rights. As we pay a final visit to Beverly and Maureen, keep in mind that Maureen is being required to stretch in her thinking, but not to a point that would put current matters beyond her reach.

> DM: If you could, would you give away some of your sensitivity?
> **Maureen:** You can't give it away.
> DM: But what if you could? Imagine if you had three wishes. Would you use one of them to be less sensitive?
> **Maureen:** No.
> DM: Why not? Isn't it harder this way?
> **Maureen:** Yeah.
> DM: Would it be better to care a little less, and that way you could still care, but not so much that Worry was able to sneak in when something hard happens? (DM intends this as a question without a foregone conclusion.)

Elements of Narrative 23

Maureen: (Mutters something DM does not quite catch.)

DM: Should I give you a minute?

Maureen: No, it's better to care. (She may be testing out this idea.)

DM: Even if it can hurt sometimes?

Maureen: Yes, because then you care more about people and they care more about you. (It is unclear to DM if she has come to this conclusion in the abstract where problems are always easier to solve.)

DM: But if you care more, how do you bear it when you lose someone? (DM is attempting to see whether the conclusion Maureen has drawn holds up in the context of her real-life experience.)

Maureen: I don't know. (This appears to strike her as a genuine dilemma and not something that affords an easy answer.)

DM: Beverly, how do you live with the loss of your father and now Jim?

Beverly: It isn't easy.

DM: Does Maureen take after you? Does caring a lot run in the family? (DM wonders if there is a legacy of sensitivity and caring.)

Beverly: She does take after me, as a matter of fact. It's not the easiest road, I can tell you. (Beverly laughs, but in a woeful tone.)

DM: And how have you lived with your sensitivity through the years? (DM senses that Beverly might be willing to join Maureen in acknowledging the complexity that comes with this gift.)

Beverly: I'd have to think about that. I wish I could give her an easy answer.

DM: I appreciate your honesty, Beverly. And I have to admit, I do not have the answer myself.

Beverly: I guess when you have that much love to give, and it's spread out among so many people who you love, and who love you, when you lose someone, there are others who gather round . . . others who come through with their love. (Beverly connects with a bit of her own wisdom.)

DM: So you take comfort in love, even as you've lost love, or a loved one has been lost?

Beverly: I think I do.

Maureen: Like when we had the funeral for Papa Jim, and everybody came.

Beverly: Right.

DM: Maureen, I want to ask you, but I don't know if it's fair to ask such a difficult question. But anyway, here goes: Is it worth it to care so deeply?

Maureen: Yeah.

DM: Can you try to explain it? What makes it worth it?

Maureen: It just is. I can't explain it. It's just better to care. (She appears to be sorting it out.)

DM: Why is it worth it to care and have the gift of sensitivity when it comes at a price?

Maureen: Because you get to have love. (She appears to join with her mother's sentiment.)

DM: Beverly, do you agree with your daughter? Is this the bottom line? Is it all about love, even when there's a cost?

Beverly: It is. She's my girl. (Beverly looks at her lovingly, and Maureen beams with pride.)

Together, mother and daughter brought to life what matters most. DM's questions were intended to create opportunities for moral reflection as Maureen extended herself to find language for what she held dear. This kind of movement can be deeply felt and also contribute to an enduring story. Given the chance, and with our help and the support of family, young people can thrive under such conditions, seize opportunities, and encounter their own desires.

Conclusion

As plotlines ascend to peaks and advance to the cliff's edge, someone must come forward. At critical turns in a young person's life, it is often parents who become well known for their unbending will and unparalleled commitments. They can fix on a direction and act decisively. Professionals, too, may vie for the lead with their powers of persuasion, criteria for diagnosing, and manuals for treatment. It is their custom, with tools in hand, to speak with conviction about young people. When we do finally hear from young people themselves, we can sometimes detect, in their first utterances, the ventriloquist's trick as the advice of adults speaks through them (e.g., "Learning good habits now will help me in the future"). But they can be called upon for more.

We focus on the potential of young agents and find they are capable of filling the bill quite nicely. With the aid of our questions, they come to study themselves as prominent figures, at times wise beyond their years, and at other times sensible beyond what might be expected of their sensibilities. They are locked in dramas that not only test but also prove their abilities and are given chances to improve on those abilities, even as they are proving them. By turning to Maureen, and pursuing an understanding of what she gave greatest value to—even at a cost—we achieved a clearer image of not just who we were dealing with, but who Worry would have to contend with. Next, let us see how we come to know young people ahead of any problem that would hope to have the first say.

CHAPTER TWO

In Pursuit of Children's Virtues
The Wonderfulness Interview

When young people come to therapy accompanied by a parent or two, it is typically not because there is an excess of good news in need of a professional audience. Something has gone wrong, especially from the perspective of adults. And even on those occasions when things are seen to be amiss from the standpoint of a young person, it is still the adults who carry the concern forward and ultimately decide it is time to consult a professional. They arrive at our offices prepared to provide an account of their children's troubles. Their daughters and sons, who are in tow, often sense their lesser standing and reluctantly lag behind, their eyes glued to the floor or perhaps scanning the room for possible escape routes.

Picture 10-year-old Patricia in a family therapy meeting, outnumbered by adults three to one, sitting quietly while her parents describe the problem: "She's shy and needs to learn to socialize. When we pick her up from school, she's usually standing alone while the other kids are interacting. We try to encourage her to reach out, but by Friday afternoon we're scrambling to find something for her to do so she doesn't end up sitting in front of the TV all weekend." They turn to their daughter and ask her to contribute now that they have established the focus for therapy. Patricia shrugs. Turning back to the therapist, they express their hope that this experience will give her "the necessary tools" to make her way in the social world.

Young people are rarely consulted in equal measure about matters that are critical to their lives. If they were, they might take exception to their parents' descriptions. Under the guidance of therapists, parents assert their rights over their charges. This is certainly not to exploit them but to care for and protect them. Still, this inadvertently contributes to a paternalistic approach to parenting and perhaps to therapy as well.

It is not that young people, if recast in the role of protagonist, would be found wanting during the therapy hour. On the contrary, our experience tells us that they would most often give it their all. Nevertheless, when brought into such places as a professional office, it is often assumed that if there is some figuring out to be done, young people are best found bringing up the rear, especially with respect to voice and strategy. Ethicist John Wall maintains that "Children perhaps more than any other group are prone to having their 'saying' capabilities overshadowed by what is 'said' by others about them. They are the most easily marginalized segment of society" (Wall, 2006, p. 537). In spite of the goodwill conveyed by the therapist and the abounding love felt by parents, "children have only half-membership . . . and adults dominate the conversational floor in family therapy" (O'Reilly, 2006, p. 564). We see this power differential play out in the unfolding therapeutic dialogue, where in overlapping speech, privileges are accorded to adults and denied to young people. This manifests subtly in how attention is paid, time is allocated, and speaking rights are secured:

> When the therapist interrupts the adult clients, there is an orientation to the interruption and a politeness strategy is set in motion. When the therapist interrupts the children, however, no such acknowledgement or apology is given. Interrupting a parent functions as a way of orienting to the nature of therapy in that the interruption announces to the parents that attention has been paid to what has been said. . . . Not recognizing the interruption of a child, in contrast, helps to construct the child's lower participation status and also suggests that the children's talk is somehow less important. (O'Reilly, 2008, p. 520)

In Pursuit of Children's Virtues

Given this inequity, it is no wonder young people seem to lack inspiration and have little to say. Ask them where they would rather be and they are likely to reply, "Anywhere else!"

When Problems Have the First Say

The potential negative effects of privileging adult voices are amplified when young people are introduced by way of the problem (e.g., "She's fearful"; "He disrespects us"; "She's been stealing"; "He's wetting the bed"), exposing them at their least commendable. The ensuing impressions would not inspire awe, let alone recommend them as capable of a prominent role in any discussion. But parents are well oriented to the occasion. They dutifully report what is wrong with their children and even speculate about the problem's dynamic, often in line with current popular discourse (e.g., "We need to get at what's underneath his anger;" "She seeks attention, even if it's negative"). They do their best to provide a coherent rendition, along with a record of their own efforts at remediation. As they recount their tireless attempts to solve the problem, their devotion is evident, and so is their exhaustion. Consider one loving mother's attempts to rectify matters and preserve a sense of her own competence in relating her concerns about her 12-year-old son to a professional:

> He's gotten himself into trouble at school. He was caught cheating on a test and lied when his teacher confronted him. And since then, he was caught again, this time cutting class. It's not like him. This is not the son I raised. Look, I understand he's developing. And he's getting older and entering adolescence and testing limits. I'm aware of what to expect. I make room for that. I understand he needs more privacy. Maybe I've given him too much room. I guess I thought we might bypass a few of these struggles. It's not easy being one of those parents who needs help with her kids. . . . What can I say? . . . We need help. I'm not really sure what's going on with him.

In her remarks there is the obligatory description of her son's indiscretions and also an understandable effort to save face, given how problems like cheating and dishonesty will implicate not just her son but her as well. After all, wasn't it her job to teach him right from wrong?

Consequently, parents do their duty by providing all the essential details, giving the family therapist what would seem needed to plan a course of treatment and bring about necessary change. In spite of the fact that parents may feel no shortage of love, they are often obliged to convey matters of weight by confessing the worst, offering what can amount to disparaging accounts of their children. All the while, young people sit idly by, perhaps lobbing in an occasional objection from the sidelines. But they are outmatched, their peripheral location making their views less persuasive. The resulting experience can be one of failure for a parent, and for a young person, embarrassment and even humiliation (Freeman, Epston, & Lobovits, 1977). And such an introduction certainly does little to strengthen family bonds of love. Whatever distance or friction might have existed prior to entering the office will likely increase as young people hear themselves described, often in detail, according to the problem and in front of someone who is a virtual stranger. It is not that caregivers are averse to providing rich introductions based on young people's best qualities (e.g., kindness, grit, humor, imagination, trustworthiness). It is simply understood that when one visits a problem solver, one is expected to talk about the problem. In fact, anything to the contrary might be considered distinctly beside the point and reserved for visits to doting grandparents.

Another challenge in attempting to meet young people on more respectful grounds is not just the disregard shown by adults, especially when problems are weighing in, but also the obstacle of their own indifference. Children come to understand that the problems that enter their lives reside outside their scope of competence and are consequently not their concern. It is not uncommon to be met by the all-too-familiar phrase "I don't know" in response to questions directed their way, as if higher thinking is above their developmental pay grade. However, this may also be the result of the kinds of questions they are asked (e.g., "What were you thinking when you . . .?" and "How does that make you feel?"). Such questions can reflect the interests of adults and only serve to alienate young people further. As with any subjugated group, they can find that their position in the social hierarchy fosters a sense of resignation. In the end, they may even come to adopt a preference for their own subordination. One study of young people in Bogotá, Colombia, exemplifies just such an attitude:

> They felt better when they were treated as recipients of knowledge rather than as knowledge producers, or as passive and subordinated units with little initiative rather than as intelligent youngsters, able to innovate and help solve their own problems. They preferred to be seen as persons who accepted indiscriminate orders, simply because these derived from positions of authority. (Salazar, 1991, p. 58)

We read their resulting self-abrogation as a consequence of domination. Following Michel Foucault, we trace this passivity through an analysis of power with respect to who is vested with the right to know and who is exposed to an evaluative gaze: "He who is subjected to a field of visibility, and who knows it, assumes responsibility for the constraints of power; he makes them play spontaneously upon himself; he inscribes in himself the power relation in which he simultaneously plays both roles; he becomes the principle of his own subjection" (1995, pp. 202–203). Young people can be made complicit with their lower rank, playing the part of both subordinate and enforcer of the status quo. In a world tailored to the perspective of adults they can see to their own submission.

The Wonderfulness Interview

We are cognizant of the potential negative consequences of learning about problems ahead of any appreciation of a young person's virtues. Without first knowing, in some detail, about the moral character of young people, we are unprepared to meet any problem effectively. We do want to know about problems. They are simply not all we want to become acquainted with and certainly not the first thing we want to hear about. Getting to know young people according to their virtues guides our interest to matters that might otherwise be considered extraneous. It is during such introductions that all parties begin to consider what young people might bring to bear on problems. Before we begin to make the problem's acquaintance, we turn to parents and ask them to introduce their daughters and sons to us according to their wonderfulnesses—that is, those special qualities that distinguish them and make them who they are at their most exemplary. We begin by addressing young people in the following manner: "If I were to ask everyone to tell me what is wonderful about you, what might they say? Would you like to tell me what is so wonderful about you and answer for yourself, or would you prefer that your parents offer an initial description?"

Very few young people ever volunteer. Most often they demur and willingly hand the reins over to their parents, not just because of the customary expectation of their passivity in professional settings, but because of the awkwardness most of us would feel in tooting our own horns. Nevertheless, they are typically keen to hear what their parents have to say. Consider the potential impact on both parent and young person when engaged by the following questions:

- What is it about your daughter that serves as a reminder that you are a wonderful mother to her?
- What is it about your son that would give you the impulse to brag about him when you're out socializing with old friends?
- Is there something about your daughter that warms your heart when she comes to mind during your commute?
- Is there anything about your son that is like a dream come true?

We assure parents that what we learn will not go to waste and is intended as much more than flattery or a joining technique. Of course, it has the likely benefit of invoking an image of an endearing daughter or son, but it does more. Given that we intend to turn our attention to the problem within the hour, we are careful not to find ourselves empty-handed. We convey to parents that the virtues documented in the wonderfulness interview will prove most advantageous in any close encounter with the problem later on. It is often young people's wonderfulnesses that are translated into the most enduring initiatives. Such merits seem to have far greater stamina in addressing problems than institutionalized or manualized interventions.

Getting to know young people according to their wonderfulnesses achieves many aims:

- It challenges the conceptualization of young people as empty vessels.
- It conveys to young people that they will be counted on as vested members of the team.
- It establishes their talents as admissible to therapy.
- It documents what is of importance to young people, thereby bringing within reach their sense of purpose.
- It increases the odds that young people and family members will hold the advantage in their engagement with problems.
- Most importantly, it allows transport down the rabbit hole into Wonderland where young people are found to be capable of most anything.

In addition, making young people's talents known serves many ends for parents:

- It aids in the restoration of parents' dignity, which has often been compromised by having to confess the worst about their daughters, their sons, and themselves.
- It genealogically links young people's wonderfulnesses to their parents, forbearers, and the communities and cultures from which they come.
- It revives the playful creativity and good humor that may

have worn thin by the deadly seriousness that so often accompanies the arrival of problems.
- Most importantly, it provides the opportunity to follow after their children down the rabbit hole into Wonderland.

Illustrating the Wonderfulness Interview

DE received a telephone call from Audrey, the mother of 12-year-old Francine, who was abused by an older cousin when she was very young. Audrey described her efforts to comfort her daughter and preserve their bond, but of late noticed less positive impact. Adding to Audrey's concern was Francine's recent weight gain. She had always been "a big girl," and this never worried Audrey. But Francine seemed to be "turning to food more and more and away from people." At home, she retreated to her room and rarely came out anymore. Francine seemed increasingly wary of the world and kept her distance, making no connections at school and, when asked, insisted that she no longer had any interest in friendship. This constituted a dramatic shift, as she had always been someone who cared about people. "Now," Audrey fretted, "it's as if she's given up on life." She had taken Francine to meet with a therapist years ago following the discovery of the abuse and more recently to a physician concerning Francine's "excessive food consumption." Audrey's alarm only increased as Francine grew bigger despite medical attention. Concern turned to crisis when Audrey discovered that her daughter was spending time (and her mother's money) on phone sex lines. All of this was conveyed to DE leading up to a first appointment.

As they settled in for an initial conversation, before a word was spoken, DE glanced at Francine and gathered that she was expecting the very worst. Surely, without the wonderfulness interview as a resource, DE would be facing a much tougher challenge.

> DE: Do you mind if we go about this conversation in a way that could be very different from what you each might have anticipated? (Both mother and daughter appear apprehensive.) I

was wondering if I might get to know you, Francine, through your wonderfulnesses—or what the people who know you best might say is wonderful about you.

Audrey: This is not what I expected. (She seems surprised but not displeased.)

DE: Well, here's my thinking. I have to assume that the problem, whatever it might be, is no pushover. And we might have to join together if we are going to do anything about it. But before we can even think about teaming up, it would be good for me to know what Francine's wonderfulnesses are, so we can all see what she has going for her and consider how to put that against the problem.

DE intends to get to know the problem in detail soon enough, but first he focuses on the establishment of Francine's virtuous reputation. Once she has become known for her worth, any number of problems can be approached with a degree of confidence, no matter how daunting they may appear at the outset of therapy. However, Francine's suspicions do not seem to have been allayed.

DE: Francine, would I be putting you on the spot if I asked you directly about your wonderfulnesses? (Francine says nothing but seems to convey that this would undoubtedly be the case. It is rare that a young person, or anyone for that matter, would be prepared to act as her own promoter or press agent.)

DE: In that case, do you mind if I ask your mother to speak about your wonderfulnesses?

Francine: I don't care. (Though she indicates indifference, she appears at least minimally engaged and has desisted from the dirty looks that appeared meant to command her mother's attention and perhaps draw it away from the interview.)

DE: Audrey, if you are up for it, can you begin to fill me in on what might be important for me to know about Francine's wonderfulnesses? (In contrast to the fatigue DE detected during their initial telephone conversation, Audrey now appears relieved, seeming to welcome the opportunity to come to her daughter's defense. She peers at DE expectantly.)

DE: If Francine and I were shipwrecked on a desert island, what would I come to respect about her, and what would I depend on her for over time as we got forced into each other's company and couldn't ring anyone? Audrey, what would I come to respect about Francine? (DE conjures a stirring scene in which Francine's skills would be required.)

Audrey: Hmm. I think she'd be fair in divvying things up, whatever you had between the two of you. (She readily speaks to Francine's interest in fairness.)

DE: So if we only had one box of supplies, she would share it with me and not take it from me?

Audrey: There's no doubt.

DE: Do you have any understanding how she came to learn fairness as a virtue? (DE attempts to trace the history of Francine's interest in fairness.)

Audrey: She has very clear positions about what she thinks is fair.

DE: Is that fairness in the sense of justice for all, or fairness along the lines of "I deserve my share, now you go and get your own"?

Audrey: It's more of a sense of justice for others as much as herself.

DE: So if some kid were being mistreated, she would stand up for that person and not go along with the unjust treatment?

Audrey: I have seen her do it. And whoever it is, she doesn't quit on them. (Although it may have been some time since Audrey saw Francine in this light, her eyes are now glistening.)

DE: Have people counted on her?

Audrey: In the past they have.

DE: Francine, does that ring a bell for you—a reputation for justice and fair treatment? Are you on board with your mother's description?

Francine: Yeah . . . sort of. (She sounds bewildered but, turning her head, she stares at DE with what appears to be considerable curiosity.)

DE: Why not just make sure to get your own share? Why worry about others? Have you ever heard the expression "every man for himself"?

Francine: (Sarcastically) I'm not a man!

DE: Of course. Will you accept my apology?

Francine: Okay. (A wry smile sweeps across her face.)

(DE is not about to leave matters there. He seeks elaboration of these claims by calling forth an account in which Francine's attributes are embedded in a story.)

DE: Audrey, would you be so kind as to tell me one story from among the stories you could tell in which Francine goes about her fairness? And when I hear it, I will begin to understand how she practices such fairness.

Audrey: (Squinting and gazing upward, as if searching for something.) Okay. . . . (Starting slowly) It was just after her seventh birthday, maybe a week or two later. She was at another girl's birthday party. They had a piñata, and one of the girls must have arrived late. But anyway, by the time she got there, all the candy had spilled out and there wasn't much of anything left. (Now looking at DE, seeming to have fully locked onto the memory.) Francine was the only child who offered her some from her own small pile. She walked right up to her and handed her a few pieces. A couple of the parents convinced their kids to do the same, but I'll never forget how Francine was the only one who just stood up and went over to her. No one had to prompt her.

DE: About how many kids were at the party, Audrey? Do you remember? Were there just a few or were there more than that? (DE imagines there may have been a good number of children there, which would have made the step Francine took even rarer.)

Francine: No, there were a lot! It was all the kids from my class and some others, too. (Francine states this with discernible pride, having joined the conversation for the first time without any prompting. Perhaps this is due to the place of honor that is being established on her behalf.)

DE: Why'd you do it, Francine? Why did you share from your own small pile when nobody made you? After all, anyone knows that candy is to a young person like gold is to an adult. (DE wants to learn more about Francine's interest in fairness and at the same time make it more available to her as a principle.)

Francine: It wasn't fair. She didn't have any. (Francine seems fully engaged in the conversation, perhaps with a growing sense that it will not be at the expense of her dignity.)

DE: Francine, how would you describe your interest in fairness—as a belief, a wish, or a hope?

Francine: It's a dream.

DE: Really! It's a dream? What do you mean by "it's a dream"? I want you to know how interested I will be in your reply. (Now it is DE's turn to be somewhat bewildered by Francine's response.)

Francine: (In a sincere tone) If everyone was fair to everyone, it would be like the dream came true.

Audrey: I have shown her Dr. King's "I Have a Dream" speech. Is that what you're thinking about? (Audrey comes to DE's and Francine's aid by providing the likely context for her dream.)

Francine: Uh-huh.

DE: Is this something you watched recently?

Audrey: Maybe five or six months ago.

DE: Have you held onto it all this time, Francine? (Attempting to provide for an experience of self-agency.)

Francine: Yeah. (She beams with pride but is still somewhat reserved.)

DE: But what if you're living in a world where people aren't fair or kind a lot of the time?

Francine: You have to try anyway! (She states this with conviction.)

DE: Is it hard to try to be fair in a world that can be so unfair at times?

Francine: Yeah. (She appears momentarily subdued.)

DE: Who is standing with you or beside you in spirit? (Seeking partners who might share her vision.)

Francine: My mom. (She looks to Audrey, who generously indicates her support with an endearing nod.)

Audrey: That's right. I'm right here. And Dr. King is with us, too, in spirit. (They smile and nod at one another.)

DE: Why did you make this your dream, Francine? Why didn't you just dream of becoming famous or having everything a person could dream of?

Francine: Because I'm not selfish.

DE: That's what I'm wondering. Why not? Why not be selfish? You wouldn't know this, but there was a film called *Wall Street* that was a big hit back in my day, and the main character, Gordon Gekko, had this saying: "Greed is good! Greed is right!"

Francine: Greed isn't good. Greed is gross.

DE: Is that right? (DE is impressed by her clever reworking of the phrase.)

Francine: That's right! (She states this firmly.)

Audrey: Wow! (She wipes tears from both eyes.)

DE: What is it, Audrey? What are you reacting to?

Audrey: It's good to see her with such spirit. It's been a while.

DE: Has the problem tried to rob Francine of her spirit?

Audrey: There's no question.

DE: Whatever the problem is, Francine, does it play fair? Does it believe in the dream, or is it out for its own gain whatever the cost to you? Would it care at all to know that your commitment to fairness dates back several months to you and your mother watching Dr. King's speech, and further back to the age of 7 when you were the only kid at the birthday party who stood up for fairness, and possibly even further back than that? (With these questions, DE lends support to a worthy identity description founded on Audrey's testimony and Francine's own contributions.)

Only now is DE prepared to turn to the problem with a sense that a start has been made in substantiating Francine as much more than a victim of abuse. Consider the potential in bringing her forward as an agent of change rather than investing in an overriding view of her as a lonely and damaged figure. The latter would necessitate concentrated efforts by others on her behalf, while inadvertently treating Francine as fragile. But what if she were further distinguished for her interest in justice for all? Is it possible that a girl who acts as a guardian of Dr. King's dream might live with a prevailing sense of purpose even if the road ahead presents inevitable challenges? How might her interest in fairness help confront whatever disparagements abuse would heap upon her? Of course we cannot know in advance exactly how she will fare. But we can anticipate that encountering herself as a moral figure ahead of any talk of abuse and its effects will only improve her chances in what may very well be the fight of her life.

A Wonderfulness Interview Guide

How we begin to get to know young people through their wonderfulnesses as a necessary prelude to approaching problems can be challenging, especially when adults have been well trained in the protocols of therapy. But the therapist's earnest interest in a wonderfulness interview is often enough to move matters forward. We find the following steps useful for guiding the process and also assuring parents that we are setting the stage for their concerns.

- *Ask parents and caregivers for their permission to postpone any discussion of the problem for 20–30 minutes.* "I know you have come with serious concerns about your son—concerns that I want to make sure we get to today. But I'm wondering if, before we turn our attention to the problem, you might consider something a little different."

This is meant to intrigue parents and prepare them for something unexpected. They are often more than willing and even relieved not to have to lead off with a negative report or amateur diagnosis.

- *Invite parents and caregivers to introduce the young person according to her or his wonderfulnesses.* "I'm wondering if you could introduce me to your daughter's wonderfulnesses—those gifts that really stand out about her . . . the qualities that others may appreciate . . . those virtues I might come to admire as I get to know her and that might offer a preview of what she already has in hand to meet the problem with."

Delivering this slowly and deliberately can give parents a chance to shift into a reflective space and to focus on what may have faded from view. Most often they welcome the opportunity to speak highly of their children and to renew their roles of loving parents. Though it is rarely the case that parents and caregivers do not enjoy the chance to offer a rich account of their children, a little reassurance can go a long way: "I promise you that this will not go to waste, and that we will put to good use whatever it is that I learn about her once we turn our attention to the problem."

- *Ask parents for a story or two that illustrates the young person's wonderfulness* (e.g., "He's kind-hearted"; "She doesn't miss a beat"). "As you describe John, is there a story among many you could tell that will help me deeply understand what you mean when you say, 'He's kind?'"

"Can you tell me a story that illustrates Ava's humor, one that really paints a picture and exemplifies this quality, one that would help me understand what her 'great sense of humor' involves and contributes to?"

We often ask for representative accounts in order to begin to fit them into a story line. We might check the accuracy of our understanding by summarizing. This also assists in maintaining the momentum of the story under development: "I think I'm beginning to get the picture. And this is one story that captures the spirit of her talent for finding the humor in things. If Ava hadn't said, 'Well, at least the dog won't go hungry tonight' at just the right moment, you might have ended up in a pool of tears. Instead you laughed so hard you cried. And you weren't the only one. The whole family, including Uncle Rick, who never laughs at anything, was in stitches. Have I got this right? Ava, do you agree with what your mom is saying? Is she right in describing you as 'naturally funny'? And is it true that you have impeccable timing?"

At this point in the interview, it is not uncommon for young people to appear more engaged and interested in joining the conversation. They might pull their chairs closer, sit up straight, and join in spontaneously, as if promoted from the lowly status of passenger to copilot or even flight instructor. We readily accept their contributions and respond by extending our inquiry and further invigorating the story under construction. In the process, they shift in attitude, no longer subdued by office etiquette or inhibited by the dread they felt prior to the interview getting under way.

- *Trace the young person's wonderfulnesses through time.* "When did you first notice Olivia's ability to bounce back from difficulty? If we could travel back in time, what moments in history would we visit for early glimpses of this gift? What were the first indications that Olivia could find her way back up after something had gotten her down? Was it even before she started school?"

Wonderfulnesses can be further substantiated as they are traced back in time. Just as problems depend on long histories for their legitimation (e.g., "She's always been a difficult child. As a baby she would cry and cry, often for no apparent reason"), so too do wonderfulnesses rely on detective work. They can lend themselves to the same kind of tracking to remote locales, where we are likely to find evidence of their first appearances. Such sightings serve as plot points that contribute to a well-storied account of a young person's character. Here again, it can be helpful to draw the question out to give a parent enough of an interval to cast back in time.

- *Recruit a wider audience by populating the story under development and invoking the presence of loved ones. Remember that identities and reputations are held collectively.* To the young person: "Do your friends see this in you as well? How might they describe it? Relatives? Neighbors? Are there others who, if they were here with us, would have something to say about this? What might they tell me in the way of a similar story?"

  To the parents: "Who else has noticed Max's ability to express himself? How did others come to learn about it? In what ways have they been impacted by it?" "Who, among all your family members, might be most appreciative of this gift? Why? Who, of all those who have known Max over the course of his life, would be the least surprised that you have acknowledged him here today for his way with words? Why?"

- *Attempt to trace the lineage (or genealogy) of the young person's wonderfulnesses.*

  To the father: "By any chance does her kindness come from her mother and the family she comes from? Is she a chip off anyone's block in her mother's maternal or paternal lines?"

  To the mother: "By any chance did it come from her father or the family he comes from? Did it get passed down to her by learning from one or more of them?" "What would she have seen her paternal grandma do in terms of 'being a giver' when she would stay with her over the summer holidays that she might have just soaked up by being 'the apple of her granny's eye'?"

To the father: "Would you think the fact that the Irish value hospitality and always bend over backward to make a guest feel at home has anything to do with the way she befriended some kids who were new to her class until she was sure they felt at home there?

To the mother: Would you think the fact that you are a Westy [from West Auckland] as are your mom, dad, and grandparents on your mother's side—and we all know the saying: 'Never mess with a Westy if you know what's good for you!'—had any influence on your girl sticking up for her mates when they were being picked on by the bigger kids on the school playground?"

Genealogy refers to inquiries that trace a moral virtue backward through the generations to more distant sources. Most often, such attributes are located in the families that each of the parents come from and from the communities or cultures to which the young person and the family belong. This contributes more than anything else to a sense of never walking alone when the going gets tough and the problem gets going. The child is made out as a representative of the moral virtues of the family through the generations and other lineages particular to her or his community and culture.

- *Inquire about the possibility of a reverse genealogy.* To the father: "By any chance, do you consider that having your son in your life these past nine years has inspired you to lead your life differently than if he weren't here? Can you give me an example of what you have come to do that you might very well be indebted to your son for?"

Young people can be similarly interviewed for the ways they have contributed to the lives of their parents: "Do you know what your dad is talking about? Do you think it is a good thing or a bad thing that watching you dance and play

In Pursuit of Children's Virtues   **45**

>gave him the chance to experience a second childhood, since, for the most part, he missed out on his first childhood?"
>
>"Were you aware before we got talking today that you have been an inspiration to your dad to have so much more happiness in his life than he had ever thought possible before you came along?"

It is not unheard of that legacies of wonderfulnesses can flow from young to old. Young people can hear testimony about the ways they have affected the lives of their elders and thereby achieve a greater sense of pride and place in the world by virtue of their own unique contributions. If young people were not already fully engaged by the conversation, they are sure to be interested in learning how they have added to others' lives.

The experience of a wonderfulness interview inspires young people and families as they are reacquainted with who they are at their best, and with our further assistance, it makes their best accessible during future encounters with the problem.

The Wonderfulness Interview as Story Development

We would never want to lose sight of the wonderfulness interview's importance in the service of characterization. As discussed in Chapter 1, characterization is a key element of story development. A wonderfulness interview replaces "the generalizable child," who can be spoken of in the broadest terms (e.g., "At this age, children need . . ."; "The thing about children who have suffered abuse is . . ."), with a young agent who lives according to particular values and is capable of responding to events by specific means. Having established what might be referred to as the moral character of a young person, we begin to orient to an emergent protagonist. This shift in understanding opens lives and relationships to a sense of promise. Young people can intrigue not only their parents but therapists as well. Children in possession of skills and with increased awareness of their moral intent are poised to move the plot forward in ways we would be hard pressed to anticipate but not challenged to appreciate.

In the dramas of young people's lives, it is not about finding solutions to their problems, as if they were readily foreseeable, or providing tools as if young people came in universal sizes and were adjustable. These could prove to be worse than fruitless efforts. They could rob the moment of expectancy (Morson, 1994) and inhibit young people, denying them a sense of place and overlooking their capacity to face adversity. A wonderfulness interview offers more than empty praise. It lays the foundation for the development of preferred identity descriptions that would have young people at the ready in fateful moments.

In certain corners, there is political advocacy for young people's active involvement in civic life with an "emphasis on participative aspects of knowledge production" (Salazar, 1991, p. 61). Denying young people influence consigns them to bland roles and single-storied identities (e.g., "at risk," "rebellious"). As Chimanda Adichie (2009) cautions during a TED talk:

> So that is how to create a single story. Show a people as one thing, as only one thing, over and over again, and that is what they become. . . . The single story creates stereotypes, and the problem with stereotypes is not that they are untrue, but that they are incomplete. They make one story become the only story. . . . The consequence of the single story is this. It robs people of dignity. . . . Stories matter. Many stories matter. Stories have been used to dispossess and to malign. But stories can also be used to empower and to humanize.

Gaps can be found in any problem account. Rather than picking up the carpenter's tools and spackle and sealing shut the cracks and crevices through which we might catch sight of new worlds and unexpected views of young people, we open them widely enough to fit through and see what wonderfulnesses await us on the other side. In this previously undetected space, the problem can be subverted.

Conclusion

A wonderfulness interview is meant from the outset to challenge the problem and to reveal young people as multistoried. Though it may take considerable effort, given the subordinated status young people have often grown accustomed to, we draw them to the center of deliberations and find them capable of intention and action. But first we must achieve an understanding of what it is they bring to the table. Once catalogued, their wonderfulnesses show how such endowments as honesty, courage, quick-wittedness, creativity, humor, compassion, and so on, can be applied to what has gone wrong. In consideration of young people and what they have in hand, we are now ready to turn our attention to the problem.

CHAPTER THREE

Meeting Problems in Wonderland

Problems in Wonderland are made up in very different guises than they are in a world where pathologies vie for the lead with their "doctored" language and padded prescriptions. On the other side of the looking glass, they can appear altogether transfigured, not unlike the chimeras and apparitions encountered by young heroes in classic tales. Think of your own favorite storybook characters and the proving grounds on which they find themselves. Who awaits them in a faraway land—a wicked witch, an evil queen, a dreadful giant, or a dreaded pirate with a foreboding hook for a hand? In children's literature, it is often the antagonist who is most memorable. As readers, we are enthralled by their charismatic personalities, sordid histories, and contemptible schemes. Their place in the story not only draws us in, but also establishes the terms by which young protagonists must make their reputations. Thanks are due, in large part, to the reprehensible pirate, James Hook, for *Peter Pan*'s acclaimed ranking. Captain Hook is made menacing "with his flourish, his poses, his dreaded diabolical smile! That ashen face, those blood-red lips, the long, dank, greasy curls; the sardonic laugh, the maniacal scream, the appalling courtesy of his gestures" (Hanson, 2011, p. 25). Add a full measure of murderous intent and we are primed to meet Peter at his very best, in epic battle, a defender of lost boys, and forever our young hero.

In therapy, we would do young people a disservice to domesticate problems by draining them of dynamism or underestimating their capacity to frighten and befuddle. It is the colossal size of problems, along with their cunning plots, that warrant heroic and noble responses by young champions. If we are to achieve maximum engagement on the parts of children, little is to be gained by supplanting what their imaginations would provide with such contrivances as sweeping generalizations and standardized treatment plans. Instead, we look up from the data, wipe our eyes clear of color-coded brain scans, and greet problems with our own sense of wonderment (e.g., "What on earth could this be?"). And when we do, we catch sight of problems parading in all sorts of get-ups.

Envision 9-year-old Lexy refusing to eat and complaining of exhaustion and dizziness. Her mother explains, "Lexy is worried about getting sick. We've all just had the flu, but I told her, it's a virus and has nothing to do with the food being spoiled." Lexy wants to believe her mother, but she simply cannot. It is as if she is under a spell! Could it be? Is she spellbound? Might this brand of Worry know wizardry? Lexy looks up, her interest piqued. "I know," she blurts out, "It's Wizzy! It's a cross between Worry and Dizzy!" Think of her mother's renewed faith, and Lexy's sense of urgency to break Wizzy's spell now that she knows what—and who—she is dealing with.

Picture a problem like the Bug getting under the skin of 7-year-old Berto and creeping along muscle and sinew before finally reaching his fingertips. Imagine it using his finger and thumb as tiny pincers, pulling at his full head of hair as if of its own volition. Before long, it has torn out clumps, leaving an odd patchwork. Upon further scrutiny, we discover that the Bug is jealous of Berto's lush black tresses, seeing as how, like most bugs, it is completely bald except for an unruly hair or two darting every which way. The Bug could not tolerate the sight of his shiny mane. At difficult points in Berto's life (e.g., his parents' divorce, when his mother traveled for work, when his father's impatience showed), the Bug would crawl into his thoughts, tempting him with sweet-sounding words: "Pull at your hair. You've got plenty anyway. It will make you feel better and much

Meeting Problems in Wonderland 51

calmer, too." But this, we discovered, was a lie born of the problem's jealousy.

Visualize Unfairness enlisting 10-year-old Phillip in daily surveillance, noting any occasion when either his sister or brother is the beneficiary of an offering or privilege, large or small, that has not been extended to him in equal measure. Consider the hollering that ensues each time Unfairness convinces Phillip that he is being cheated or overlooked by someone in the family. These are crimes, Unfairness maintains, that call for severe punishment. And so Unfairness sends him into a rage, seeking retribution, all the while convincing him that he is on a righteous path. Imagine it leaving him with nothing but the empty promise that his devotion to constant monitoring will eventually pay off. Someday, he will be proven entirely right and all others wrong.

Finally, imagine Comparison showing up in the life of 12-year-old Patty, disguising itself as her new friend and mentor. To this point, Patty had been content with her books and the solitude she coveted, along with time spent in the company of childhood friends and family. She had little interest in such trifles as fashion and cool crowds ... or so she thought. Almost without warning, her contentment turns to self-contempt. Under the guidance of Comparison, it is the people and clothes she collects, rather than the ideas she confects, that matter most. It is as if, in an instant, name brands, accessories, and popular friends become the gauge by which her worth is measured. Comparison makes her body conscious and critical of her newfound faults. Boys supplant books as her great interest, and her hungry mind, which was previously insatiable, seems to have lost its appetite. The constant preoccupations that Comparison fuels become her paltry food for thought. It draws freely on images from popular culture to degrade Patty for lacking the essential qualities that connote a young woman of value—things she can only long for but never attain (at least that is what Comparison would have her believe).

Young people cross paths with a range of problems, including those that can heat them up when they might hope to keep their cools. Others can terrify in the dark hours, leaving children drenched and drained by morning. Still others can lead them down a path of trouble. And whenever they can, problems recruit parents and caregivers, ushering them down roads of professional appraisal (e.g., evaluation and diagnosis) where the terms of engagement are impressive enough to declare young people powerless. As a colleague warned DM upon sending a mother and son his way, "It is impossible to successfully resolve trichotillomania without the use of medication." DM had no doubt she was right. A young person would indeed be hard pressed to address such a psychiatric disorder, let alone pronounce its name—but dealing with the Bug would prove an entirely different matter.

Bringing Problems Within Young People's Range

Problems often demonstrate a capacity to overwhelm, but we can reduce their bewildering effects by seeking them out in a realm where young people's imaginations are poised to greet them. In our meetings with children, problems are divested of their sashes and gowns and dispossessed of their rank in the ivory tower. At the start of such an endeavor, the therapist may have to contribute considerably to get the imaginative ball rolling and to assure the young person that she or he is vital to such an undertaking. Problems may be spied on by all concerned in order to discover their motives and the means by which they engage in their own brand of mayhem at young people's and families' expense (White, 2007). Still, it is assumed that young people will be most gifted at recognizing their schemes. Consider the following discussion between DM, 7-year-old Berto, and Berto's mother, Alma, in which the Bug is exposed as the actual culprit for all its ill intent. DM aims to unmask the problem in a spirit that always keeps it within range of Berto's worldview and imaginative powers.

> **Alma**: People love his hair, and you should have seen it before he started pulling at it.
> **DM**: What was it like? You don't have a picture, do you?

Alma: I might. (She takes out her smartphone and begins scrolling through images.) Here's a good one. Look at the difference. And just look at his curls. (She hands it over to DM.) People used to stop him on the street just to tell him . . . (She trails off.)

DM: Oh my! Beautiful. Berto, is it true? Do people love your hair? (DM is genuinely struck by the photograph.)

Berto: They used to.

DM: Did people tell you so?

Berto: Yes.

DM: What would they say?

Berto: That I have beautiful hair.

Alma: It wasn't just his long black curls. It's the way they framed his eyes and face. Of all things, I don't know what's gotten into him. I've asked him a hundred times—what is it!? (She looks at him plaintively. Berto looks away.)

DM: Is your mom right? Is it like something's gotten into you?

Berto: I don't know. (He seems removed, or perhaps embarrassed, and besides, this is an ill-advised question and understandably beyond his reach.)

Alma: I understand his life could be easier. Who's taking him to school in the morning? Who's picking him up . . . where he's sleeping on which weekend. . . .

Berto: Yeah, because my parents got divorced (looking at DM).

DM: Are you shifting back and forth between your mom's house and your dad's?

Berto: Uh-huh.

DM: Has life gotten twice as complicated with two houses to go to?

Berto: Yeah, but it's always been that way.

Alma: We were divorced when he was a baby. (Turning to Berto) You weren't even 2.

Berto: I don't remember.

DM: How do you deal with going back and forth?

Berto: It kind of bugs me, because just when I get used to being at my dad's, I have to come back to my mom's. Or if I am at my mom's, then I have to put everything in my backpack again and go to my dad's.

Alma: And, of course, sometimes he forgets things. That's a whole other story. Let's just say we do a lot of driving.

DM: That does sound complicated, living in two houses and going back and forth, unpacking, packing up, and then unpacking again.

Berto: Yeah. It really bugs me.

DM: Does it bug you a lot?

Berto: Yeah.

DM: A whole lot?

Berto: Yeah. (He can see DM's up to something.)

DM: Hey, Berto, did you ever hear the story about the boy who was so bugged by life that he turned into a bug? (Picking up threads such as "something's gotten into him," being "bugged," etc. and attempting to link ordinary words to an extraordinary realm, where Berto may be found ready and waiting.)

Berto: No! (He appears taken aback by the very idea, but perhaps also intrigued, as if he may know a thing or two about passing into this realm. One thing is clear though. He is now interested.)

DM: Yep. And do you know what he does now that he's a bug?

Berto: What? (Showing interest in knowing the answer, not unlike a young reader anxious to turn the page to find out what happens next.)

DM: He crawls inside boys and girls and bugs them. He gives them itchy fingers and toes, and scratches their foreheads, not on the outside, but from the inside. And only sometimes, when he's done all the bugging a bug can do in one day, and if he's completely satisfied and in a very good mood, he tickles their tummies—from the inside, of course.

Berto: No, he doesn't! (Laughing, but offering an authoritative response.)

DM: Well, do your fingers or toes ever itch?

Berto: (Laughing) Yeah.

DM: And does it ever feel like your tummy is being tickled from the inside?

Berto: No!

DM: Let's have a look. (DM motions for him to come over, which he willingly does. DM takes his finger and runs it along Berto's right arm.) Are you right-handed?

Berto: Yeah.

DM: Yeah. There it is right now, headed for your fingertips! (Berto squeals with delight and pulls his arm away. It is clear that he feels at home with this form of play.)

DM: Well, it's just a story. But is it like you're being bugged a lot by a bug, and with a life that's pretty complicated? (Moving from the indicative, and what is, to the subjunctive, and what is imaginable.)

Berto: Yeah.

DM: I'm wondering, Berto, could it be (speaking in a low hush) . . . could it be that it's been the Bug all along that's been getting you to tug at your hair? I don't know if—

Berto: It's the Bug! It's the Bed Bug! (He shouts, appearing exhilarated and in harmony with this sort of imaginative enterprise.)

DM: The Bed Bug?! How do you know it's the Bed Bug and not just any kind of bug?! (DM is excited that Berto has stepped in to claim authorship rights over the problem by altering it. From this moment forward, he will turn to Berto for knowledge about the problem's tricks, for while DM knew about the Bug, it is only Berto who knows about this particular species of bug.)

Berto: Because it happens when I'm in my room. (He is able to speak directly about the problem.)

DM: Does it happen when you're in your bed?

Berto: Uh-huh.

DM: Okay! So you know exactly what it is. (Rubbing his chin and playing along.)

Berto: (Assertively) I knew it was the Bed Bug, because that's where it lives. (Berto seems to be stepping into greater authorship in regard to the developing story.)

DM: How did you know that's where the Bed Bug lives? (DM is genuinely curious.)

Alma: Sometimes when I say goodnight I'll tell him, "Don't let the bed bugs bite," don't I? (They all laugh.)

Berto: Yeah.

DM: Right. So Berto, what else do you know about the Bed Bug? Does it promise you anything, like you'll feel better, or that life will be better if you just . . .? (Attempting to map the problem.)

Berto: That I'll feel better. (He answers boldly.)

DM: And is the Bed Bug telling the truth? Is it helping you?

Berto: Umm . . . (He may be momentarily confounded, as if this is something new to consider.)

DM: Does it promise to make you feel better? Does it say it can make things easier? (DM is speculating about the problem's tactics.)

Berto: Yeah!

DM: And does the Bed Bug come through? Does it keep its promises?

Berto: What? (Perhaps the question needs reshaping.)

DM: Is the Bed Bug telling you the truth? Does it make you feel better?

Berto: No! It's a liar. (Stated with moral authority. He seems prepared now to assess the problem.)

DM: How do you know?

Berto: Because I don't like the way my hair looks now. (He may have found the freedom to speak about his hair with the blame coming off his shoulders and being reassigned to the Bed Bug.)

DM: Gosh, Berto. Thanks for sharing that with me. I really appreciate it. Would you call what it is doing a trick, or a dirty trick, or something else?

Berto: A trick! (Said with conviction.)

DM: I guess that would be a trick. By the way, what kind of hair do you think the Bed Bug has? (DM attempts to further invigorate the conversation by making the problem more lifelike.)

Berto: It doesn't have any hair because it's a bug. (Berto takes over the narrative here. Alma and DM are both caught off guard by this clever comment.)

DM: What do you think the Bed Bug wants to do with all the hair it stole from you?

Berto: It wants to glue it on his head. (Berto appears thrilled with this realization and with himself. They all laugh. The counterstory is gaining momentum.)

DM: Do you think the Bed Bug was planning all along to trick you and steal from you?

Berto: I won't let it! (Said with considerable bravado. He appears intentional.)

DM: Oh gosh. I just thought of two questions. Should I ask them together, or one at a time?

Berto: One at a time.

DM: Of course. Now that I think about it, it's impossible to ask two questions at once. Okay. Question number one: What would the Bed Bug say that a 7-year-old boy should do if he's really upset about something, and he's in his bed, all tucked in?

Berto: What's the second question?

DM: Question number two: If the Bed Bug isn't bugging you and you're just deciding on your own, what do you think a 7-year-old boy ought to do if he's really upset about something?

(DM wonders if asking less directly might afford room for reflection.)

Berto: Talk to his mom or dad about it.

DM: How come, Berto? Why talk to them instead of listening to the Bed Bug?

Berto: Because they love me and the Bed Bug is just a bug. (He personalizes his response.)

Alma: That's right! You can always come to me and talk to me about anything. (Spoken in a heartfelt manner.)

DM: Do you think the Bed Bug thought you were just another kid all on his own who it could trick?

Berto: I'm not! (In such a simple utterance, Berto starts to redefine his moral identity as one that will no longer countenance a trick being played at his expense.)

DM: Do you have your own ideas about how to deal with the Bed Bug?

Berto: I'll tell it to go jump out of the window, or I'll step on it and squash it. (He stands up, lifting his leg and then bringing it down with force, and grinds his foot into the carpet to demonstrate what would happen if he and the Bed Bug ever crossed paths.)

Alma: Why don't we wash your sheets and blankets when we get home? What do you think? (Joining in the spirit.)

Berto: Can I get new sheets? (He smiles at his mother.)

Alma: First things first. Let's start by throwing the Bed Bug into the washer and dryer. (She shoots him a playful look.)

Berto: Yeah, we'll get his mouth full of soap! (Laughing and returning her look.)

Berto's imagination soared as he detailed a plan of action with ease, having no shortage of ideas now that the terms for the problem's reform have been reinvented.

We will leave any further discussion of young people's responses to problems for Chapter 4. For now, we will simply say that both Alma and DM assisted Berto as he determined what was necessary in the way of a response to a problem as smug (and snug) as the Bed Bug. Even when problems find their way into young people's lives as a result of family conflict, children are never to be left out or simply treated as injured parties. While we make room for them to speak to their distress, we create equal opportunity for them to take decisive action founded on their own moral grounds. Rather than turning to parents and requiring that they alone handle matters, as if that were even possible, we count on everyone's engagement. But first, problems must be made fathomable to young people. Countering psychiatry's rationalization for a shared medical taxonomy to help professionals effectively name and address problems, we reserve a space for unique problem descriptions that give young people the vernacular edge.

Externalizing the Problem

We will speak to the practice of externalizing only briefly since this linguistic turn has been discussed at length in a number of published works (Freeman et al., 1997; Madigan, 1992; White & Epston, 1990; White & Morgan, 2006). Our interest in externalizing language represents more than technique. This semantic alteration allows for the potential establishment of at least two perspectives—one belonging to the problem and a second belonging to the person. At the very least, by virtue of externalizing, we bring to light the problem's agenda and make room for what may ultimately become known as the young person's counteragenda.

Once freed from the seductive pursuit of a single account of the problem and the sort of inquiry that would have us speaking to what is really going on, we can suspend our mountainous ascent, no longer convinced that the truth awaits us at the peak. We come down to the valleys and plains where knowledges are roughly equivalent and where one characterization of the problem, no matter its pedigree, cannot be taken for granted as ruling out another (Zimmerman & Dickerson, 1996). This is not to suggest, however, that we hold no preference. We are eager to traffic in the imaginary where there is nothing lost and much to be gained. As we move into fantastic realms, problems come alive and young people can be found exemplifying most persuasive and inspired dispositions (Epston & White, 1992).

Let us consider both internalizing and externalizing questions and their implications for the location of problems and the resulting narrowing or multiplying of perspectives.

Internalizing Questions

☐ Are you sad? Why are you sad? What (or who) is making you sad? Or the practitioner might avoid direct questioning, but still entertain the same concerns, wondering silently:
☐ Is she sad? Why is she sad? What (or who) is making her sad? The familiar design of these questions in making people and problems indistinguishable would likely be received as a natural way of thinking.

Externalizing Questions

☐ How does Sadness find its way in? Does it unpack its bags and stay the night or longer? Does it like bunk beds, or does it prefer snuggling right up to you? The unfamiliar design of these questions might leave one having to think twice before answering, but this is to be expected. Given the tendency to locate problems inside of people, such questions often require a moment's pause. Note how the internalizing questions would have us talking to a sad person, while the externalizing questions would have us talking to a person about Sadness. In the latter, there are two—the person and the problem—leading us to the by-now well-known adage:
☐ The person is not the problem. The problem is the problem. Having established the conditions for receiving young peo-

ple as uniquely gifted through the wonderfulness interview, we are careful not to collapse the space by means of internalizing language whereby people and problems would become one. We favor multiple expressions of identity over notions of a single self with internal conflicts.

Externalizing Rather Than Dividing Practices

Psychology has sliced and diced us in its untiring pursuit of essence. We have been split in two according to surface and depth and by expressions of the self that are either conscious or unconscious. Undaunted by Christianity's tripartite manifestation, Father-Son-Holy Spirit, Freud created psychology's "holy trinity" by dividing us against ourselves. The warring parties, id and superego, are best engaged in efforts at détente, brought to the negotiating table by the great mediator, the ego (Freud, 1930/1962). Nearly a century later, expressions of intrapsychic disharmony can be found in everyday parlance as we take note that "part of me feels one way, and part of me feels another," or when the self leases out space to "the child within." In any case, however we are partitioned, these characterizations aim to reveal "the architecture of man."

We are less inclined to join in an exploration of the structure of things, siding with one compartmentalizing claim over another. Instead, we are drawn to a performative account of identity (Denzin, 2003; Schechner, 1981), shaped by both actor and audience. Rather than ascertain or excavate internal pillars and posts, we engage in spontaneous and imaginative interplay that is creative, not archaic (Finley, 2011). In our practice, it is story development that shows us who we are, if not factually, then at least vividly. We are not after bedrock truth, but instead, a persuasive account that resonates. Externalizing language, employed in the service of problem exposé, contributes to this end by creating room for the young person to come forward—or come into being—as someone other than who the problem would portray (Winslade, 2009). See how such a space is created as the problem is personified:

1. Does it make sense that Sadness would show up given what you're going through?
2. Does Sadness ever try to get you down by keeping you all to itself?
3. How much of a place would you say Sadness deserves in your life?
4. How much of a place would Sadness lay claim to?

Note how questions 1 and 2 allude to two modes of living: the explicit mode according to Sadness and an implicit indication of life—and one's identity—apart from it (Carey, Walther, & Russell, 2009; White, 2000). In questions 3 and 4, Sadness is not automatically made out as an enemy, but instead something to consider allowing for, but only to the extent that the young person might deem suitable. Giving the problem limited position in relation to the young person rather than awarding it residency allows her or him to negotiate the terms of what has now become a relationship. This is in contrast to the problem enjoying all of the rights of ownership by virtue of occupancy. After all, let us not forget that possession is nine-tenths of the law.

As we pursue an understanding of the problem as separate, an opportunity arises for a response. This is made conceivable by externalizing language and the progressive widening of space between the young person and the problem. We begin by looking outward and finding evidence of problems in all sorts of places—under beds, in closets, tagging along to school, wedged in-between siblings in the back seats of cars, etc.). Importantly, it is problems, and never young people, that are objectified and placed under scrutiny. Even on those occasions when problems manage to temporarily sneak *inside*, misappropriating young people's imaginations or giving them itchy fingers and toes, they are never mistaken for the young people themselves.

The following questions demonstrate our commitment to externalizing language as a means of establishing separate grounds upon which preferred intentions can be realized. In each of the three pairings, question 1 is meant to create space by exposing the problem in all its intent, while question 2 offers a separate platform for possible action:

1. If Wizzy were the queen of your imagination instead of you, what would it decree about eating and what would it tell you about your mother's cooking? When everyone's sitting around the dinner table, where does Wizzy think you ought to be? Does Wizzy have ideas about the kind of relationship you should have with your mother and whether she should be trusted?
2. If Wizzy were not directing your imagination, and you were free to use it for your own enjoyment (Freeman et al., 1997), what could you imagine doing with it? If it were up to you and not Wizzy, how much trust would you think is wise to place in your mother?

1. If it were up to Unfairness, how would it spend your time and energy? How much value would it give to family?
2. Even when Unfairness isn't front and center, would you still agree with it that family is overrated? You wouldn't be the first person to leave family behind when you are old enough and rely on friends instead. But I'm not sure if that would be your idea or Unfairness's.

1. If Comparison were to look back over your life, what would it say was a complete and utter waste of your time? Looking ahead, what new interests would Comparison encourage you to adopt?
2. Can you recall what you treasured before Comparison came around? Would you chalk it up to immaturity and conclude that you are older and wiser now? If you think about it on your own terms, rather than Comparison's, what might you say is important in life?

It is in the contrast between the designs of the problem and the desires of the young person that new possibilities arise. The distance between the two can provide the space needed to reflect on the problem's impact and to take a moral position. It is often the case, when consulted about the problem's effects—provided that it has been sufficiently externalized and its motives exposed—that a young person takes issue with it. Ultimately, this may depend on what was revealed in the wonderfulness interview and whether the young person's merits will fortify their resistance to the problem's entreaties.

The Benefit to Caregivers

Externalizing problems with parents and caregivers can be equally beneficial (Freeman et al., 1997; Madsen, 2007). Problems such as Guilt, Failure, Frustration, and Disrespect can gnaw at parents, call their characters into question, and put them at odds with their daughters and sons. Externalizing conversations can preserve and restore the reputations of parents by reacquainting them with their best intentions. In contrast to psychology's long-held penchant for parent blame, and especially mother blame, we hold a commitment to parents that is equal in every way to our allegiance to young people. They are welcomed into conversation and trusted to possess the heart and will to unite with their daughters and sons in addressing any problem that comes their way—or comes between them. The following questions illustrate how parents' aims can be distinguished from those of problems.

1. Does Guilt keep a record of your most regrettable moments as a mother? Does it haul the list out at the most inopportune times to try and discredit you?
2. When you shine your own light on the past, instead of Guilt spotlighting it, does it look any different? What do you see in the way of your efforts as a mother that Guilt would have to blind you to?

1. What would Disrespect have you do if you were faced with disobedience (e.g., if your instructions were blatantly ignored)?
2. If Disrespect called for a stern response, would you be on board? If you did not adopt the attitudes Disrespect would recommend (e.g., a preference for authority, domination), what mood would you hope to find yourself in?

Who Is Responsible for the Problem?

If we externalize problems, aren't we discouraging responsibility? This is a frequently posed question. In fact, we would suggest the opposite is the case. We conceive of responsibility as having less to do with accepting blame for what has gone wrong (e.g., "You need to take responsibility for what you've done!") than with taking the initiative to intervene where problems occur. When we externalize, young people can observe problems, evaluate them from a distance, and assume positions as moral agents (versus guilty parties). When we ask, "Is the problem right or wrong in leading you down this path?" instead of "Are you right or wrong in heading down this path?" there is less risk of incrimination. Young people are free to join in deliberation, whereby they may confront the problem on their own terms.

This is not to suggest that there is no place for blame. Calling someone out for destructive behavior may very well be a principled act in the name of justice. But blame can be distinguished from responsibility in how it would apprehend young people at their worst, while responsibility is made possible by engaging people at their best. In a call to blame, little is needed of the person at fault beyond her or his availability for censure. And it is a good thing since, at our worst, we tend to be capable of very little. Blame rarely fosters much in the way of a response beyond confession, or worse, anger and defensiveness. Under the aegis of blame, our connection to compassion is faint and any higher aspiration may be put beyond reach. Even a simple request for an apology (e.g., "The least you can do is apologize!") can be vexing and produce an inferred bitterness as the accused spits out the phrase, "I'm sorry!" Responsibility is not typically achieved by means of confrontation. Such an approach puts the confronter's values on display, while the confronted is caught red-handed, devoid of any salutary intent.

Responsibility involves intention that must give way to action, while action that lacks intention can be more rote exercise than anything of a more meaningful nature. Connecting young people to the purposes of others simply will not do. If it is an intention hatched in the minds of adults and delivered from above, whether in the form of instruction or admonition, it is likely to enjoy little more than the half-life of a mayfly. It is the purpose behind action, born of reflection, that allows for a heartfelt response (White, 2011). And it is the intention, and the degree to which it is embodied, that makes responsible action sustainable.

In the following conversation with 9-year-old Brett and his grandmother, Peggy, the question of responsibility is taken up as Temper comes face-to-face with Brett's interest in the golden rule. With the use of externalizing questions, DM creates an opportunity for Brett to consider two potential roads and where each might lead.

> **Peggy**: I think he has good intentions but he's so impulsive he doesn't follow through when it comes to me and Abby. (Brett's younger sister by two years)
>
> **DM**: So, you don't think there's a problem with his intentions? Do you think his intentions are good?
>
> **Peggy**: (Nodding.)
>
>> (DM is keeping in mind Peggy's earlier description of Brett as kindhearted. This was illustrated in an initiative Brett devised to collect money for a community of orphaned children. This stood in stark contrast to a description of his temper.)
>
> **DM**: Do you think that Temper or something grabs hold of him ahead of his intentions? (Continuing to distinguish the problem's intentions from Brett's.)
>
> **Peggy**: I do.
>
> **DM**: (Turning to Brett) Is Temper faster than anything you could think up?
>
> **Brett**: I don't know.
>
> **DM**: You think . . . .
>
> **Brett**: Maybe it's a tie.
>
> **DM**: A tie? So you think you might be as fast as Temper?
>
> **Brett**: (Nodding.)

DM: So Temper's fast. . . .

Brett: Even though I get mad, I can slow Temper down and solve things.

DM: What kinds of problems are you interested in solving? (DM is careful not to steer the conversation in "the right direction.")

Brett: Maybe why some of my friends don't appreciate me like some of my other friends do. (Although he admits this, he seems embarrassed to have done so.)

DM: I know the feeling. (DM is quick to join him and spare him any possible humiliation.)

Brett: You do?

DM: Oh yeah, some friends seem to care more.

Brett: (He seems steadied.) My best friend, Charlie, he goes to my church. He's really, really nice to me.

DM: And other friends are less considerate or show less interest?

Brett: One of my friends who's not very considerate is my friend—almost not my friend—Giorgio. But another friend, Abra, treats me pretty well too.

DM: Abra?

Brett: Abra. He's from India. It's spelled A-B-R-A.

DM: A-B-R-A. He's from India. (Jotting it down accurately.)

Brett: He's really nice to me.

DM: He's really nice to you too. So you have two good friends—Charlie, your best friend, and Abra. . . .

Brett: And my third best friend, Gary, is really nice to me. G-A-R-Y.

DM: Yeah, I figured that one out.

Brett: (Laughing.)

DM: You seem to be able to spot niceness. (Giving attention to what may become known as a personally held value.)

Brett: Yeah.

DM: Do you have a pretty good eye for that?

Brett: (Nodding.) I can easily spot someone who's pretty nice.

(Brett goes on to explain how he can discern niceness in people who dress well and are polite. As he elaborates, DM wonders whether Brett's interest in niceness might provide him a vantage point from which to examine Temper's interests.)

DM: And this is probably going to be a ridiculous question but I'm getting the sense—you might tell me it's obvious—I'm getting the sense that you are more interested in niceness than meanness.

Brett: (Turns to look at his grandmother.)

DM: Why did you look at your grandma?

Brett: (Smiling shyly) She has the answer to that. . . . I do too. I'm more into niceness than meanness.

DM: I gather I've hit a nerve.

Brett: Often I am nice to people, but sometimes I can get a little upset.

DM: Is that when Temper takes the lead?

Brett: Yeah.

DM: Before Temper gets in the way, what is your interest in niceness? So far you've highlighted niceness in Charley, niceness in Abra, and niceness in Gary. Tell me about your interest in niceness. (Brett deserves a platform from which to describe what appears to be a genuine interest. It is especially important that he have the opportunity to affix his value, given that Temper would seem to have an interest in getting a fix on him.)

Brett: I like being nice to people and people being nice to me, because I follow the golden rule. (Brett may be giving expression to a value, though it is not yet clear if he is indicating a position of his own or merely echoing a hollow axiom taught to him by adults.)

DM: Tell me your version of the golden rule. Let's see if it matches up with what I think you're going to say.

Brett: (He seems hesitant. Perhaps he feels put on the spot.)

DM: Or should I tell it to you?

Brett: You can tell it to me.

Meeting Problems in Wonderland

DM: I'll give you two versions and you can tell me which one you're more interested in, or maybe you'll come up with your own version. (Brett nods in agreement.) One version of the golden rule would be: Do unto others as you would hope they do unto you. That's one version, and the other version—or maybe Temper's version would be, I'll only be nice to you if you're nice to me first.

Brett: A lot of my friends do that—the second one.

DM: And what about you? Which one interests you more?

Brett: (Thinking.)

DM: Or is that a tough question?

Brett: That's kind of a tough question. (It is not uncommon, once we have found our way into territories where problems have no permit, to find young people capable of moral deliberation. Here, Brett appears sincerely struck by the profound implications inherent in the first golden rule.)

DM: That's a tough one, yeah.

Brett: (Shifting in his seat.)

DM: I don't want to put you on the spot. Would you like to think it over?

Brett: Yeah, I'll think it over.

DM: Should we come back to it?

Brett: Yeah, I'll think about it. (This is stated earnestly.)

Contrary to popular conceptions of children, Brett appears no less able at age 9 to consider a question that confounds many adults, who can be heard bellowing at intimate partners, "If you don't want me to get mad, don't push my buttons!" This sentiment would seem to indicate a capacity for, or interest in, niceness, but only under ideal conditions in which they perceive themselves as being treated fairly. Under such circumstances it may be less a moral conviction that keeps them calm, and more their partners' willingness to manage Temper for them by treading lightly. For many adults, trying to hold onto niceness, even when provoked, may be more an aspirational goal than something attainable in any permanent sense. In any case, it is not something one comes to easily.

DM: I appreciate that—that you're willing to think it over, or think it over seriously. It's not an easy question. I guess it would be easy to fake it.

Brett: It would be easy to fake it, but I don't want to fake it.

DM takes Brett at his word and near the end of their first meeting returns to the question of the golden rule:

Brett: She makes unfair rules in the house (pointing to his grandmother).

DM: Okay, so this comes back to the golden rule. Should we come back to it and see if you're ready to piece it together? (DM is keen to see if Brett might apply himself to this difficult question.)

Brett: (Nodding.)

DM: So there's the one version of the golden rule: "I'd like to be nice to other people if only they would do things fairly"—that would be one way of putting it. And another way of putting it is, "I'd like to treat people the way that I would hope to be treated."

Brett: (Thinking.)

DM: In the first one, "You're making me act this way. I'm mad because you're forcing me into it . . . because you're screwing up so much." Are you with me so far?

Brett: (Nodding.)

DM: And in the second one, "Whether you're screwing up or not, I want to follow the golden rule. I want to be a nice person no matter what."

Brett: I want to follow the golden rule.

DM: That's a tall order—isn't it? You want to be nice no matter what? (Wanting to see to the strength of his conviction.)

Brett: I do that to my friend—my ex-friend, Adam.

Meeting Problems in Wonderland 71

DM: Yeah?

Brett: I tried to be nice to him but he still won't be my friend.

DM: And has it turned you mean?

Brett: No.

DM: You're nice anyway?

Brett: I'm still nice to him even if he doesn't want to accept me. (Brett appears to be carving out a moral position.)

DM: Why are you nice even if he's not being so nice?

Brett: Because I don't want to fall into his trap of making me mean.

DM: Is Temper making you fall into a trap with your grandma or your sister? Is it trying to turn you mean with your grandma or your sister? (DM is challenging Brett to identify his intention in the realm where Temper has often had the first say and the final word.)

Brett: I don't know. I don't know about that.

DM: Is it a fair question or is it the wrong question? (DM wants to be sure he hasn't gotten out in front of Brett or gotten in the way of his deliberative process.)

Brett: It's a fair question—I just don't know.

DM: Is it an interesting question? Is it a worthwhile question?

Brett: That is an important question.

DM: What's important about it?

Brett: That I make sure I'm not going to be mean just because of that. (He seems to be alluding to Temper.)

DM: It's important, huh?

Brett: It's important.

Though he may still be undecided, it would appear Brett has begun to consider where he might hope to stand in relation to Temper. He has also tentatively entered into negotiation with it, according to his own interest in niceness and as a reflection of what had been determined from the outset with respect to his kind heart. It is on such bases that a young person's character is further animated, a felt sense of responsibility is embodied, and opportunities for meaningful deliberation and action are revealed.

Conclusion

What if, instead of consulting children, we sent them out to waiting rooms when it is time to get down to business? Imagine young people being written (or charted) into story lines as patients or amateurs with no capacity to engage in their own methods of appraisal. Even if circumstances began to take a favorable turn, the ultimate credit would belong to the adults for having settled on the problem and effectively conditioned the young person's response. It is the consideration given to young people's interests and their inclusion or marginalization in therapy that can either set events in motion or grind them to a halt. Now that we have met the problem on imaginative and moral grounds, let us see what a little mischief can yield in the way of problem redress.

CHAPTER FOUR

Where's the Fun in It?

Fun is a highly valued and indispensable activity for children. Unlike adults, who attempt to schedule it around the main activities of their lives, most young people would prefer to give it central location. As parents know, it is no easy task explaining why all fun must be set aside when there is work to be done. When pressed, adults might be apt to recite a version of the maxim, "Life is not all fun and games," perhaps followed by a short sermon enumerating the greater merits of hard work. But why is work given privileged status, while fun must wait patiently for its turn? If we hope to engage children at their best, we might do well to seek them out in dispositions of mirth and mischief. While they are undoubtedly capable of solemn deliberation, fun can pay its own hefty dividend.

Time Is Money: The Language of Capitalism

Living in a capitalist economy that rewards industry, we are predisposed to discount the value of fun and instead attribute greater significance to productive endeavors. "Because play, in effect, produces nothing, neither material goods nor works of service, it is often described as basically empty, sterile, misspent or lost time, rather than as time well applied" (Meier, 1980, p. 27). It may be acceptable for certain groups like retirees to be the fun-loving sort, but only after they have earned the right to relax through years of sustained effort. Fun is justified in light of the dedication to work that preceded it. It is the fruits of one's labors that are to be savored with the understanding that such treats are made delectable by having been acquired through toil. The gratification that can be felt from fun, we are told, is much sweeter when it is delayed. But try pitching that concept to a young person.

This is not to say that adults do not appreciate children's interest in fun. Play is even encouraged as long as they have attended to work first (e.g., "Get your homework done and then you can play!"). Still, it is understood from an adult perspective that as young people mature they will waste less time, learn to appreciate the value of work, and sustain industrious efforts for lengthier periods. This kind of work training is considered necessary and in the best interests of children. How would they otherwise survive and ultimately thrive in the world if they did not learn to value work over play?

From an economic standpoint, fun has no bearing on performance reviews or other measures of productivity. At most, it provides respite from profitable or gainful pursuits. If given any value, it would be in the service of making possible new bursts of energy, resulting in greater focus and readiness to resume work. Or, in the case of children, value may be conferred on play if it serves the purpose of building and fortifying habits that are critical to healthy development. But this is an adult view. According to Rhonda Singer, when young people were asked about their interest in playing basketball, their answers were relatively straightforward:

> Not a single player said, "I started playing because I wanted to be socialized" or "because I wanted to learn the value of healthy competition and teamwork." These are adult reasons, the kind we give at coaches' meetings, in our talk with other adults, in our articles and pamphlets about the value of sport, and in our well-intended speeches to players. If you ask kids why they play, they are most likely to talk about how much fun it is. (2003, p. 207)

Young people's talent for fun is not wasted on us. We are careful to avoid configuring a work space and infusing it with professionally intoned knowledge. Though they arrive at our offices with the idea (usually someone else's) that they work something through, the opportunity to play their way there can hold greater appeal (Freeman et al., 1997). And so, we put on pause "the development and aggrandizement of the orderly and hard-working spirit" (Meier, 1980, p. 26) that is automatically embraced in most locales, in favor of a mischievous brand of fun—a neglected and undervalued endeavor in most professional contexts (Rieber, 1996).

Making Mischief in Everyday Life

You will remember that when we first meet young people, introductions are meant to bring their best foot forward. Sometimes, the talents we learn about take us in the direction of mischief, where children's spirit and creativity are on display. Young people often appear exalted by their mischief. Consider the irresistible satisfaction that Matilda, the heroine in the eponymous Roald Dahl novel, must feel while exacting revenge (by mischievous means) upon the cretinous figure who is her poor excuse for a father:

> Now, in the early morning privacy of the bathroom, Matilda unscrewed the cap of her father's OIL OF VIOLETS and tipped three-quarters of the contents down the drain. Then she filled the bottle up with her mother's PLATINUM BLONDE HAIR-DYE EXTRA STRONG. She carefully left enough of her father's original hair tonic in the bottle so that when she gave it a good shake the whole thing still looked reasonably purple. She then replaced the bottle on the shelf above the sink, taking care to put her mother's bottle back in the cupboard. So far so good. (1988, p. 59)

Disclaimer: Make no mistake that in our work with young people we do not encourage harmful brands of mischief at parents' expense.

Instead, it is problems that find themselves on the receiving end of such antics.

Young people can be found dreaming up mischief even when there is no apparent reason for it or identifiable antagonist. Any parent knows all too well, all you have to do is leave two children alone for a few minutes to get them rolling. Still, it might never occur to adults that these same talents can be relied on in overcoming onerous problems. Listen in, as we happen upon the tail end of an ordinary conversation between a young sister and brother, who are roughly 7 and 5 years old, in a Studio City, California, café:

> **Brother**: You launch her but she's unbreakable.
>
> **Sister**: I want to invent a potion.
>
> **Brother**: Okay, I'm going to think of another one.
>
> **Sister**: You have to have a certain food in your inventory and you launch it at somebody.
>
> **Brother**: Like a potato? (He seems to be getting the gist.)
>
> **Father**: Less talking, more eating! (Having arrived moments earlier.)
>
> **Sister**: That doesn't make sense. Less eating, more talking! (A shrewd retort.)
>
> **Brother**: Ooh. I got one! Invisible water balloons. (He maintains the spirit of innovation.)
>
> **Sister**: Yeah, and when you launch it, it hits the person but they don't know what's going on, because it's invisible. (She is on an inventive track that requires more attention before anything else, even the tempting grilled cheese sandwich that sits before her, can be considered.)
>
> **Brother**: I lost my tooth last night.
>
> **Father**: (Joining the conversation.) You lost a baby tooth. An adult tooth is going to come in and replace it. You'll have the new tooth your whole life. (He goes on to explain the difference between baby teeth and the permanent teeth that

come in behind them. This is the kind of rational dialogue he appears to have a greater talent for. The children listen dutifully.)

To the father, the plans undertaken by his daughter and son may have seemed like nonsense, thereby lacking any substantive value. After all, what good could come from launching potatoes and invisible water balloons? But we have found it is just these sorts of plans and conversational threads that can weave a rich tapestry in therapy, and sometimes even a flying carpet.

Mischief seems to emerge from a blend of imagination in full flight and irreverence on the part of the child. Perhaps such irreverence arises from a developing understanding of adult-made conventions and children's talents for flouting them: "Children's games challenge the world of adults, punctuating the pompous shams of authority through play" (Chaudry-Fryer, 1995, p. 320). An "emancipatory laughter" (McKenzie, 2005) escapes young people's lips as hierarchy is disrupted and the top position becomes theirs. The social activist and scholar Kembrew McLeod, himself a prankster, traces the creative inspiration for the Apple computer back to Steve Jobs's and Steve Wozniak's early efforts at mischief making. Before they ever conceived of engineering a device as complex as a PC, they engineered pranks: "Jobs started in elementary school, where he countered his boredom by making 'Bring Your Pet To School Day' posters. 'It was crazy,' he recalled, 'with dogs chasing cats all over, and the teachers were beside themselves'" (McLeod, 2014, p. 9).

Parents can be caught by surprise as they are sometimes the intended audience and target of such mischief and, for that reason, young people's delight can be spontaneous and infectious. Picture 7-year-old Lucy placing a plastic spider on her father's pillow, carefully remaking the bed, and then lying in wait. Upon hearing him shriek, she jumps out from behind the curtain, squealing with excitement and asking wide-eyed, "Did I scare you, Daddy? I mean, did I *really* scare you, or were you just pretending?" Young people relish these rare "rituals of reversal" (Turner, 1969) when power is subverted and the higher ground is seized, if only momentarily. Children set the trap and wait impatiently for adults to enter the scene as unwitting foils, wholly unprepared.

Assuming their pranks stay within the realm of good-natured fun, young people can be recognized for their mischief. In contrast to a case of misdeeds, most parents recall stories of mischief with pride and pleasure. Because of the entertainment value associated with mischief making, relatives and family friends often seek these youngsters out for further accounts ("Have you been up to any mischief lately?"), perhaps because "there is vicarious pleasure in watching him break the rules, and potentially fruitful fantasizing, too, for listeners are invited, if only in imagination, to scout the territory that lies beyond the local constraints" (Hyde, 1998, p. 12). It is at the edges, far beyond the bureaucratic bounds of goals, skill building, homework, and hierarchies, where life becomes animated.

An inversion of roles is frequently found in children's literature. Dr. Seuss knew when he wrote, "PAT CAT, Pat sat on cat" (Dr. Seuss, 1991) for toddlers, that they would already be poised to take in the action with full recognition of the value to be found in such larks. And for those more accomplished in mischief, he delivered his magnum opus, *The Cat in the Hat* (Dr. Seuss, 1985), in which the titular Cat turns what had been an orderly household upside down. He is found balancing goldfish bowls on the handles of umbrellas and even birthday cakes atop his top hat—tilting precariously to one side and then the other. And while Sally and her brother suffered anxious moments in anticipation of their mother's imminent return, we can be certain that devoted readers, sitting at a safe distance from any impending calamity or consequence, experience no such ambivalence and recognize immediately the pleasure to be had in such an indecorous occasion. And was there ever really a Cat in the Hat? Or was he conjured up one rainy afternoon, the property of two bored children who tumbled into their very own wonderland and applied their imaginations to mischief making?

A Proposal for Making Mischief at the Problem's Expense

What if we were to see young people as intentional and their mischief as admissible to venues conventionally established for the diagnosis and treatment of problems? And what if we sought to mobilize everyone to follow suit and engage the problem in the same spirit for the purpose of undermining it? Because this spirit is aligned with the most enthralling imaginative play a young person has been known to undertake, it is likely she or he may be at the forefront of such an endeavor. After all, mischief is one of the first arenas of young people's lives in which they are acknowledged for something that might be considered their intellectual property. The following story illustrates how a serious problem can be met with such inspiration (Freeman et al., 1997).

Harry, a 4½-year-old boy, was brought to meet with DM following a disturbing incident. He had been frightened outside his prekindergarten classroom by four older boys who knocked him down and threatened to beat him up. Harry escaped unscathed but was reluctant to return to school, preferring instead to keep close to home, never venturing far from his mother's or father's side. Two weeks passed during which time he grew more fitful, attending school only when accompanied by one parent or the other. His father, Morris, explained in an initial e-mail,

> He's been very stuck with asking over and over again if he has to go back and doesn't seem calmed by us saying we will help the bad feelings go away. I think now he's having anticipatory anxiety, possibly more afraid of the feelings he may have when at school than any of the initial fears of the boys who scared him.

In order to help him regain his confidence, Harry's parents and teacher made every conceivable effort on his behalf, speaking with the parents of the guilty parties, designing a safety plan, assuring Harry that he would be all right, reminding him how much fun he used to have at school, keeping laughter in the house, and, beyond all of this, attending to him in innumerable loving ways. The passive recipient of such soothing efforts, Harry was momentarily comforted, even becoming temporarily brave, but before long found himself overcome by Fear once again. With each step forward, Fear spun him about and marched him back to square one.

As the days passed, Fear began taking hold of the adults who loved him. They wondered, "Is there something we should be doing that we haven't thought of?" They felt discouraged, and worse, they were sure they were failing Harry. As they came together for a first meeting, it was DM's intention to see if Harry could be found in relation to the bravery and fun that seemed, if not entirely banished from his life, like kindly relatives who rarely visited anymore. He would need to assist Harry in traversing the space from dependence (where he appeared ill equipped to take on life's challenges) to a counterworld, where he might find himself a most formidable figure, his mind awakened to new possibilities.

At the start of their first meeting, Harry was friendly, if slightly wary. He seemed to appreciate his parents taking the first turn and providing DM with an initial impression. In response to DM's interest, they listed with ease Harry's many talents and ideals.

> **Evie**: He's funny. He has good dance moves. He's creative. He has an excellent vocabulary. He's good at rhyming . . . (If not for Morris chiming in, there was every indication Evie could have easily continued.)
>
> **Morris**: (Joining in with pride) He's smart, he's good at sports and hitting a baseball, he's goodhearted, he's kind, he likes to do nice things for people, he's aware, and he has a good memory.
>
> **DM**: Gosh, where to start—I've always loved good dancers. I grew up watching Fred Astaire movies as a boy, but that was a hundred years ago. What kind of dance moves are kids doing today, Harry? Do they have a name, or are the ones you do your own original moves?
>
> **Harry**: They're my own. (He states this without bluster.)

DM: Is it too soon to ask you to show me a few? Should I wait until I know you a little better?

Harry: Yeah. (He appears understandably cautious.)

DM: And what is it about Harry's mind and the way he uses it that tells you he's smart? (DM needs to learn more about Harry's gifts. He knows from experience there is no telling which among them will prove most useful as they turn to face the problem.)

Morris: He's already an amazing reader. And he follows adult conversations and can join in on a range of topics. (Morris goes on to further substantiate his claim of Harry's intelligence with stories about school assignments and his advanced vocabulary. Both Evie and Morris respond with ease and provide supporting evidence for their abounding claims about Harry. Before long they are fortified and ready to turn their attention to the problem. But first they revisit the story of the disturbing events on that unfortunate schoolyard day . . . and more.)

Morris: Harry's been through a lot in a short period. We don't think it's just about what the four boys did. We talked to their parents, and they're not going to bother Harry again. We've seen to that. There are other things he's had to adjust to. I returned to work recently. His best friend, Isaac, got sick about a month ago, and we're hoping he's going to be okay. And we go out weekends, lately, without him, on Mommy and Daddy date nights and he has a babysitter, which he's still getting used to.

DM: Wow, that does sound like a lot. I'm sorry to hear about your friend Isaac. (Turning to Harry. He looks down.) Did all of this happen in a short period of time? And is that when Fear came knocking? Is your dad right, Harry? Was it a lot all at once that seemed to bring Fear into your life? (DM relies on externalizing language to separate Harry from the problem.)

Harry: Yeah.

DM: With everything I'm beginning to understand about what you've been through, Harry—the four mean boys at school and Isaac's illness—I suppose it would be enough to bring Fear into anyone's life. (DM is careful to acknowledge that Harry, even at 4½ years of age, is no less subject to real stresses than anyone twice his age, or 10 times his age for that matter. He would never want to diminish Harry by minimizing or overlooking the difficulty of his situation.)

DM: Has Fear stolen fun from your life, Harry? Has it tried to get you to stop dancing and running fast and jumping high and having fun?

Harry: I can still run fast! (This is stated with enthusiasm.)

DM: You can? (DM is taken aback by what might be an act of defiance by Harry in the face of the problem.)

Harry: Do you want to see?

DM: I'd love to see. (In mapping the effects of the problem, we are bound to discover the limits of its reach and, importantly, the areas it has not yet intruded upon that are still reserved for people's own influence [White & Epston, 1990; Winslade & Monk, 2007]. In this instance, Harry asserted his right to run, thereby precluding Fear from giving him the runaround.)

(Harry opens the office door, which leads to a short hallway, and with little warning, runs down the hallway and back.)

DM: That *was* fast—only, could you do it again so I can time you? (DM sees that Harry is emboldened and wants to prolong the moment.)

Harry: Yeah. (He leans forward, readying himself.)

DM: Ready? Go! (Harry speeds to the end and back, not a long distance.)

DM: Five seconds!

Harry: Do it again! (DM complies, asking Harry to hold on until the second hand reaches the top of the dial.)

DM: Ready? Go! (He runs even faster.) Four seconds! (Harry seems satisfied with his time. In fact, to this day it remains a record for the Miracle Mile Community Practice hallway. He jumps back on the couch with his mom and dad. Harry appears invigorated by his feat—and by his feet. He had arrived at the meeting in good enough spirits but is now enlivened. DM wonders if he is prepared to address the problem.) Harry, your dad told me in a note he sent that you already had a couple of ideas for dealing with Fear before we even met. He told me how one time you used your bravery to get rid of Fear, and then how another time you told Fear to get lost. And what I'd like to know is, how'd you do it, Harry? How did you come up with these ideas? And how do you still manage to have fun and run, which you proved right here today in my office? (DM underscores actions Harry has already taken in order to challenge any single-storied account of him as helpless.)

Harry: I just did it.

DM: The thing is, Harry, isn't Fear sneakier than that? If it were up to Fear, wouldn't it decide kids should have no fun at all—that they should spend all their time at home keeping Fear company, maybe even dreaming about Fear while they're sleeping, and listening to it first thing in the morning when they wake up? (DM attempts to arouse an image of a personified problem who is up to no good. He had been clued in by Morris and Evie that these were some of the very effects Fear was having on Harry's life.)

Harry: No! (He shouts this indignantly.)

DM: Has Fear ever tried to sneak into your dreams, Harry? Does it wake you up in the morning instead of your mom and dad and tell you it's going to be a bad day?

Harry: (He says nothing at first, appearing to have a germ of an idea, and then suddenly stands straight up and begins to speak.) You know what we could do?! We could . . .

At that point, DM had to hold onto his seat with one hand while writing as fast as he could with the other. He was heard repeatedly asking Harry to slow down, unable to keep up as Harry fired off one idea after another, each intended to exile Fear. The following e-mail, sent to Harry the next day, summarizes their first encounter, including a record of his inspired plans. Whether sooner or later—and in this case it was admittedly sooner than DM was accustomed to—we can expect mischief to make an appearance. It is a matter of establishing the therapy office as both a welcoming site for fun and an inhospitable venue for Fear and for the professional claims it might foster.

To Harry and the "Harricanes,"

It was super great to meet you all today. I knew from our phone conversation that I was going to be meeting with a 4½-year-old boy with a good mind, but I had no idea just how good his mind was going to be. Harry, your dad told me that you'd already come up with two good "team Harricane" ideas on your own before we even met:

1. Telling Fear to get lost
2. Getting your bravery to kick Fear out of your life

But when I saw you put your mind to work in my room, I couldn't believe how many good ideas you came up with—so many ideas in less than an hour. I took notes but my hand couldn't keep up with your mind. Hey, Harry, is your mind faster than Fear, too? Your mind was certainly faster than me. Here is a list of what I was able to get down. Could you write me back with your parents' help and let me know what I missed?

3. Creating a plane-box to send Fear flying away from your life
4. Shooting Fear out of a cannon across the ocean and onto an island with pirates
5. Putting a button on Fear to turn it into a flag
6. Making Fear false hair so someone will take it and put it on someone else's head
7. Putting Fear in a tissue box

Harry, did I get these right? Or did I mess something up? Please help me and correct any mistakes I made.

Where's the Fun in It?   **85**

I asked your mom and dad to tell me 10 wonderful things about you. It was so easy for them to think of 10 things and they even thought of not just 10, but 11. They told me about:

1. How funny you are
2. Your good dance moves
3. How creative you are
4. Your excellent vocabulary
5. How good you are at rhyming
6. How smart you are
7. How good you are at sports and at hitting a baseball
8. What a good heart you have and how kind you are (I guess this is two things)
9. How you like to do nice things for people
10. How aware you are
11. How you have a good memory

I know you are using your mind to outsmart Fear. Tell me, Harry, are you planning on using any of your other talents and special qualities from this list to deal with it?

For example:

- Have you ever used your sense of humor to cheer Fear up, or would it refuse to laugh?
- Have you ever used your vocabulary and talent with words to say things to Fear that would make it give up and leave you alone?
- Have you ever used your ability at sports to run faster or jump higher than Fear and leave it far behind?
- Have you ever used your kindness to teach Fear a lesson in how to be good Fear rather than bad Fear?

Good luck this week, Harry.
Your friend, David
P.S. Just one last question. Now that we've had a meeting and are putting our heads together to kick Fear out of your life so you can grow up and be

a big boy, does this mean that I get to join in and become an official Harricane (a member of Harry and the Harricanes) myself and part of this incredible team?

In spite of his efforts to be a faithful scribe, DM knew he was inadequate to the task and made himself answerable for any errors. Harry, like anyone delivering dictation on an important topic, valued his own creative input enough to see to it that every detail was in its proper place. Now authorized to entertain his own ideas as a valued form of knowledge, Harry had more than a thing or two to say in response to DM's e-mail. With Evie's help, he provided necessary guidance:

Dear David,
    Thank you for your letter. You made two mistakes, so please correct these. This is Harry.
    Please push the button on fear to turn it into an EAGLE. (This is a correction for number 5.)
    Number 6 should be: Make a statue of me with fake hair so the fear will think it's me and go to that statue, but it's not me, it's just a statue of me.
    Your letter made me smile and I need to bring it to school cause it's gonna help other kids with their fears. They don't even know what a fear fighter is!
    By the way, you are definitely part of Team Harricane, and I am part of Team Harricane. I'm Harry.
    Bye Bye. See you next time. If you need any help, then call up the police or Harry. Bye.
See you Soon.
Harry

We see Harry undertaking the work, or perhaps more pointedly, the play involved in addressing the problem. What is most salient about these ideas is that they are of Harry's own making. Though he was actively supported in ways that speak to the collaborative nature of

Where's the Fun in It?

this approach, he was drawn to the center of the action where his skills were recognized as most salient. It was his brand of knowledge that was accorded full value. We have learned from young people that if we do our part by removing a few props from the rostrum of canonized knowledge and resetting the scene for the performance of their scholarship, they too can assume the role of lead instructor, less with the weight of pressure or expectations and more with a sense of opportunity.

DM encountered an emboldened young protagonist once Harry had come to know that it was his range of talents that were pivotal. They all met again two weeks later, but not before DM had received the following e-mail from Morris:

David,

Thank you so very much for your wonderful way of talking with us and Harry. He really connected with you as you could likely tell. Harry went to school all day today without his mom there. He had a little fear in the evening, and a little in the morning that made him think he didn't want to go to school. But we were able to remind him of how he is smarter and faster than Fear and how he is able to make Bad Fear go away. This morning, he went smiling into his classroom and had no trouble at all separating and came out of school with a happy face at the end of the day. His teacher said he was like that all day! We are delighted and very proud and look forward to seeing you again next week.

By the time they arrived, DM was primed with the good news he had received from Morris. He asked Harry if it was true that he had returned to school.

> **Harry**: Yeah. (He states this matter-of-factly.)
> **DM**: How'd you do it?
> **Harry**: We put two pencils down and Fear can't get over them.
> **DM**: Huh? What did you do?
> **Evie**: We figured out that if we laid a pencil at the front of the entrance to his class, and another one just before you get

inside, Harry could jump over both of them, no problem, but Fear could not.

DM: Is that right, Harry?

Harry: We trapped Fear so it can't get in. (He seems quite proud.)

DM: Where did you trap Fear? (Still trying to comprehend the exact method.)

Evie: It gets trapped between the pencils.

Harry: Yeah, because I can jump over, but Fear can't.

DM: You can jump right over in one big leap?

Harry: Yeah!

DM: You can jump all the way over and into class, but Fear can't jump like you? So it got stuck in the door? (Finally getting it. This is the challenge with original knowledge. Given that it is newly invented rather than recycled, it is not automatically recognizable.)

Harry: Yeah, so it couldn't come in.

DM: I get it now. Are you saying that you figured out how to go back to school without Fear by trapping it?

Harry: Yeah.

DM: How great is it to be a kid who's good at running and jumping?

Harry: It's good.

DM: What's it like to be back in school, knowing that Fear can't ruin your fun?

Harry: It's good.

Harry was unmistakably pleased with his reclaimed freedom and triumphant return to school, a place he had always loved before Fear's unwelcome incursion in his life. Morris and Evie were clearly relieved. The fact that Fear still lurked at the edges was worth keeping an eye on, but all three adults acknowledged that it was no different for any of them. Fear could sometimes encroach, especially late at night after a bad day, and when work deadlines loomed, keeping them up rather than letting them drift off to a peaceful slumber.

Where's the Fun in It?

They decided the news of Harry's rapid comeback was worthy of recognition and celebration.

While Harry had Fear on the run by rather unconventional means, his methods would be comprehensible to most anyone his age. It was only after adult efforts were exhausted that his parents turned to a professional, perhaps expecting measures of an even higher order. But this was not what they found. By resisting the allure of practical wisdom in favor of the implausible, they found their way—or rather, Harry led the way, so invigorated by his own prolificacy, it was all they could do to keep up with him. As a result of his comeback, Harry was invited to apply for membership in the Fear Fighters' Society,[1] a group comprised of people, young and old, who had gotten the best of Fear, after it had initially gotten the better of them. It is especially in instances when people have suffered experiences that result in lost affiliation that we look for ways to establish and strengthen bonds of connection. And though Harry had recently found his way back into his school community, the disruption to his life was not forgotten.

In lieu of the availability of younger society members from his generation, a meeting was arranged with senior members (counselors in training at Miracle Mile Community Practice) to consider his application. His parents were also in attendance, and though a successful outcome could not be guaranteed, they had baked cookies for what they hoped would be a winning vote by the society's representatives. After warm greetings and introductions all around, the society members settled in behind a one-way mirror to listen in and consider the evidence as DM and Harry and the Harricanes presented their case. An account of the work and examples of Harry's ingenuity in taking his life back from Fear were presented. The following talents, tricks, and decisive actions were recounted:

- Harry's aptitude for running and jumping
- The mischievous tricks and strategies he designed in their first meeting
- The unprecedented solution he and his mother devised to trap Fear in the doorway so that only he could leap, Fear-free, into class

Harry, Evie, Morris, and DM rested their case, satisfied they had provided sufficient testimony to merit membership. Afterward, they traded places to look and listen from the other side of the mirror. Harry's nose was pressed to the glass as the facts were considered surrounding his victory. Though there was some discussion and even a moment's doubt expressed by John—the most senior and sometimes cantankerous member of the group—it was not long before they voted unanimously to welcome Harry into the fold. They presented him with a gold medallion with the engraving FF #134 to signify that he was the 134th and, notably, the youngest member ever admitted to the Fear Fighters' Society. Harry could not have been more pleased. Fortunately, the cookies his parents baked were most appropriate to the occasion and did not go to waste. DM was so happy he ate two in Harry's honor. As they all sat together, the society members reached into their pockets and purses and, one by one, showed him their own prized medallions. They described their contentious relationships with Fear and took pride in telling their own comeback stories. All agreed that a lifetime membership in the Fear Fighters' Society was the best thing of all, especially given that none of them was immune to Fear. It was a comfort to know that on those occasions when it crept back in, there would always be society members to call on. Harry readily offered to make himself equally available for consultation.

Outsmarting the Problem by Mischievous Means

Harry's story illustrates but one of many playful approaches (Freeman et al., 1997) in which the practitioner maintains a safe distance from traditional person-problem assessment and focuses instead on fun in one form or another. As a consequence, more opportunities are found for young people to become increasingly relevant to their lives at times when problems enter the picture. Consider the following eight constructions of young person-problem relational engagement, not as an exhaustive list by any means, but rather as an invitation to spur further creative development:

1. Playing a joke on the problem: If the young person has helped us understand that the problem has merely been playing a joke with relatively benign intentions and should not be taken seriously, then, in a lighter atmosphere, she or he might consider playing a joke back on the problem in the same spirit. "If you came up with the perfect joke to play on the problem, would it be similar to the one you played on your brother when he was sound asleep, all peaceful and dreamy, and not suspecting a thing? How did you come up with it at the time? What inspired you?"
2. Trick-or-treating the problem: If, under scrutiny, it is found that the problem, despite having promised the young person a treat, has in fact delivered a trick instead, it would be justifiable for the young person and her or his family to even the score. This allows for the trick to be countermanded by a more clever one. Sounds of laughter can fill the air as the young person is supported in thinking up tricks she or he never would have dreamed adults would tolerate, let alone take delight in. "When you've gone trick-or-treating and knocked on people's doors, were you ever tempted to play a trick? What might be the best trick to play on this kind of problem? In my day, we might have gone down to the prank store for a whoopee cushion for the problem to sit on, or fake barf for the problem to step in, but I don't know if those tricks have gotten old after all these years."
3. A case of mistaken identity: Here we rely on a familiar trope to infuse the conversation with mystery as we review the young person's wonderfulnesses and find ourselves baffled by a problem that would pick on such a wonderful kid. By the end of the interview, it becomes clear that the problem was misinformed about the young person as the reputation it has spread is so different from what the parents and others hold to be true. The version of their child they champion and to which the young person would have to consent is often sufficient grounds to prove the problem wrong. In instances when a young person does not seek alliance with

the problem and now claims to have been miscast, a case can be made that the problem just plain got the wrong kid. We may ask, "Did the problem mistake you for someone else? Could it be that you look just like someone the problem might have on its list? Should your parents take you to the office where they give out identification cards so that you can prove you are the person we learned about in the first meeting, and not who the problem mistook you for?"

4. Proving the problem a bad arguer: If it is found that the problem's claims about a young person are at considerable odds with the portrayal offered by his parents, we can invite her or him to prepare for a hearing in which the case will be argued. "Did the problem think you were just going to sit idly by while it did all the talking? Should we compare what the problem has to say about you with what you have to say for yourself? Who else should we call upon to testify on your behalf?"

5. When the problem doesn't play fair: This engagement takes place in an ethical realm with respect to what the parents and young person consider to be fair play. The ethics of the problem are put under examination. If everyone reaches the same conclusion that the problem can be indicted for unfair play, the family can decide to play unfairly, or conversely, stick to fair play despite the unlikelihood of the problem upholding the same standard. If the young person takes a gentler or more ethical stance, further story development might be undertaken as to her or his finer qualities (e.g., honesty, decency, generosity of spirit). "Although you have a strong interest in fairness, is it right to expect you to be fair to a problem that has been so unfair to you? What might be the best approach? Fighting fire with fire? Or do you see yourself sticking to fair play even if the problem deserves much less? Would it benefit from a lesson or two in the values your family stands for?"

6. Casting doubt on the character of the problem: This engages the young person in speculation about the problem's motives

in going to such lengths to recruit her or him into a life of trouble in the first place. The problem's own background and temperament can be investigated in order to come to an understanding of what makes it tick. For all we know, it might have started out as a Puppy Lover, a Homework Helper, or a Giggle Grower before things soured and it became the problem it is today. On the other hand, it might have been a fusspot from the start. "What kind of childhood would you guess the problem had? What company might it keep? What would you guess the problem believes in and values most? What kind of interest does it take in young people? What is it ultimately after?"

7. Exposing the problem as clueless: This engagement can be undertaken in a fun-loving manner. The young person and family are invited to consider how clueless or misguided the problem might be in bothering a kid it really has no cause to mess with. They might wonder whether the problem has begun to realize what it is up against and whether it is having second thoughts about messing with a family who goes by the credo "all for one and one for all." Some thought is given to the kind of work the problem might be better suited to (e.g., used car sales, movie critic), or whether it should consider an early retirement (e.g., in Boca Raton, Florida). "What on earth was the problem thinking to mess with a family like yours? Do you think it has any idea what it's gotten itself into? If it could find a way to back out without losing face, would it pack up and head as fast as it could in the opposite direction?"

8. Discovering the problem is jealous: In characterizing the problem as jealous, an opportunity presents itself not only to review all the special qualities about the young person that have already been documented and that might provoke such a petty response, but also to cast aspersions on the problem as lacking character and succumbing to spiteful feelings. "Have you ever wondered if the problem is jealous of you? How would you guess the problem took it when we first

met and your parents described you as [e.g., good-hearted, smart, creative, funny, loyal, sensitive, clever] and told wonderful stories about you to back up their claims? Would you care to guess how the problem might have reacted when your mom told the story about how brave you were the first time you flew on an airplane?"

When the mood is light and imagination is solicited for these sorts of spirited endeavors, there is an overall air of goodwill. Once unbound from the strictures of convention and let loose to originate rather than duplicate knowledge, young people are often revealed as virtuosos. At the same time, they come into view as noble in their intentions to rid their lives of problems (even if by ignoble means). And we see parents begin to relax and even join in the fun. Perhaps they appreciate being relieved of the mandate to work harder, along with the unpleasant (and often fruitless) task of convincing their daughters and sons to do the same.

Conclusion

Mischief is a most fitting ploy given that it calls young people forward at their nimble best. The moral intent that can be summoned and the creative means by which they achieve their aims can lead to some very amusing turnarounds. While most often children have few reservations about joining in and playing along, we are always at the ready. As Chapter 5 illustrates, when young people momentarily reach the limits of their own imaginations, we are only too happy to infuse the space with a little mischief or magic of our own before stepping aside to see what might happen next.

CHAPTER FIVE

The Therapist's Imagination Lends Inspiration

Although our work is built on a belief in the transformative potential of young people's imaginations, this does not mean that we simply sit back and wait for the magic to happen. If only it were that simple (e.g., "Okay, show me what you got!"). While young people can surely impress, it is not their limitless creative powers that we count on. Child psychologist Lev Vygotsky (2004, p. 15) tells us that "every act of imagination starts with [the] accumulation of experience" and this gives adults a distinct advantage in their capacity to conceive of much more. But children can retake the lead and amaze with their "greater faith in the products of imagination" (p. 34). It is their unabashed trust in what is made imaginable, either with our assistance or on the basis of their exposure to the world so far, that heightens the senses and moves the work along. For unlike adults, who can envision vastly more but only half-heartedly, children can be found to believe with their whole hearts.

It can be incumbent upon us as practitioners to animate the conversation by means of inventive proposals and sleights of hand, especially during moments when conversations flag and imagination has gone missing. In such instances, sprinkling a little fairy dust over all concerned parties can help with lift off. After all, we learned from Peter Pan long ago that traveling to Neverland is impossible without it: "for no one can fly unless the fairy dust has been blown on him.

Fortunately . . . one of his [Peter's] hands was messy with it, and he blew some on each of them [John, Michael, and Wendy], with the most superb results" (Barrie, 2005, p. 34). Contrary to popular belief, thinking happy thoughts can only take us so far.

The following two stories illustrate the benefits of imagination via each therapist's (DM and DE) readiness to turn an ordinary space into one that is magically real (Faris, 2004) with a sprinkling from the practitioner's own reserve of fairy dust. Despite being a hemisphere apart, there was a synchronicity in the work that unfolded as DM and DE each set off imaginative charges in the hope of reviving two young people, both of whom appeared listless and resigned to dull and dreary lives. DM and DE hoped the ensuing blasts would be powerful enough to rouse their spirits.

First Things First: Getting to Know What Matters to Young People

On a cold winter's day (at least as cold as it gets in Los Angeles), DM received a telephone call from Alex, the father of 10-year-old Danny, prompted by frustration over his son's "laziness" and "constant fears" (Marsten, Epston, & Johnson, 2012) He explained that Danny had been living with him from the time of his mother's death 4 years earlier and since then, "all he does is sit around and read his books or watch TV. If we go out, I have to drag him along." Alex went on to describe how Danny "has bad dreams and wakes up in the middle of the night convinced he's in danger and someone's breaking in or hiding under his bed or in the closet." As DM hung up the telephone, his thoughts drifted to memories of young people who had been prematurely confronted by the death of a parent. In each instance, one or more special gifts appeared. He wondered what he would sooner or later discover about Danny. If, at night, his imagination was vivid and freighted with fear, might this be an indication that it could, under less duress, take flight? If that turned out to be the case, it would not be the first time Fear had appropriated a young person's imagination, invading his sleep and turning dreams to nightmares.

Alex walked through DM's office door the next day, turning and waiting on Danny, who trailed behind with a book tucked under his arm. When DM asked him what he was reading, he silently held it out. It was *A Series of Unfortunate Events, Book the Ninth: The Carnivorous Carnival* (Snicket, 2002). The drawing on the front cover was reminiscent of Daniel in the lion's den and enough to give anyone distressing dreams. DM learned that the books in the Snicket series were his favorites. Danny asked if he had ever read them. Wishing he could say yes, DM admitted he had not. Eager to understand something about Danny apart from any further portrayal that Laziness or Fear might offer, DM asked him for a detailed description of the book series. He wondered what he would find out about Danny in his appreciation of the book's protagonists, the Baudelaire children, and hoped it might shed light on what was at stake for him. Might they all find this information useful in engaging whatever problems they were about to encounter? But first he would need to do a little reading up on his own.

Violet, Klaus, and Sunny Baudelaire (from the Lemony Snicket collection, *A Series of Unfortunate Events*) made it all the way to *Book the Ninth* (2002) and counting, in spite of facing one perilous predicament after another, all the while carrying heavy hearts over the loss of their parents in a tragic but suspicious fire that left their home and family in ruins. Their talents for problem solving and escaping deadly traps with ingenuity and courage were, by now, legendary to their readership. The dangers they faced were not the usual kind, or at least not akin to those DM had any recollection of from his early years, whether in real life or in what he watched on television. What he saw depicted long ago in Saturday morning children's shows and after-school reruns offered no window into the hazardous circumstances of the Baudelaires' lives.

Violet, Klaus, and Sunny are suddenly orphaned. And in hot pursuit of them is their diabolical and dubious distant relative, Count Olaf, and his lover and accomplice, Esme Gigi Genevieve Squalor. Literature has rarely produced, through the ages, two more menacing characters, with their designs on the Baudelaire inheritance, not to mention plans for the orphans' premature demise. And did Olaf have anything to do with the deaths of the children's devoted and loving parents? One can only surmise that he must have.

The first thing Danny explained about the Baudelaires was that, though they were always in the custody of one adult caregiver or another, it was invariably someone who lacked any of the requisite skills for delivering care. Consequently, in every practical and important way, the children were totally on their own when threatened by whatever fiendish scheme Count Olaf was surely hatching. Danny took pains to ensure that DM understood just what the Baudelaire children were up against in their dealings with the count. He described Olaf as "a bad person" and explained, "He's like the worst person you could ever meet." In contrast to his antipathy for the count, Danny's sympathy for the Baudelaires was boundless. Since the death of their parents, they faced risk at every turn, and it was only through their combined efforts that they managed to survive one harrowing plot after another.

Unlike Danny, the Baudelaires had each other to turn to in the event of danger crossing their paths. Danny was still sorting out his relationship with his father, and since migrating to Los Angeles, found himself at a distance of more than 100 miles from the people who had previously been central to his life. He had his father, of course, but their contact had been limited until his mother's shocking death turned his world upside down. And even still, father and son had not found their way into each other's hearts. To Alex, Danny was a riddle. He was "baffled by him." Danny was withdrawn, seemingly keeping his own counsel, or perhaps adrift and even lost to himself. It might have been, at that point in time, that Danny knew the Baudelaires better than he knew himself. He was most fervent when discussing them. His keen interest in their imagined world was at odds with his lethargy at other times and seeming disinterest in his own real life and surroundings.

The contrast raised questions for DM. What did Danny's interest in the plight of the Baudelaire children suggest about his commit-

The Therapist's Imagination Lends Inspiration

ments and purposes for his life? What was it in those pages that awakened his senses? What did Danny feel or know at these times? How might the rift be mended between this imagined world and the everyday world in which he seemed to be living a kind of half-life? These questions floated through DM's mind as his own imagination began to come alive.

Meanwhile, halfway around the globe, DE received a telephone call about a 10-year-old girl facing a very different sort of problem. Jan and Rob were gripped with concern that their daughter Kelly had an "obsessive-compulsive disorder." They based this on the fact that she was spending hours on end in the bathroom and requiring them to buy toilet paper by the case. All their efforts to talk her out of the problem, let alone out of the bathroom, failed, as she would become "hysterical" if they tried to interfere with what they referred to as "her rituals." Because this was a one-toilet family, when Kelly locked herself in the bathroom and would not come out, her parents were extremely inconvenienced and had to get a bucket for their own use. But this was a mere frustration compared to their concern for what was becoming of their kindly and "sweet-hearted one." Their worry was shared by Kelly's schoolteacher, who beseeched them, "Get some help for her before it's too late."

DE learned of a recent occasion when Kelly's girlfriends came over on a Saturday afternoon to hang out. For a shy girl, Kelly cherished days when she was able to entertain friends at home. Her mother described her as "beside herself" an hour before they were to arrive, peering out the window and continually asking for updates on the time. Jan recalled previous visits when she would overhear the girls giggling and talking excitedly. At such moments, her fears about Kelly's future were allayed. However, what Jan had put so much hope in came to a seeming end in the blink of an eye. On that fateful day, even with her girlfriends on hand and ready to play, Kelly was irresistibly drawn to the bathroom. After waiting for an inordinate amount of time, her girlfriends called their parents to come and pick them up. From that point on they were reluctant to return and Kelly was equally averse to inviting them back. No amount of encouragement could budge her. She was adamant that she had "no time for friends." Jan and Rob were heartsick over what they saw as the "last hope for Kelly coming right," and they despondently conceded, "This is beyond us." They had exhausted every possible remedy, along with Internet searches, nutritional approaches, and good old-fashioned soul searching.

The first meeting began with Jan dutifully informing DE that he should not expect Kelly to say a word. "You don't speak to strangers, do you, darling?" Kelly seemed relieved by her mother's offer of initial cover from what, to her mind, promised to be a mortifying experience. One would guess that Kelly might have expected to be appraised according to the problem rather than according to her wonderfulnesses. Seemingly relieved by the initial line of inquiry, Kelly was at least willing to nod or shake her head to indicate her agreement or disagreement with her parents' accounts.

About 45 minutes into the first meeting, they turned their attention to the problem, but not before learning, among other things, about Kelly's penchant for fun. This had been traced all the way back to her ancestral home of Ireland through her father's line, but more proximately to her Auntie Sarah, who was regarded as "a laugh a minute." Jan and Rob were sure that if Sarah had pursued a career in stand-up comedy, she could have made a go of it. But by one turn and another she ended up a primary schoolteacher and proved herself "a natural with kids." Jan and Rob had never visited her classroom but were sure, knowing her as they did, that Sarah must sometimes feel the temptation to address her budding young students as if they were a nightclub audience.

Whenever Auntie Sarah visited, no matter how reticent Kelly had been beforehand, they were soon "falling about laughing," with Kelly usually laughing loudest. By the time Jan and Rob brought the loss of Kelly's girlfriends to DE's attention, her reaction stood in stark contrast to the image of a fun-loving girl who could hoot and howl with the best of them. Despite her parents' wonderful descriptions, Kelly sat with her head bowed and her hands folded over her lap, appearing to DE like a repentant sinner. This was a very poor match for her parents, who looked pained in their inability to do anything to palliate her suffering. DE sat back, took a deep breath, and, with the seed of an idea, began to contemplate how the distance between these two impressions of Kelly might not need reconciling, but rather could present an opportunity for action.

A First Attempt to Invigorate the Conversation

It is sometimes the case that a young person's imagination and that of family members has been run ragged by the problem to a point of near collapse. And questions meant to intrigue and resuscitate, though earnestly delivered, do not always reach their intended recipient. DM was keen to ask Danny what it was about the Baudelaire children that had him sticking with their story through book nine rather than leaving them behind in book three or four. Surely one would know all one needed to by then. Danny rolled his eyes. It was clear DM had a lot to learn. He pursued a more detailed understanding of the Baudelaires from Danny's perspective, hoping to learn more about him and his aims along the way. Danny introduced them to DM, each in turn.

> DM: All right, let me see if I've got this straight. When Violet puts her hair up, you can tell she's thinking and putting her mind to work. Is that right?
>
> Danny: Yeah, and Klaus reads and has lots of information and Sunny can bite through anything, not just like a rope or something easy, but like hard, metal things. (His interest is obvious.)
>
> DM: But I thought you said Sunny was a baby.
>
> Danny: Yeah, but she has really sharp teeth and she understands a lot, even though she can't really talk. She can talk, but only baby talk, but Violet and Klaus can understand her.
>
> DM: Okay, I think I'm beginning to get the picture. These are pretty special kids with special talents for living and for facing difficult problems, even life-and-death problems. Am I on track here?
>
> Danny: Yeah. (He seems to appreciate DM's efforts to understand something about them.)

> **DM:** Do you know anyone in real life who reminds you of the Baudelaires?
>
> **Danny:** Um, I don't know. (He appears annoyed by the question.)
>
> **DM:** Any relatives, or anyone at school maybe, or someone from your neighborhood?
>
> **Danny:** No.
>
> **DM:** Anyone with really sharp teeth? (A feeble attempt to reengage him with humor.)
>
> **Danny:** No. (He shuffles his feet, finding nothing funny in DM's question.)
>
> **DM:** Is there a special kind of link between you and the Baudelaires?
>
> **Danny:** Um . . . no . . . can I use the bathroom?

Danny may have needed a restroom break, or perhaps he was generously giving DM some time to get the conversation back on track. In retrospect, this was an ill-conceived attempt to connect real and imagined worlds. A sturdier bridge would be needed. DM went back to the proverbial drawing board.

Back on New Zealand's emerald shores, DE had every hope that the wonderfulness interview would get things rolling in a preferred direction. He anticipated that, in addition to helping him consider how Kelly might effectively meet the problem, it could offer her protection from the shame that might otherwise intrude. But it turned out, this was not (yet) the case.

> **DE:** Kelly, what did you think of the problem shutting you away in the toilet and having your girlfriends miss out on the fun you usually have together during a playdate? (Attempting to establish a separate platform from which Kelly might evaluate the problem.)
>
> **Kelly:** I don't know. (Speaking in a disconsolate tone.)
>
> **DE:** Say you were on your own playing with your girlfriends. What do you think would have happened? (Taking another tack, as obviously the previous question was insufficiently designed to attract her attention.)

The Therapist's Imagination Lends Inspiration

> **Kelly**: We would have had fun. (She becomes minimally engaged.)
>
> **DE**: What kind of fun would you have—play fun, talk fun, joking fun, or just plain 10-year-old-girl fun?
>
> **Kelly**: Ten-year-old-girl fun. (She now appears to be coming out of a trance.)
>
> **DE**: I am so much older than you. What do 10-year-old girls get up to these days to have fun? (DE assumes a learning position and seeks out Kelly's knowledge.)
>
> **Kelly**: I don't want to talk about it. (She appears embarrassed, perhaps reminded of the lost friendships.)

DE was not unaccustomed to this sort of interim setback. He would take Kelly's reluctance to heart and find another way.

Reaching out to young people from a distance can be daunting for professionals who are attempting to close the gap. The encounter traditionally locates them on an upper ridge and young people and their perspectives far below. Such an arrangement can produce a strained posture for those peering upward, and for those looking down, a less than inspiring view.

If at First You Don't Succeed

When Danny returned from the restroom and settled back in, DM made another attempt to bridge the two worlds.

> **DM**: Is there something in particular about the Baudelaires that interests you, Danny?
>
> **Danny**: I don't know. I just like them and the way they can get out of anything. And they're smarter than the grownups. (He looks up as he says this, seeming to wonder if DM can take it. Not all adults are enthusiastic about being upstaged.)
>
> **DM**: Is that right? Do they live in an upside-down world where kids are smarter? Because in this world, don't we treat adults as smarter than kids and knowing what kids need? In the world of Violet, Klaus, and Sunny, is it kids who know what

kids need? (Attempting to support a worldview in which young people, and perhaps by extension Danny, might know best.)

Danny: Yeah. (Smiling.)

DM: Is that one of the best things about the books?

Danny: Yeah. (He seems pleased with how the conversation is proceeding.)

DM: Is there something special about kids' knowledge? Can kids' ideas fit into kids' lives better than adult ideas some of the time? (DM hopes this will be a more suitable connection.)

Danny: Yep! (Stated with obvious pleasure. Danny seems to move toward a more explicit understanding of young people as knowledgeable, an understanding that may have only been implicitly appreciated previously.)

DM: Do you relate with your mind to the way that Violet uses her mind? (Attempting, once again, to bridge the two worlds.)

Danny: What?

DM: Let me try that again. Can you use your mind to understand the way Violet uses her mind?

Danny: I guess so. (He seems hesitant, a possible indication of how foreign Danny's own skills are to him at this point. Or perhaps the question still needs revising.)

DM: Do you like putting your mind to work or giving your mind a good workout the way Violet does? (Finally getting the question into better shape.)

Danny: Sometimes.

As the end of their first meeting approached, DM wondered what more there would be to learn about Danny's mind along with any additional talents that might be revealed. As they said their goodbyes, DM mulled over how he might continue to solicit the help of the Baudelaires.

Speaking of help, "down under" it was clear to DE that Jan and Rob were Kelly's finest allies. It is most often the case that parents love their children best and are faithful collaborators in addressing problems that have invaded the lives of their daughters and sons. In spite of what popular misconceptions would have us believe about helicopter mothers, enmeshed relationships, and the like, DE realized long ago that with the help of parent partners, the task can be cut in half. And so he turned to Kelly's parents for aid.

DE: (Giving Kelly some breathing room) Jan, what kind of fun would you have expected Kelly and her girlfriends to have?

Jan: I can't tell you in words how much fun they might have had but they would be chirping away like a box of birds.

DE: What kinds of birds, Jan?

Jan: Canaries, budgies, perhaps even tuis. (Laughing) [Tuis are colorful and clamorous birds indigenous to New Zealand.]

DE: As Kelly's mum, did it do your heart good to overhear this "box of birds" chirping away under your roof?

Jan: Did it ever! (The smile that creases her face must come from this reminiscence.)

DE: How about you, Rob?

Rob: For me it was more than their chattering; it was their laughter. We don't hear Kelly laugh much lately, so it filled my heart with joy to hear her and her mates laughing out loud.

DE: Kelly, do you mind me asking you if this problem killed your joys with your girlfriends? (Picking up on Rob's use of the word "joy" and preparing to bring the problem to life.)

Kelly: What do you mean?

DE: Do you not know what a "killjoy" is? (She looks blank and perhaps embarrassed by her obvious unfamiliarity with the word. DE turns quickly to her parents for assistance.) Jan and Rob, do you know what a killjoy is?

Rob: Yeah, sure! A killjoy is someone who hates people having fun and I guess "kills their joys." (Readily coming to DE's rescue.)

DE: That sounds about right, but should we look it up in the dictionary? (DE consults the *Oxford Concise Dictionary*, which he has handy for just such occasions.) Here it is: "One who spreads gloom over social enjoyment." What do you think, Kelly?

Kelly: Yeah, I suppose so. (Somewhat more engaged as this conversation has now taken an unexpected tack.)

DE: By the way, everyone, is that a good way to refer to this problem? Or can you think of a more apt description? (DE attempts to lend inspiration by offering a novel description of the problem, but he does so tentatively, in case anyone has a different idea.)

Jan: That's really good, David!

Rob: Spot on, I'd say!

DE: How about you, Kelly?

Kelly: I suppose that's right. (Perhaps carried away by her parents' enthusiasm.)

DE: If after giving it some thought over the next week or two, you come up with something better, will you e-mail me and let me know?

Kelly: Okay.

DE: (Returning to the wonderfulness of caring for others that was meticulously elaborated, first her practice of it and then its genealogy. David consults his notes to provide a thorough recap.) Kelly, your mum and dad have just told me with such regard about your wonderfulnesses, especially your virtue of caring for others, including those younger than yourself and smaller than you, like cats and dogs, and goldfish right down to spiders, despite the fact that so many people, even adults, are freaked out by spiders. I really appreciated the story they told about how you went along with your young cousin, Amelia, when she had to go to the outdoor toilet while you were camping on the beach last summer. And how you rescued all the spiders and freed them outside so no harm would come to them, and so she wouldn't be frightened to use the "dunny" (a slang term used in New Zealand and Australia for toilet).

And I learned that your care and love for others have been passed down from your grannies on both your mum's and dad's sides of the family. Both grannies are well known for lending anyone in need a helping hand at their churches and in their neighborhoods. And so it would seem, you are an exact chip off your grannies' blocks. Your mum and dad said this caring missed out on their generation, but I am not so sure I should take their word for that as they seem like pretty caring parents to me. (DE regularly summarizes, weaving together wonderfulnesses and events as a means of giving the nascent story line initial lift. In spite of the fact that the story under construction is based on long-standing values and events, it may not have been sufficiently woven or cogently told until now. And even still it is an early draft.)

I mention this because I am feeling sorry for the Killjoy as it must be full of gloom and not have a clue about having any sort of fun. In fact, as your dad suggested, this problem seems to hate people having fun like you and your girlfriends. Can you imagine what it must be like for your problem to know only gloom and doom? Kelly, do you in any way feel sorry for this Killjoy? (DE is careful to shore up the developing story with Kelly's values as supports.)

Kelly: I guess so. No fun at all would be no fun. And killing other people's joys isn't good. (Now speaking with a newfound measure of authority, buttressed by the story of her wonderfulnesses.)

DE: That's for sure. Would you be willing to lend the Killjoy a hand and help it have some fun?

Kelly: I guess so, but what do you mean? (She tilts her head to the left. Her query is quizzical rather than querulous.)

DE put his own imagination to work on Kelly's behalf, but was, at the same time, careful to create possibilities for action that were founded on her practices (e.g., fun, caring, helping) and on those of her family across the generations. They had a lengthy discussion about how she and her parents toilet trained their dog, Martha, by showing her where to go and where not to go. And how she once helped her younger cousin make chocolate-chip cookies. What seemed common to each story was showing the person (or animal companion) in need how to do something. They arrived at a pedagogy of showing rather than telling, or at least showing first and telling later. Kelly came to the fore, and Rob and Jan were readily available to back her up with their own accounts of lending someone (or something) a hand. Here they were adumbrating the engagement Kelly and her family might have with such a problem, but rather than toilet training the Killjoy, she might instead, out of the goodness of her "sweetheartedness," show it how to have fun.

On further jocular inquiry, they concluded that although the Killjoy might "get around," it mainly seemed to live in the toilet. This told them where Kelly might best undertake her mission. There was something absurd in the very notion. Still, they could not help but feel curious as to *what exactly* DE had in mind.

The Therapist Sets an Imaginative Charge

Back in Los Angeles, things were about to heat up. At their second meeting, which took place a week later, DM pursued a more detailed understanding of Danny's mind and the uses to which it might be applied. Among other things, he learned that Danny had "the ability to focus in on something if he cares about it," at least according to Alex. In addition, there were two late-night occasions in his room when he was able to get a good night's sleep after Fear had made a sudden appearance. DM asked Danny if it was this talent for focusing or refocusing his mind that had him secure a peaceful night's sleep. Danny wasn't sure but thought it might be possible. While he did his best to answer DM's questions, he seemed to labor over them. This supported DM's impression that, rather than anything in the way of an ordinary interview, Danny was in need of something different—something outside the realm of the familiar.

Just then, there was a noise. They glanced over in time to see an envelope sail through the mail slot in the door. DM retrieved it immediately, only to discover that it was addressed to Danny. He handed it over and watched as Danny first examined it, then slowly opened it and read in silence, appearing transfixed. Then he read it again, this time out loud. Here is what it said:

Dear Danny,

Your current *plight*—a word used here to mean a challenging circumstance someone is facing—has come to my attention. Given that I am unable to visit you at this time—as it will be no surprise to you that we currently have our hands full, to say the least, with none other than Count Olaf—I immediately decided to put pen to paper and write to you. I hope to have more time to write in the future, but for now, just a quick note of support and appreciation. I have felt very lucky to have a mind that works in my favor and helps me deal with plights in my own life, not to mention the importance of being able to come to the aid of my brother, Klaus, and sister, Sunny, both of whom are very dear to me. Though I have only recently learned about you, I have an early hunch and wonder if I am right. Are we—you and I that is—*like-minded*? Have you ever put your mind to something and found that your very own thinking provided the answers you were looking for? If so, isn't it a wonderful feeling? I made the exciting discovery some time ago that I had the kind of mind that could be put to good use for all sorts of things.

But I'd be interested to know more about you, Danny. Have you ever thought back to early signs of your mind trying to tell you something clever or brave? Is there a favorite story about you that your mother or grandparents used to love to tell whenever the whole family got together?

That's all I can say for now. I hear heavy footsteps on the staircase and they're getting louder. Unless I'm mistaken, they are the footsteps of YOU KNOW WHO! Wish me luck, and the same to you (of course, if I'm right about you, we both have a little more than luck going for us, don't you *think*?)

Keeping you in mind, *Violet B.*

Upon finishing the letter, Danny promptly looked up at DM with what appeared to be equal parts astonishment and suspicion and asked if he had written it. DM assured him he had not. Danny turned to his father, who likewise denied any knowledge of it. And while Danny appeared largely unconvinced by their denials, he seemed only too willing to suspend disbelief. Maybe this was the wake-up call he needed, the one his imagination had been waiting for. Danny had been stalled for some time in a liminal space (Turner, 1969; van Gennep, 1960), having been wrenched from the world he knew, without having yet achieved a sense of arrival at a new destination. Languishing between worlds, he experienced little in the way of resonance. What was dependable and stationary had been set adrift. It was more the imaginary to which his attention seemed drawn, and so DM hoped to seek him out there. An imagined space might be just the locale where they could meet and where Danny might find himself. Time would tell.

But for now, let us head back to the bathroom, an unlikely place for inspiration and fun. With the aid of DE's imaginative subsidization, Kelly and her parents began transmogrifying her wonderfulnesses into a family practice. They all agreed that living in the bathroom was not the most likely place for anyone or any problem to meet friends or have fun. By the same token, they concurred that bathrooms are pretty lonely places, since they are typically visited by only one person at a time.

> DE: Kelly, do you think we just have to go where the problem lives? We can hardly expect it to come out in the lounge for you to show it how to have a good time. (DE is hopeful that, having learned about the family's predilection for fun, this might represent the kind of response to the problem that they would find fitting—even if it was a tight fit.)
>
> Kelly: I suppose so. (Seemingly intrigued, not quite knowing where this conversation is headed, but perhaps with some sense that it might be in the direction of the bathroom.)
>
> DE: Rob and Jan, how many people do you estimate could squeeze into your bathroom?

Rob: Three of us, but it might be tight. (Getting the gist of this conversation. By now, the parents' pained expressions are long gone.)

DE: Is it possible to invite Auntie Sarah and fit her into the fun making? (Jan and Rob can't help guffawing.)

Jan: She actually lives in Tauranga. (The town is a 3-hour drive to the southeast.)

DE: If she knew everything we had been talking about, do you think you could call her on the phone so she could tell some jokes to you three and the Killjoy? This way you would be feeding two birds with one worm. Do you know that saying, Kelly?

Kelly: Dunno. (Somewhat perplexed but trying to catch on.)

DE: Don't worry about it. I just made it up. But let me tell you what I mean by it. You could catch up with your auntie and laugh yourself silly and at the same time show the Killjoy that life is not all doom and gloom. Would you be willing to lend it a hand so it doesn't have to go through life as a kind of "misery guts"?

Jan: (Somewhat anxiously awaiting Kelly's response) Will you do it, darling?

Kelly: Okay! (Smiling at Jan's approval and what DE guesses is the anticipation of the hilarity awaiting them.)

Jan and Rob said they would have no problem connecting with Auntie Sarah and arranging a suitable time to show the problem how to have fun. As Rob said about his sister, "Whenever Sarah is around, fun is sure to follow!" They discussed her style and wit and how the "Irish sense of humor" went back generations all the way to Kilkenny. Rob regaled them with sidesplitting tales that were part and parcel of his family's history. The one DE remembers still is about a legendary great-uncle who went around one night after a protracted visit to the local pub and nailed all the doors to his neighbors' outhouses shut—to everyone's consternation.

DE could not wait to meet them the next time. Sarah indeed had been riotous. Rob explained how she "plunged right in," showing the problem how to have a good time and "busting everyone's sides." "Even the toilet flipped its lid," Jan reported. And Kelly was far more animated than DE had ever seen her.

> **Kelly:** We laughed so hard we almost peed! Good thing there was a toilet! (Everyone laughs. Until now, DE has not witnessed Kelly's humor firsthand.)
>
> **DE:** (Catching his breath) Kelly, can you guess if the Killjoy has lightened up a bit since you and your family have shown it your Irish humor? What do you think?
>
> **Kelly:** I think so. (There is a hint of pride in her tone.)
>
> **DE:** Why do you say that? Has it been able to go out of the bathroom and get around a bit more and perhaps meet some other problems it could befriend? There are sure a lot of problems around these days, aren't there?
>
> **Rob:** Sure are! (Joining in the spirit of fun.)
>
> **Jan:** And you know, David, Kelly is having a lot more fun, too.
>
> **DE:** Kelly, now that the problem isn't living in the bathroom all the time and killjoying your fun, do you find you don't have to spend as much time in there keeping it company? Have you heard the saying "misery loves company"?
>
> **Kelly:** No. (Baffled.)
>
> **DE:** Jan or Rob, can you explain that saying to her?
>
> **Jan:** What it means, I think, is misery doesn't like fun company, it just likes miserable company.
>
> **DE:** Kelly, have you been showing the problem how to be fun company by having some fun and showing it how you do it, so it can follow in your footsteps? (DE attempts to reserve the lead position for Kelly by further conceptualizing the Killjoy as unseasoned and in need of counsel.)

She was bemused by DE's query, but Jan and Rob were quick to point out myriad examples of their daughter getting out and around a lot more and regaining some of her old friends and, indeed, making a few new ones. DE could tell from the looks on their faces that they were experiencing considerable relief. They reported having two or three more "comedy shows" in the bathroom. They might have considered selling tickets to future performances if only there had been more room and conventional seating available.

DE wondered aloud if the next step should be a mixture of showing and telling. Of course, everyone wondered how to go about this. DE knew that Kelly loved animals, and while he was in the Auckland Central Library one day, a book practically leaped off the shelf in front of him. When he noticed the title, he realized why. It was *The New Yorker Book of Dog Cartoons* (New Yorker, 1992)—a perfect rejoinder to any ideas the Killjoy might sponsor.

Everyone decided that although a funny 10-year-old like Kelly could understand quite a few of the cartoons, it might have to be a family affair to figure out others so Kelly could explain them to the Killjoy. They would head back to the bathroom on regular occasions, especially if the Killjoy just wasn't getting a joke. And some cartoons would have to be saved for a while until the problem grew up and could understand more. In the meantime, they enjoyed looking at each one and puzzling out together what was so funny about it. Kelly was relieved to learn that there was also a *New Yorker Book of Cat Cartoons* (New Yorker, 1990). She felt sorry for cats being made so much fun of in *The New Yorker Book of Dog Cartoons*. Jan promised she would stop by their local library to order the cat cartoons book because she was worried, like her daughter, that the dog cartoons were somewhat prejudiced against cats.

Imagination in the Realm of Life and Death

While imagination can be a perfect partner for any variety of antics, it can be as fittingly relied upon to provide relief from what is incomprehensible. Danny was cruelly confronted at a young age by the brutality of life. DM was concerned that he might have quietly determined existence to be unbearable, not only as an outcome of his mother's violent death, but also having been wrenched from the family and community who knew and loved him best. At their next meeting, the conversation turned to Danny's mother and the sad telling of her passing. Danny recounted how his uncle and grandparents first told him that she had been struck by a speeding car as she stepped off a curb, the victim of a drunk driver. Alex explained that Danny never showed any emotion over his mother's death, either at the funeral or since. Danny added in a distant voice, "Everyone was crying at the funeral but me." Avoiding any professional impulse to hypothesize about what Danny's dry eyes meant, DM undertook to assist him in establishing meaning that might hold resonance for him. Of course, given that Danny was not an "authorized meaning maker," DM anticipated that it would take some doing on his part to clear the center position for Danny's potential occupancy.

> **Alex**: He hasn't cried or shown any emotion since. It's like he's numb.
> **DM**: Is your dad right, Danny? Is there a kind of numbness that's taken hold of you?
> **Danny**: Kind of . . . I don't really know. (He appears distant.)
> **DM**: I wonder who would know. Who knows you best, Danny?
> **Danny**: I'm . . . I don't know.
> **DM**: Do the Baudelaires talk much about the loss of their parents?
> **Danny**: Not that much. (He seems wary.)
> **DM**: Do you have a hunch about why that is?
> **Danny**: It's not easy to talk about.
> **DM**: Do you think their parents would understand anyway, how much they are missed, even if Violet and Klaus don't say much? (Calling on the Baudelaires to share in Danny's experience.)
> **Danny**: Yeah.
> **DM**: What would their parents understand?
> **Danny**: That they miss them.
> **DM**: What about your mom? Do you think your mother would understand, even though you didn't show much outwardly? (Perhaps the Baudelaires will once again offer passage.)
> **Danny**: I don't know. She's not here. (He states this lifelessly.)

The Therapist's Imagination Lends Inspiration

DM: Do you believe your mother is watching over you? (Trying to engage Danny's imagination or perhaps his faith.)

Danny: I don't know.

DM: If she were, would she be surprised about the numbness you've lived with these last 4 years? (Posed subjunctively as speculation.)

Danny: No. (He pauses, seeming to consider the question.)

DM: Did your mother know you best? Would she understand what this numbness is all about? (Attempting to establish an alliance between mother and son that would begin to unriddle Danny. One's sense of identity is often made vivid with the benefit of an audience to one's experience. Lost loved ones can be called upon on such occasions [White, 1988; Hedtke & Winslade, 2004].)

Danny: Yes. (His tone is serious.)

DM: What would she know? What would she understand about how numbness took hold? (Here Danny is being relied upon to help them, and perhaps himself, reach some understanding.)

Danny: That it was hard. (His voice is thick with emotion. Danny seems to be moving toward a position of knowing. Perhaps he is becoming more known to himself through his mother's eyes.)

DM: Are you talking about your mother's passing? Is that what was so hard on you?

Danny: M-hm. (He is choked up.)

DM: Was this a deep loss, Danny?

Danny: M-hm. (Struggling to maintain his composure.)

DM: Do people feel deep loss especially when they have felt deep love? (Danny is being acknowledged for an experience of numbness that is profound rather than being mistaken as unfeeling or heartless.)

Danny: Yeah. (Holding his breath.)

DM: (To Alex) Did Danny and his mother love each other deeply? (Inviting Alex to bear witness to this developing account.)

Alex: They had a good relationship. They were very close.

DM: Was she a good mother to Danny?

Alex: She was. She was very involved in his life. She was devoted to him. (Alex is invited to contribute to the story under development.)

DM: (To Alex) And was Danny a good son to his mother?

Alex: Yes, I think so. (Danny looks up.)

DM: Danny, is it possible that the numbness that came into your life was proof of your deep love for your mother?

Danny: Yeah. (There appears to be relief in his tone, as tears begin rolling down his cheeks.)

DM: Do you think your mother knows and understands this even now, from where she is?

Danny: Yes . . .

Here Danny was engaged in an experience of active meaning making as he reconnected to his mother with a little help, once more, from the Baudelaires. We have found that people can, at one and the same time, describe an experience and the meaning it holds and encounter that meaning for the very first time. We resist structuralist accounts of such experiences and think of it less as the uncovering of something that was there all along, awaiting discovery, and more as an evocative "performance of meaning" (Bruner, 1986, p. 25). It might have been that Danny was living in a state of disconnection from his mother and himself, entrusted to the readiest metaphor in circulation—one of letting go and moving on (White, 1988). By bringing the spirit of his mother into the conversation, not just as a faded object but as a trusted aide and consultant (Epston, 1989; Epston & White, 1992; Hedtke & Winslade, 2004; Marsten, Epston, & Johnson, 2011; White, 1988), Danny seemed able, through her loving eyes, to entertain a rich account of himself.

It was at the start of their third meeting that a second letter sailed through the mail slot in the office door. Again it was addressed to Danny. This time he opened it, less amazed but no less delighted and, as before, read the following to himself and then aloud.

The Therapist's Imagination Lends Inspiration 117

Dear Danny,

    I was in the middle of reading a book on reptiles this morning when Violet came rushing in and interrupted me. I tried to make it clear to her that I was busy and did not wish to be disturbed. I am sure you know how *absorbed*—the word is used here to describe the pleasure that can be felt in losing oneself in a riveting text—and contented one can become while engaged in a gripping story. This was just such a story, specifically one about poisonous snakes that are common to the Americas. Would it interest you to know, Danny, that there are 32 species of rattlesnake? But that is beside the point. Violet insisted that we speak right then and there. She rarely interrupts me without good reason. As a result, I have learned to trust her in such instances, so I closed my book and gave her my full attention. When she told me your story and how you suffered the loss of your mother, I was really moved. Of course, there is no avoiding the sadness I feel over the loss of my parents and I know Violet and Sunny suffer, too . . . especially Violet. Sunny is still very young. I have imagined both my parents watching over me from heaven, and sometimes I am convinced that this is absolutely the case. Sometimes they are closest to me in the moments before I fall asleep and also in my dreams. I think of those experiences as the most special, holding bits of magic, at which times anything is possible. Have you found ways of reconnecting to your mother, Danny? It is a most wonderful feeling. At times I cry and cry over the loss, but Mr. Snicket doesn't say too much about that in the book series. This is in keeping with my request for a degree of privacy. Violet knows better than anyone how I have struggled with the loss. I have turned to her many times for comfort. It is sometimes a great mystery to me how to face the loss of my parents and, at the same time, still hold them close in my heart.

    I want to thank you for your interest in our sad story and for sticking with us through book nine. My thoughts are with you, Danny.
In sympathy and friendship,
Klaus B.

    Klaus joined Danny in the saddest of all human experiences, the loss of a loved one. Once again, Danny was summoned to an imaginary place where he could take to heart the letter from Klaus and envision his mother, constant in her love. All it took was a little imagination and a token of camaraderie from a cherished figure, who knew all too well the sorrow Danny bore. In these ways Danny was seen and understood.

The elements of narrative structure gave form to Danny's developing story. It was infused with drive by the arrival of a letter. Danny came into sharp relief against a backdrop of tragic loss, numbness, and fear, for his adroit mind and imagination. The story became heartfelt with the affirmation of his tender connection to his mother. The sense of one's identity relies on both the performance of meaning and on those who bear witness to that performance (Denzin, 2003). Family and friends, some real, others in spirit, and still others conjured from the pages of his favorite book series, served as an appreciative audience (Madsen, 2014; Madsen & Gillespie, 2014; White, 1995).

What a Little Toilet Humor Can Do

DE continued to meet with the family monthly to review how things were going with Kelly lending the Killjoy a hand. She was doing such a good job of it that the problem had been downgraded from a Killjoy to a Worry by the fourth meeting. Kelly came up with the new name without hesitation. Jan, now seemingly delivered from her burdens, spoke of her daughter in very different tones.

> Jan: We are seeing this year which sport Kelly really likes. She is enjoying tennis and doing very well at it. From my point of view, it is really lovely to see. She is so enthusiastic and although the Worry is still there, it is nothing like it was. And we tend to forget just how far you have come, Kelly. I think she has done very well! (Turning to Rob, who nods in agreement.) Now her friends are coming over again and she goes to the bathroom and just comes out.
> (Kelly, who appears to be intently following the conversation, joins in.)

The Therapist's Imagination Lends Inspiration

Kelly: I probably come out of the bathroom quicker when I am having fun. I just go in when I need to go. (Later in the conversation, Kelly is even more assertive regarding her ability to handle Worry.)

Kelly: I think it is really annoying when the Worry is trying to annoy me when I want to go outside and play.

DE: Given that the Worry is taking up a lot less of your time, does that mean you are having more fun and the Worry is no longer killing your joys?

(Kelly assures one and all that this is definitely the case.)

DE: Do you think the Worry was trying to punish you for something or other? (Helping to distinguish the problem as having a rather contrary motive.)

Kelly: Yeah, kind of.

Jan: And it makes you say, "I can't . . . I can't do this!" all the time, doesn't it? Whereas we all know you can!

DE: Jan, do you have any suspicions why the Worry doesn't want Kelly to express all her abilities and talents to the fullest?

Jan: I don't know about you, but it looks to me like the Worry is getting afraid of her.

DE: Can you see any signs of her worrying the Worry?

Rob: (Amused by the concept) The fact that she is playing tennis, having her friends around, and getting out and about surely must mean the Worry is getting worried.

DE: Do you think you might now have to lend the Worry a hand to coach it in how to be calm, cool, and collected? (Kelly's grin indicates that this might be something to put on her to-do list.) Kelly, if there were 100% of your life, what percentage would you say is fun filled and what percentage is Worry filled?

Kelly: Half of the time it's good and half of the time it's bad so it is getting a lot better than it was. When I get tired, Worry tells me I am not making any progress and I can't do it.

DE: Say, before you go to bed at night, have you ever told Worry off? I remember your mum telling me that she was very angry that Worry was stopping you from reading.

Kelly: Well, with the reading, it is getting better, because, "Oh no, I want to keep reading. The book is too exciting!" (Everyone laughs uproariously.) And it's the same when I am having fun. I want to have more fun!

(Jan asks Kelly to tell DE about her friend's visit recently.)

Kelly: (She happily launches into her account.) My friend Rosy and I were playing Pictionary and I went to the bathroom and I got out pretty quickly. And then we just carried on playing.

DE: Did this have to do with your preference for fun and friendship? Did it have to do with you teaching Worry to have more fun, or a bit of both?

Kelly: Maybe. I think it was more the fun because Rosy and I were playing and having fun.

DE: Did the Worry still try to make you worry?

Kelly: Well, I think it tried. Even when I am having fun it still tries to make me worry and not come out.

DE: What did you do so it didn't kill the joys you were having with Rosy? (Providing an opportunity for Kelly to know herself as an active agent.)

Kelly: I think I might have been ignoring it a little bit so it was still there telling me I should use more toilet paper. But I didn't listen to it because I just wanted to get out and play. Because that is what I do. I will be thinking what I can do when I get out, kind of.

DE: If the Worry knew you like Auntie Sarah knows you and your mum and dad know you, do you think it would realize it got the wrong person, and admit to a case of mistaken identity? What about when it sees you as a worrywart but your dad sees you as "full of life now" and your mum thinks of you as a "sporty girl"? Who do you think knows you better—Auntie Sarah, your dad, your mum, or the Worry? (Summarizing and drawing a further distinction between the problem's story of Kelly and a preferred story that is supported by family.)

Kelly: They do! (She turns and meets her parents' eyes, which are filled with pride.)

DE: Do you think you also might have to lend the problem a hand by bringing it up to speed about you as a caring and fun-loving friend and daughter? (Kelly smiles at the prospect of yet another humanitarian mission.)

Several months passed before they met one last time. In a detailed discussion, Kelly decided, thanks to her charitable nature, that the Killjoy was no longer a killjoy and the Worry was no longer so worrisome and that she was far better suited to fun than fretting.

DE: Kelly, now that the Killjoy has retired from killing your joys and your family's joys, do you think you should tell the problem off for doing what it used to do? Or do you think you should forgive it?

Kelly: No, I want to forgive it. (She answers without hesitation.)

DE: Kelly, why do you want to forgive the problem? After all, it spoiled a fair bit of your 8-year-old, 9-year-old, and 10-year-old girl fun, didn't it? At least that is what your mum and dad told me when we first met. (This question may afford Kelly the opportunity to take a moral stance.)

Kelly: It didn't know what it was doing. It didn't really mean it. (Kelly brings her own imaginative spirit to a characterization of the problem.)

DE: Really! You don't say! Jan and Rob, have you heard that before?

Jan: No! (As puzzled as DE.)

Rob: No! (Answering at the same time.)

Kelly: I have forgiven it. It didn't know any better! It just didn't know how to have fun. (Kelly is out in the lead with respect to original story development.)

DE: Kelly, do you think a day will come when this retired problem will offer you thanks for lending it a hand?

Kelly: Yeah, I suppose so! (Grinning.)

They all parted company in the best possible good humor, agreeing that if there was a time in the future when a problem tried to "kill anyone's joys," they would just have to teach it a similar lesson—even if it meant packing in the bathroom again in order to do so. And if that didn't work, they would gather together in DE's more spacious office and have a good laugh together.

From Sorrowful Silence to Signs of Life

As a rich description of Danny began to take shape, DM turned to Alex to see how he was impacted and what might be possible in the way of a stronger connection between father and son.

> **Alex:** I'm learning. A lot of his behavior has been hard to understand. (DM is listening for an entry point that would be in service of the emerging story. The first fragment of Alex's comment about learning seems to offer possibilities.)
>
> **DM:** When you say you're learning, what comes to mind? What have you begun to learn?
>
> **Alex:** Well, when I think about it or take a longer view, he's been through a lot. (He may be shifting in the direction of the preferred story.)
>
> **DM:** Are you describing two different perspectives? (Not wanting to rush or get out in front of Alex. Better to follow him as he makes the turn to a story line that holds promise.)
>
> **Alex:** Yeah. When I'm in the middle of it every day, it's frustrating and I'm thinking, what's going on here?
>
> **DM:** And now, taking the time here, you're tapping into another view?
>
> **Alex:** I am. I mean . . . I've always known he's been through a lot, but I feel more aware in a way. In a way it makes sense that he's had such a hard time. I guess I kept thinking he should be over it by now.
>
> **DM:** And now?

The Therapist's Imagination Lends Inspiration

Alex: Now, I think he's doing pretty good considering. . . .

DM: When you consider what he went through, what is it you're appreciating?

Alex: He's doing his best.

DM: What's telling you he's doing his best? (Inviting more of a detailed description.)

Alex: He did a little better last semester. And I think he's trying, even if it's a little hard to see sometimes.

DM: Are you finding a way to see things that could be otherwise overlooked?

Alex: I guess so. It's all baby steps, right? But he's trying. School is getting better. I think he's doing better this semester. Aren't you? (Turning to Danny for confirmation.)

Danny: Yeah.

Alex: And we're spending a little more time together. He's not *always* in his room. We watched some TV together last night and he helped me with dinner. (Alex is contributing to a more promising account.)

DM: Is that right, Danny? Did you help out last night?

Danny: Yeah.

DM: How come?

Danny: I don't know.

DM: Is your dad right that some things have been better, like school and some things at home with you and your dad?

Danny: Yeah.

DM: Would you agree with your dad that, considering what you've been through, you're doing pretty good? (Seeing if Danny is engaged by the alternative story and aligned with his father's description.)

Danny: Yeah.

DM: With what you've been through, would you agree with your dad that you're doing pretty good or doing your best?

Danny: Yeah, because I've been through a lot, and after my mom died I just didn't care about anything and was just kind of in shock. I just missed her and didn't want to move, and I didn't really care about anything, school or anything. (Danny joins in the telling of his long road back quite easily.)

DM: Okay, so you've been caught in this state of shock for years . . . since your mother's death, and it's not the kind of thing a person can just snap out of, especially when it's a deep two-way love we're talking about. Is that right? (Summarizing and keeping the story afloat.)

Danny: Yeah, but I'm coming out of it. (He moves into the lead.)

DM: How can you tell?

Danny: I care more.

DM: Is caring an important sign?

Danny: Yeah, because before I didn't care about anything.

DM: Okay, I'm starting to get it. And what are you caring more about? Things you used to care about that you're caring about again, or are there things you're caring about for the first time?

Danny: Everything. Like school and just everything.

DM: What's it like to care again after all this time?

Danny: It feels good.

DM: For somebody who knows deep love and is capable of giving it and receiving it, is it even more important to be able to care again? (Further establishing caring as a value.)

Danny: Yeah.

DM: Can you explain why, Danny? Do you feel like you know something about love and caring and what's important about it?

Danny: Because if you don't care about people or if they don't care about you, then what's the point? (This was not an easy question to answer, but Danny seems prepared now to take an active role and step forward as lead agent.)

DM: Yeah, that makes sense. And this has come back to you, this awareness?

Danny: Yeah.

DM: And how can you tell? What's been happening, or what have you been up to that's making this clear to you? (Inviting Danny to give more substance to the story under development.)

Danny: I'm starting to spend more time with my dad.

DM: Has spending time together been important to you?

Danny: Yeah. It's just the two of us.

DM: Alex, did you know that Danny's been caring more about caring, in a way, and that he's bringing caring back into his life and relationship with you?

Alex: Yes and no. As I said, he's been hanging around more, but I didn't know he's been thinking about it or really caring about it. (Alex seems surprised.)

DM: (To Alex) How is it affecting you to know this? What would it mean to you to see your son caring about you and about his life again?

Alex: It would mean everything to me. (He is clearly moved.)

DM: Do you think the two of you just might make good partners in caring?

Alex: I'm sure we will. We're gonna be okay. (He looks at Danny tenderly.)

Danny: Yeah! (There is unmistakable warmth between them.)

With an eye toward constructing a story that drew upon Danny's imagination and the properties and scenery that made up his world, including the players who populated it, Danny found his way. And then there was the matter of making a little magic permissible. With the help of the Baudelaire orphans, Danny was able to cross the divide when needed from the real to the imaginary and back again.

One Last Imaginative Charge

Father and son returned for three more meetings over a span of 6 months, and in that time Danny held to his commitment to reengage with life, disavowing any interest in numbness or a passive existence. Fear still made an occasional appearance in the middle of the night but without the same virulence it once possessed. Danny reached the conclusion that, given the circumstances of his mother's dramatic death and his awareness of how suddenly life can end, it was more a matter of figuring out how to live with Fear than undertaking any goal to overcome it. Alex and DM readily agreed and allowed this to inform their thoughts on the matter. Alex realized the significance of Danny turning to him now, in moments of need, much in the way the Baudelaires turned to each other. He trusted his son's judgment, and on those nights when Danny's mind was overrun by thoughts too strenuous to bear, Alex lifted up the blankets as Danny crept past the hallway shadows and slid into his father's bed and under the covers where he would be safe.

At their final meeting, one last letter floated through the mail slot in the door. Danny jumped up to retrieve it, familiar with the routine by now. He opened it without hesitation and read its contents, grinning from ear to ear. He showed the letter first to his father and then quickly walked over, handing it to DM. It was signed, Sunny, in cursive form, bearing some resemblance to Violet's curved signature, though it could have been in Klaus's hand. At the bottom of the page there were six symmetrical indentations in a semicircle, appearing to be sharp teeth marks. You will recall that it was Sunny's razor-sharp teeth that could puncture even steel and had saved her older siblings from many a menacing predicament in Lemony Snicket's books one through nine. This was undoubtedly her mark. The brief missive read as follows:

Grrox!—Most likely meaning, "Danny, thanks for teaching me so much about caring."
Sunny

Conclusion

Although this chapter is meant to highlight the role of the therapist in providing imaginative charges, it is still the talents and heartfelt commitments Danny had in common with the Baudelaires, as well as the special gifts Kelly shared with her parents, Auntie Sarah, and her forebears, that were drawn upon in yielding desired outcomes. The imagination conscripted on behalf of both young protagonists was not recycled, but rather born from the contexts of their lives, based on their interests, and informed by the values and talents with which they were closely aligned. In recognizing the role of others in bringing to fruition what became possible for Danny and Kelly, we do not intend to diminish their achievements. After all, it is rarely the case that any of us acts alone, especially in hard times. Instead, it is our affiliations with loved ones, whether earthly or heavenly—along with an imaginary friend or two—that hold the greatest potential for helping us find our way.

CHAPTER SIX

The Relational Composition of Identity
Letters, Testimony, and Ritual

During her trek through Wonderland, when the Caterpillar asks Alice a seemingly straightforward question—"Who are you?"—she is baffled and fumbles for words. Perhaps her confusion is the result of having been "so many different sizes in a day" (Carroll, 2000, p. 42). But it is more likely due to the sudden and dramatic changes in her social world. Above ground, Alice is surrounded by those who are "older and wiser"—not to mention taller. Down below, she experiences a reversal of fortunes. There is no denying her relative wisdom among Wonderland's rare and aged ranks. And the more Alice is found to be knowledgeable, the taller she grows, and the greater her authority. Even the Caterpillar, who is rather conceited, can do with a lesson or two in the finer points of metamorphosis, which Alice gamely delivers.

Given that meaning is negotiated relationally, how we comes to know ourselves is more a consequence of social engagement than the result of private meditation (Sax, 2006). The notion that self-esteem is found within may be alluring. But any hope of pinning it down, once and for all, is no more reliable than the sighting of a Cheshire Cat in the branches of a tree—here one moment and gone the next. Ultimately, it is in the context of relationships that we know ourselves as more or less capable (Bird, 2004b; Gergen, 1994). In contemporary Western culture, however, what we achieve (or fail to accomplish) is often seen as evidence of our private properties in the form of internal resources or lack thereof. We are treated as separate units, as if the social world can be disregarded. But it is unlikely that anyone could weather a degraded reputation and thrive in equal measure with someone who is upheld for public approbation. Zigmunt Bauman offers a critique of individualism and the dangers of a privatizing account of identity:

> What is at stake then is the acquittal . . . of the awesome responsibility placed on one's shoulders—and on one's private shoulders alone—by irresistible "individualization." In our "society of individuals" all the messes into which one can get are assumed to be self-made and all the hot water into which one can fall is proclaimed to have been boiled by the hapless failures who have fallen into it. For the good and the bad that fill one's life a person has only himself or herself to thank or to blame. (2001, p. 9)

Problems capitalize on such a view by claiming to know all about young people from the inside out. Given their tendency to privatize human experience, it is often necessary, as a countermeasure, to assert who young people are in the eyes of others. As they attempt to cover the distance from problem-laden provinces to richer regions of understanding, young people travel best in convoy, not as lone riders. New territories of identity can only be scouted and "put on the map" (White, 2007) through collective sightings.

In therapeutic contexts, caregivers, teachers, coaches, imaginary friends, pets, and others are sought out to offer testimony in acknowledgment of young people's virtues. Such offerings are felt expressions of resonance, rather than calculated messages of approval delivered from above. They are meant to recognize and recount those values and practices that young people themselves have decided are the best representation of their moral character.

Acknowledgment, when delivered by letter or achieved through ceremony, can be legitimizing (Epston, 1989; White & Epston, 1990) and "re-grading" (Epston, 1989, p. 114) and possess a staying power that might otherwise fade shortly after the therapy hour ends. Though bearing a certain formality, the design of such enterprises is never so proper as to limit the chance for imagination to make an appearance. We are ever mindful to create contexts that are inviting to young people and welcoming of their particular tastes and talents.

In what follows, we propose several remedies for the negative and isolating effects of problem stories and their unsettling claims on the lives and identities of children and their families. We believe that all young people, not unlike Alice, deserve opportunities to grow into preferred story lines and recruit their own devoted readership.

A Tale of Two Friends

Five-year-old Briana woke up one day and refused to go to school. Her mother guessed she was worried about getting into trouble (and subsequently not receiving a gold star from her teacher), but Briana insisted this was not the case. Instead, her reluctance sprang from "not having a best friend." During naptime, as other girls were calling spots next to each other, Briana was left standing alone at her mat. And instead of enjoying herself on the playground, she was either hindered by shyness or "turbo-driven" straight into other children's games, disrupting whatever activities were under way. The school psychologist decided that, far from being anything original, this was "a classic case of ADHD." She had spoken with Rochelle, who admitted, "Getting Briana to slow down and focus . . . or sit still can be a challenge." To make matters worse, Briana noticed that she was the only girl at school with braided hair. Already at her young age, she was subject to exclusion among her peers on an apparent basis of race.

"I want to wear my hair down and long like the other girls," she begged her mother, Rochelle, who empathized deeply. Like Briana, Rochelle had been the only African American student in her elementary school with the exception of her brother. Rochelle spoke reassuringly with her daughter, hoping it would bring her comfort.

"Braids are beautiful," Rochelle told her. "I wore my hair in braids, and all your aunties wore braids when they were your age, and Grandma braided my hair, just like I braid yours."

Welcomed into their family home as Briana's therapist, Laurie was mindful that her own whiteness made her an outsider. Still, she was eager to help. Rochelle and Laurie shared Briana's concerns with her teacher and principal, who promised to work toward greater inclusivity within the classroom and in the broader school culture. But Laurie wondered what else she might do in the meantime. Following a trip to the library, she called Rochelle to run an idea by her. Rochelle assured her that "anything is worth a try" and said in a friendly tone, "You know I'll tell you if I don't like what you're doing!"

On her next visit to the house, Laurie brought a book called *I Love My Hair!* by Natasha Anastasia Tarpley (1998). On the cover is an African American girl Briana's age with braids swinging in the air, as if she is in motion. At the beginning of the story, the young protagonist, Keyana, complains while her mother combs her hair. But she soon realizes that the nightly ritual and the many styles she can wear connect her to a rich family and cultural heritage. The accompanying illustrations by E. B. Lewis are uplifting. On the story's final page, Keyana can be seen taking off with her two ponytails flapping like wings and carrying her high into the sky. Perhaps the image is meant to symbolize freedom from oppression—a poignant hope.

Briana happily accepted Laurie's invitation to read the story while Rochelle was helping her oldest, Ray, finish his math homework at the kitchen table. Before they had gotten halfway through the story, Briana jumped up from the couch and ran to Rochelle. "Mommy, come and read this book with us! Come and read it, please!" Rochelle was happy to oblige and offered to assume the role of narrator after assisting Ray with the last problem. Briana sat quietly, and when they got to the final page, something unexpected happened: a lavender paper heart slipped out.

"What is that?" asked Briana.

"I don't know." Rochelle looked at Laurie and gave her a wink. There was some discussion about what to do with the heart until Briana figured out that it was origami and could be unfolded. With a

The Relational Composition of Identity

little encouragement, she carefully opened it and to her delight, recognized a familiar word.

"Mommy, that's my name! That's my name," she repeated in disbelief.

"It's okay. It looks like a note. Should I read it?" asked Rochelle.

"Yes, yes!" Briana snapped to attention, and Rochelle read the following aloud:

Dear Briana,

I like your name. It's similar to mine. I heard your mom almost named you Angela. That's a pretty name, too. It sounds like angel. But I have to admit, I'm glad she picked Briana, because that makes us almost the same in a way.

Sometimes when I wear my hair in ponytails, I feel like I can take off and fly. I want to fly all the way past the clouds and to the stars and then land on the moon feet first. Have you ever had this feeling?

Check "yes" or "no"

The hardest thing of all is when I feel like I want to fly, and I have to sit still in my seat. Does this ever happen to you? If you checked "yes," what do you do when it happens? Can you tell me, please?

Okay, that's it for now.
Your friend,
Keyana
(See, it's almost like BRI-ANA!)

Briana immediately ran into the kitchen and scrambled for a pen, at which point Rochelle offered Laurie a nod of approval. With her mother's help, Briana checked the "yes" box and then dictated the following response:

"Let your energy out, Keyana!" Rochelle offered a word of caution, but Briana insisted this was the perfect advice for her new friend. When Rochelle finished writing, Briana proudly signed her own name. Then she asked Laurie for two stickers, one to dot the *i* in her name, and the other to place next to Keyana's. This marked the beginning of a relationship in which the two girls exchanged vows of friendship, as well as advice for living with Turbo energy in a world that was not always appreciative of its effects. Together, Laurie and Briana folded up the note but were left wondering what to do with it. After some brainstorming, they decided that Laurie would return the book to the library the next day, but instead of dropping it in the slot marked "returns," she would carefully place it on the shelf where she first discovered it. She would leave it there for 24 hours and then return, hoping magic would strike twice.

During her next visit to the house, Briana greeted Laurie excitedly. To Laurie's surprise, she did not ask about the book, at least not right away. Instead, she told Laurie to sit down and that she had something to show her. She ran to her bedroom and returned carrying a bag filled with plastic barrettes and bobbles. She poured them out and proceeded to show Laurie her favorites. Laurie admired the many colors and shapes and, with permission, picked out her favorites too. Rochelle joined them and reminisced about how much pride Briana used to take in her hair: "As soon as I was finished, she'd stand up and walk around showing everyone." Briana hopped up and offered a demonstration. She held her head high, her back straight, and marched around the room. Rochelle laughed: "Not too proud! But that's it right there. I just don't want her to lose that confidence. She's tall, so she needs to stand tall and walk like she's proud of herself."

"I *am* proud!" Briana answered defiantly.

"Well, okay. That's all I want." Suddenly remembering the book, Briana swung around and asked Laurie, "Did she write back?"

"She might have. Should we check?" Briana nodded expectantly. Laurie handed her the book, and when Briana opened it to the last page, she found a new note. This time it was pink and folded into a triangle. Briana quickly passed it to Rochelle, who read it aloud. Keyana expressed excitement at having made a new friend. Briana was clearly tickled by this news. But Keyana also recounted some trouble she had gotten into after letting her energy out during a math lesson. At first Briana was distressed and even shed a few tears. Laurie and Rochelle assured her that the trouble was nothing that could not be fixed. Once Briana was convinced of this, she dictated a response that included a list of occasions when it was okay to let her energy out, as well as times when it was better to "call it back in." Briana was happy to share her secret about how this was done (e.g., with the wave of her arm), which Laurie and Rochelle were also eager to learn.

Shortly thereafter, the family moved across town. As a result, Briana and Ray transferred to a new school. Laurie thought Briana might need her pen pal more than ever, but it turned out she was wrong. When Laurie visited Briana, she found her walking around the new schoolyard with a companion, another little girl about the same height with braided hair. Briana was happy to make introductions, and then the two ran off to play. Later that day when Laurie caught up to her, Briana spoke enthusiastically about the kids at her new school. Perhaps Keyana had come into Briana's life at just the right time—when she needed a friend most. It seemed for now, Keyana could return to the local library. Perhaps she is there now, trying out new origami designs and waiting patiently for another young reader to befriend.

A Letter of Full Disclosure: Addressing the Problem Directly

It is not always a young person who is the intended recipient of a letter. On occasion, we consider writing to the problem in order to clarify that the young person is not defenseless, nor is she or he alone (Epston & Marsten, 2010). We might present the idea to the young person and family as "an ethical requirement" in order to satisfy the terms of full disclosure. After all, it is only right that the problem knows as soon as possible what it is getting itself into in taking on, not just a young person, but her or his entire clan. Young people's wonderfulnesses are commonly found to be traceable across generations as part of a legacy and as proof of family, community, and cultural bonds.

In all fairness, full disclosure of a young person's abilities and affiliations might be swiftly sent to the problem by post, e-mail, or in some other dramatic fashion. There have been instances when we have dared the problem to attend meetings in our offices or at a family's home so that full disclosure could be made face-to-face. So far, none has had the nerve to show up. DE illustrates how, given its absence, a young person, with the support of family, can address the problem by letter.

Dear Stealing,

We, the Jones Family, felt it only fair that you should know who you are messing with as you might have gotten the idea that Julie was a pushover. We know you more or less caught Julie by surprise as she thought at first you were a friend and teacher. She has informed us that you told her you would look after her and make her life a lot better than how she was experiencing it at the time. But you may have thought you could just hoodwink her. It looks to us like you took advantage by convincing her that it pays to take things so she can have them sooner rather than later. You gave her the idea that she couldn't wait and showed her how getting things right away would lead to a better life, but this turned out to be what she now considers "phony baloney." Still, when she was your student and you posed as her teacher, you may very well have gotten the impression that you could keep pulling the wool over her eyes.

No wonder you will probably be surprised to learn from us that she is a very smart cookie. We thought you had better be warned just what a smart cookie she is, so we decided to tell you a lot of smart-cookie stories about her. Why would we warn you and not just let you find out the hard way? Well, our family is fair and no matter what, we play clean and, not surprisingly, we don't like players who play dirty. But even if you play dirty, and try to rob her of her good reputation, Julie decided "we should play fair because that is the right thing to do in our family."

Julie reported, "I like puzzles and hard problems." You probably didn't know this about her, but if she gets something wrong she'll stick with it until she figures it out. Her favorite book is *Harriet the Spy*. She likes Harriet "because she's smart but she's not perfect, and she tries to do the right thing, even if she makes a mistake at first." Jenny, Julie's mom, confirmed this and added, "Julie always had a strong sense of right and wrong and wasn't one to try and get away with something. That's why it was so out of character for her to take something that doesn't belong to her. In a way, we knew it wasn't her."

Kevin, Julie's dad, is convinced she has a sixth sense, especially when it comes to figuring things out with their family dog: "It's uncanny. We all agree it's as if she can read Ruff's mind. He'll be sniffing around, disturbed about something or other. Julie's usually the one to solve the mystery. She'll find a lost bone or toy; she'll play with him or just sit with him until he's calm." If Harriet (the Spy) could see Julie in action, she'd be proud to have her as a devoted reader.

Now that you know who you are dealing with, you might be wise to leave her alone. If you intend to stick around and bother her, at least you have been fairly warned. Julie is not alone, so you are in for more than you may have bargained for with us. Why? Because "we have teamed up"! And be forewarned that we would not be happy at all for you to bother another young girl like Julie. If we find out that you have, we will go and tell her family how we managed to send you packing.
Yours sincerely,
Julie; Julie's mom, Jenny; Julie's dad, Kevin; and Ruff (Ruff! Ruff-ruff-ruff!)

While Stealing may have been happy to spend time with Julie when it was just the two of them alone, DE suspected it might be averse to crowds and disinclined to stick around much longer now that it had been informed of Julie's family bonds. Time was of the essence to demand an apology from Stealing, though DE guessed its plans for a stealthy retreat might already be underway. Even if they managed to reach it before it vanished without a trace, he knew that it was highly unlikely that Stealing would oblige anyway, no matter how just the request. It turned out Stealing must have gone into hiding as soon as it realized Julie was aided and abetted by loved ones and could not be so easily trifled with. As a result of its sudden disappearance, it was up to DE to channel the problem and write its letter of contrition. Luckily, he was rather practiced at letter writing and had little trouble composing the following—with the family's help:

Dear Julie (and Julie's mom, Jenny; Julie's dad, Kevin; and Ruff),

I had no idea you stood for honesty and were such a smart cookie, but those stories your mom and dad told me were certainly convincing. I just thought I could pull the wool over your eyes and you would follow my advice blindly and steal stuff and take money from your parents' wallets. I had no idea you were a person of integrity or that you came from a family with strong values, going all the way back on both parents' sides to your grannies and their mothers before them. I must admit, it never occurred to me that you were guided by what both your parents described as "a clear sense of right and wrong." I mistakenly figured you for a naive girl who I would have no trouble convincing that wrong is just as good as right. But now I've learned you live by a strong set of values and that you even came up with a plan for how to recycle water for use in your family's garden.

I suppose if I had known all this, I wouldn't have tried to pull the fast one that "they will never miss the money," or "Hey, you need stuff. Why wait until next Friday until you get your allowance? Get it now!" If I had known what a smart cookie you are, I might have guessed you'd see through me sooner or later and even tell me off and reject me.

Well, I can fool other kids who aren't such smart cookies so it's probably a good idea to bid you adieu and head off on another assignment to the home of another girl your age. I am sorry I mistook you for the person you obviously are not. You have taught me a lesson to be more careful about who I choose. Do you think I should stick to kids a year or two younger than you are?

We are now parting company.
Your problem-from-the-past,
Stealing
P.S. As you may have noticed, I did not list a forwarding address (ha ha!) since the last thing I need is for you and your parents (and Ruff) to show up and blow my cover.

A Letter of Solidarity: Between Father and Son

Sadly, it is not just talents that can be found in evidence among family members from generation to generation. Problems, having gotten to know families, are sometimes reluctant to move on. Instead, they can wait in excited anticipation of new arrivals, relishing the prospect of cozying up with the daughters and sons of adults they previously tormented. Seeing problems travel across generations might tempt some to choose one side or the other in the unremitting nature-nurture debate, as if nailing down the cause would somehow contribute to the problem's resolution. (Claimant A: It's genetic! Claimant B: It's environmental! Claimant C: It's a combination of the two!) Problems themselves do not mind being interrogated for their origin stories. They much prefer it to the kind of scrutiny that would expose them for the tricks of their trade. But we resist pursuing how and where it all began and instead take a more practical view. Packing up and moving is such a nuisance after years of nesting. Why would any problem go to the trouble of looking for a new family and residence, when it had already gotten comfortable and made itself at home?

Rather than feeling discouraged in any way, we find that when parents or caregivers have contended with the same problem that their young charges now face, there is the added prospect of establishing a united front. It is often the case that a young person finds relief in learning she or he is not the only one to have met a particular problem. And rather than establishing the parent as the wiser of the two and relegating the young person to the role of pupil, daughters and sons are let in on their parents' own irksome histories with the problem—with the parent's permission, of course. If anything, hierarchies are leveled as parents readily admit to having been taken for their own wild ride with no shortage of highs and lows.

This was the case with 7-year-old Josh, who found himself contending with Embarrassment and frequently heeding its warnings not to engage in any fun or daring activity, no matter how narrow in scope. DM wrote the following letter after having discovered that the very same problem already knew its way around the family domicile.

Dear Josh,

Thanks for hanging in there last night. Although you were tired and rubbing your eyes and maybe not in the greatest mood, you did your best, which was plenty good enough. And I have to admit some of my questions could have used improvement, especially the one about whether Embarrassment ever gets embarrassed for embarrassing young people. Do you remember that dud? You weren't the only one who was confused by it. I practically confused myself. The most interesting thing we learned, at least the thing that struck me the most, was that Embarrassment is no stranger to your family. It is an old friend of your father's. I use the term "friend" advisedly.

Your dad explained that when he was a boy, Embarrassment used to get to him, convincing him not to ask for help. He said, "My mother and father are really smart. My mom went to Harvard and my dad went to UCLA and on to grad school at the University of Pennsylvania. I felt like I had to be really smart too and know all the answers to everything all by myself. I was embarrassed when I didn't know something and thought, 'I shouldn't ask for help! I won't ask for help with anything!'"

This got me wondering if Embarrassment might stand only half a chance if it were up against the two of you. With your imagination (which I've come to learn is excellent), and your dad having known Embarrassment all these years, do you think you'd make a good team?

Even prior to teaming up, you had your eye on Embarrassment and what it can get up to. You explained how it tries to convince you that the worst things in the world are:

- Making mistakes
- Getting something wrong
- Not knowing the answer to a question the teacher asks
- Anything less than perfection 24/7
- A new math problem

The Relational Composition of Identity

And you've already had some ideas about what to do if it tries to boss you around and get you to clam up, make you mad, or say you can't ask for help when you need it. For example, you might give it a karate chop—by the way, did you earn your green belt on Thursday?

Good luck this week, Josh. If Embarrassment has anything in mind, like swiping your good mood and replacing it with a bad one, or trying to change you from the boy who "loves life" into the boy who lost his laugh, let me know. I wonder if it will think twice, now that you and your dad have your eyes (all four of your eyes) on it.

Your friend,
David

Finding himself in good company, Josh spent time with his father comparing notes. And as it turned out, the tricks that Josh described Embarrassment playing on him were the same ones it had played on his father long ago. Apparently, Embarrassment had not learned a single new trick in all the years in between, which made it a less impressive problem than Josh first took it to be. Michael was happy to come to his son's aid and share how, even to this day, Embarrassment could make an occasional appearance. His decision to talk openly with his son was only further evidence of his love for him. It was in the context of this connection that Josh began to take his life back from Embarrassment.

In the same way a father can lend his son a hand, a son can make a similar offering to someone his junior. This well-documented approach (Epston, 1998; Epston & White, 1992; Freeman et al., 1997; Marsten et al., 2011) has been shown to benefit young people by recognizing them, not simply as recipients, but as bearers (and sharers) of knowledge. Once Josh had achieved steadier footing in relation to Embarrassment, DM turned to him for assistance, with the hope of enlisting him as a consultant.

Hi Josh,

When I told a boy I met this week, who is 6 years old, that I know a boy who is 1 year older and starting to figure a thing or two out about

Embarrassment, his eyes got wide. He asked me, "What did he tell you? What does he do?"

I said that you were still figuring it out, but that you had caught on to the kinds of tricks Embarrassment can play on a kid. I haven't shown him your list, but I'm thinking he could learn a lot from it. I wanted to get your permission first. If Embarrassment were your boss, here's what you said it would order you to do:

1. Don't ask for any help!
2. Don't stop reading. You'll never get started again.
3. Don't do math homework. You'll make a mistake.
4. Don't try new things. You can't do them.
5. Don't have new friends over. You're not good at playdates.
6. When you are changing clothes for gym, worry that people are looking at you.
7. Don't do your spelling. The words are too hard.
8. When you make a mistake in soccer, Embarrassment says, "YOU STINK! DON'T PLAY ANYMORE! JUST QUIT!"
9. Don't share your feelings. Don't say what you need. You'll be sorry if you do.
10. Embarrassment can make you unhappy and then it can make you mad. (This is its favorite trick.)

I have gotten to know this boy a little and think it would be a real help if I could tell him about numbers 1, 3, 4, 5, 8 (he's playing tee ball), 9, and especially 10. Embarrassment is giving him an awful time and making him keep to himself and avoid almost everything that could bring fun into his life. I wouldn't bring up numbers 2 or 7 because he's not reading or spelling all that much on his own yet.

Do you think it would help him to see how Embarrassment sneaks around in a kid's life? If I tell him about the kinds of tricks Embarrassment can play on a boy who now knows how it operates, do you think it would make a difference? I'm hoping he would be able to stretch and find his way into a 7-year-old understanding, with your help, even

The Relational Composition of Identity

though he's only 6. Even if all he can do for now is hold onto your ideas until he's old enough to more fully understand them, do you think it might give him some hope in the meantime?

I'll be meeting with him in two days. If there's any way to let me know before then, I would really appreciate it. I know he would, too. Of course I wouldn't tell him your name or anything about you unless you told me to tell him. But even then, I wouldn't give him your last name or e-mail address.

I hope you had a good week and that Embarrassment didn't spoil too much of your fun—especially now that you've decided that taking chances and having more fun is part of what makes life worth living. Whatever you decide, thanks for teaching me lots and lots about Embarrassment.

Your friend,
David

Josh proudly assented to having his 7-year-old knowledges shared with his new 6-year-old protégé. It is most likely that his status as a consultant contributed to his own advancement in life and in relation to the problem. There is the potential for transport in such a request: "In consulting the young person on behalf of those who may find themselves in near identical predicaments, the young person finds her/himself in a new role as young expert and veteran of the problem" (Marsten et al., 2011, p. 62). In a final document DM and Josh cocreated, Embarrassment was put on notice as Josh listed the areas of his life he had taken back in full or in part from the problem. DM acted as faithful scribe.

Things Have Gotten a Lot Better
By Josh (in His Own Words)

1. At home:
    - I am moving past my fears.
    - I am in charge of Temper.
    - I am more independent with homework.

2. At school:
      - I am going to play tennis.
      - I am more in charge than Embarrassment.
   3. About our impending move out of state:
      - I am excited about the move and being closer to my grandparents.
   4. With friends:
      - I am more outgoing.
      - I will try to become friends with new people when we move.
   5. In general:
      - I am more comfortable.
      - I am proud of myself.

Josh approved the list for its accuracy and commended DM for his skills in taking dictation. Like his father before him, he did not expect that he would henceforth live a life totally free of Embarrassment. He suspected that in difficult moments the problem would do its best to take advantage and try to lure him into a colorless life. But he had every reason to believe that, before long, he would manage to tug back and carry on, according to plans of his own design. And besides, if he was capable of advising others in need, he decided, the least he could do was take his own advice now and then.

Restoring a Mother's Place in Her Son's Heart: A Mother Appreciation Party

Given that mothers are often derided for their perceived shortcomings and even for the tragic circumstances that can befall them and their children, it is sometimes necessary to come to their aid by calling on friends and family for support. This can include helping their daughters and sons retrieve what may have seemed forever lost in the way of love for their mothers. Although DE was well known for his vast experience as a family therapist, he was nevertheless taken aback upon meeting Mary and her 13-year-old son, Joey, and hearing their sad tale. Despite having only recently reached her 40th birthday, Mary looked as if she was weary of life itself. She immediately set about telling DE what she considered to be the backstory to her son's fits of temper.

Mary met and married Joey's Kiwi father overseas and then immigrated to New Zealand to make a home with him. He was an international businessman whose travels took him away from New Zealand for extended stays. From the very beginning of their marriage, and even more so after the birth of their son, Joey's father would yell and beat her if any of his whims were not immediately indulged. Her fervent desire for her son to grow up in a home with a father, which she herself had been denied, overruled any concern for her own safety and well-being. And so she decided there was nothing she would not endure to see this dream of hers come to pass.

During her husband's trips abroad, she breathed a deep sigh of relief and then braced herself to receive him each time he returned. Mary described how Joey "hid himself away" when his father would come home. However, around the time of his 11th birthday, he changed course and, as Mary put it, "started standing up and having a say about things." As a result, his father turned on Joey in the worst way, chastising him for each and every perceived breach of conduct. Mary did everything in her power to deflect her husband's attention but was told in no uncertain terms to "stay out of it" with the absurd claim, "It's got nothing to do with you!" To her dismay, he started beating Joey. This was unbearable, given her immense love for her son and her wish to protect him. Despite her husband's threats of dire consequences should they attempt to leave, they fled to a women's refuge during one of his trips. As DE might have expected, mother and son looked very kindly at each other throughout a review of these events. But this was soon to change.

As Mary proceeded, her direct manner of speaking was replaced by hesitation, as she took pains not to rile Joey. DE quickly learned that she had good reason for such trepidation. She explained that ever since they had been on their own, Joey had begun threatening and beating her if his requests were not instantly met. "In fact," Mary explained, "he calls me the exact same names his father did!"

DE was disturbed by Mary's description and then startled when Joey suddenly erupted with such intensity that DE's first thought was for the safety of the children and families in the adjoining therapy rooms. He leaped from his seat and rushed to Joey, imploring him, "Quick, give me your hand! This is an emergency! You are frightening the young children in the other rooms!" Completely surprised, Joey temporarily desisted and allowed DE to take his hand. He recovered his equanimity enough to assure DE they could safely proceed. Mary explained, while keeping a close eye on Joey, that such events "occur somewhere between 10 to 15 times a day." This provided DE with fair warning. There were four more incidents of uncontrolled screaming during that very hour in which Joey was appalled by one or more of his mother's comments and intended to censor her. In each instance, DE succeeded in employing his "emergency response" to reasonable effect.

In between Joey's fits, Mary spoke of a vow to which she had remained faithful: "I decided never to say a bad word to Joey about his father." DE turned to Joey and asked whether he could bear to learn his mother's truth, even if it might be very different from his own or his father's. DE wondered whether it might have some impact to know more about what Joey's mother had endured. He tentatively agreed. With his consent, DE interviewed Mary about her mission to protect Joey by "taking the blows" that were intended for him and seeing to it that "he got away unharmed" whenever possible. DE observed Joey listening intently. He turned to him and asked, "Did you have any idea before this moment that your mother went to such lengths to protect you?" He admitted that he did not. DE then asked, "Do you mind telling me if knowing this changes your mind about your mother?" Joey admitted that it definitely did. "Would you be willing to tell me what kind of mother you thought you had before knowing her 'truth'?" DE asked. "Say what you really think."

Joey shamefacedly admitted that he thought his mother "was just plain dumb." In response, DE asked, "Has your mother's 'truth' given you second thoughts about her stupidity?" Joey nodded. DE then turned to Mary and asked, "Is it the case that you played dumb to protect Joey?" She admitted to having done so. "Joey, I had to keep it from you," she reassured him. Regarding his tantrums, Joey pledged, "I will never have another tantrum as long as I live."

When they returned in a few weeks' time, he had indeed lived up to his promise. Mary wept with joy, exclaiming, "I have my son back. I thought I'd lost him forever!" Joey was more than willing to acknowledge that he was deeply concerned for her well-being. He had never considered her as sacrificing herself on his behalf but merely paying a penance for her own blunders. DE sought Mary's permission to speak with Joey "privately for the time being," and then added, "Mary, I give you my word that in due course absolutely everything Joey and I discuss will be revealed to you." Mary readily gave her consent and hastily left the room.

DE asked Joey to draw his chair closer. He looked at him kindly and tentatively inquired, "Are you worried about your mother's well-being?" Joey agreed. "Have you come up with anything off your own bat to provide some relief from her distress?" He hadn't. Given Joey's interest but uncertainty about what could be done, DE submitted the following proposal: "Have you ever heard of a surprise mother appreciation party?" He hadn't but did know about surprise parties, so DE asked, "Would you be willing to consider a 'surprise mother appreciation party'?" Joey agreed but wondered how to go about it.

In the conversation that ensued, they easily covered such essentials as invitations, decorations, and the choice of food and drink for the party. With respect to the guest list, Aunt Jenny stood out as a strong advocate for Mary, having assisted in their flight and rehousing. By the end of the meeting, they had a list of invitees, whom Joey promised to contact between sessions.

At their next private meeting, DE learned that Aunt Jenny and Mary's best friend and former neighbor, Beth, insisted on helping with the preparations. Joey had indeed kept the party a secret, and he smiled mischievously as he described all the subterfuges he had been up to in avoiding detection. Conspiring with DE had allowed them to draw even closer and become at ease with each other. Still, DE had some reservations about his next question: "I suppose you have been wondering how you go about 'appreciating a mother' at a surprise mother appreciation party." Joey admitted, "I don't have a clue." "Well, the only way I know how you can show your appreciation for your mother at her surprise party," DE explained, "is by giving a 'mother appreciation speech.' Hey, don't worry about it! I will ask you mother appreciation questions, and you will reply with mother appreciation answers. I will take notes and then type them all up as your speech. You might even give it to your mum afterward as a keepsake." When they let Mary know that they would need one last secret session, she laughed aloud and said, "You can have as many secret sessions as you guys need. Joey has been such a help lately. You must be doing something right."

Three weeks passed and, as promised, Joey called DE his first chance to report that all had gone as planned. Anxious to hear about the party, David invited them to meet one last time. The highlight of the session was Joey agreeing to reread his surprise mother appreciation speech to DE in Mary's presence. He asked his mother for it. She reached into her purse, pulled out a protective sleeve, and opened it to reveal the letter. She carefully handed it over to DE in the manner of a member of a persecuted religion secretly showing a relic to a coreligionist. DE asked Joey if he might stand up and face his mother. He hesitated, clearing his throat, before he commenced:

To everyone here, I want you to know why I planned a surprise mother appreciation party for my mum—with Aunt Jenny and Beth's help. I am so grateful to her for doing everything she could to see to my care and protection. Most of you know that my father would scream at my mother, call her terrible names, and beat her up for just about anything. She had to follow his orders, and if she didn't jump up right away and meet his exacting standards, he would use it as an excuse to beat her. I was so scared but, at least for a time, Mum managed to keep me safe and hidden away in my room when my father lost control. When he was overseas, I now realize she did everything she could to help me believe in myself. She brought me out of my shell and doted on me when he wasn't around. She must have feared how I would be treated once I got older if I didn't follow my father's orders. Sure enough, he started screaming at me and calling me names. And it wasn't long before he would beat me up, too, even if it wasn't as bad as what Mum got.

This is about the time that my mum started getting stupid. Or at least that is what I thought at the time. She would do really obvious things that would get her a beating. Just a month ago, my mum told me she did it on purpose to draw the attention away from me and keep me as safe as possible. I was ashamed because after we lived at the women's refuge and then got this apartment, I was the one screaming and calling my mum the same names he used to. And I hit her, too.

One reason for my speech is to tell you how ashamed I am and how I want my mum to know how much I respect her for saving me from my father's violence as much as she did. She suffered blows that otherwise would have been meant for me. Now, can anyone here think of a better reason for a son my age to hold a surprise party to appreciate his mother? When I am older and maybe have a son of my own, I hope my mother will be as wonderful to him as she has been to me. Everyone lift a glass, and let's sing, "For she's a jolly good mother!"

DE didn't ask what happened at the party, but, from the tears the three of them shed during this second public reading, he could easily imagine there was not a dry eye in the house. Joey's public contrition and renewed appreciation for his mother not only restored their mutual love, but also provided a basis for him to separate from the legacy of his father's cruelty. DE had every reason to believe he would continue to find his way forward as a different sort of young man. They parted company with warm embraces all around, but before they were out the door, Joey remembered a promise he had made to DE. He turned back and shared one final detail, as if he hadn't already proved himself a devoted son: "Mum didn't do a lick of work at her party."

When Odds Are Long and Stakes Are High: Letters to Foster Hope

We end this chapter with Laurie's efforts to recruit an appreciative audience (Madsen, 2007; Madsen & Gillespie, 2014; White, 1995) on behalf of Rafael, a 10-year-old boy, who found himself on a collision course with Trouble and at risk for school expulsion. The penultimate straw involved a "fire sale" of candy bars he had stolen from a younger boy. This was followed by an incident of "borrowing" sports equipment from the gym office without permission. Although he returned it all the next day, his punishment, a two-day suspension, was not revoked. In the tradition of narrative letter writing, Laurie created a document to circulate among those people at school (e.g., the principal, his guidance counselor, his teacher, and the school psychologist), who might support him in finding a more promising path (Winslade & Monk, 2007). To offset the cumulative effects of these events, she included stories that spoke to his good character, hoping to pave the way for a preferred story line.

To Rafael's School Allies:

As most of you know, Rafael returned to school last Friday after a two-day suspension. The day before his readmittance, several of you offered encouraging words. Mr. Potts [his teacher], you told Rafael that in your book, "Everyone deserves a second chance." Mrs. Garrett [the principal], you assured Rafael that you are looking forward to "getting to know him on better terms." Rafael was moved by your words and told his mom, "I'm tired of getting in trouble. I promise I'll try my best not to get kicked out of school." Rafael's mother believes in him and told me, "I know my son can do it."

But as anybody knows, Trouble doesn't give up easily. For this reason, Rafael hopes you will help him remember, should you see him falter, all that he has to live for—and who he is—apart from Trouble. First and foremost, Rafael has a strong heart and is determined to do good. We could list any number of representative examples of his strong heart, but for now, we'll share just two:

1. Rafael comforted his younger brother, Frankie, in the midst of a dramatic scene when they were both really scared. As the police were banging on their front door, Rafael's first thought was to hide his brother under the bed they shared. He draped a sheet low to conceal him and whispered just loud enough

for Frankie to hear, "Everything's going to be all right." When the two boys were removed from their home, Rafael reminded Frankie that their mother would know just what to do. During a distressing two-month separation, while she worked to bring her sons back home "in record-breaking time," Rafael looked after Frankie "because he was the only thing that mattered."
2. Rafael remembers the moment he saw his baby brother, Manny, for the very first time: "He opened his eyes and looked up at me." And from that day on they had a special bond—so special that even when they were separated for a time, his baby brother never forgot him. Rafael describes their reunion: "He looked at me and started hugging me, and I was so happy." Rafael could not believe it when Manny called him by name, "Rafa." He learned Rafael's name before anyone else's, which proved their relationship was beyond compare.

When I asked Rafael why "being good" was important to him, he talked about his love for his tia, Maria, who died three years ago, and his devotion to his mother. He also talked about his love for God. Rafael told me that when he is doing his best, God looks down from heaven and thinks, "That's my son, and he's doing great." When I asked him what else God sees in him, he said, "The light in my soul and that I'm trying to make it and trying to do right." Rafael knows that God, his tia, and his mother have hopes and dreams for him. Some of which are:

1. Doing all his work
2. Looking after "the little ones"
3. Never gang banging
4. Going to college
5. Treating girls right
6. Staying alive

Rafael realizes all that he's up against. People with less firsthand knowledge of Trouble might try to offer well-meaning advice like:
"Just turn your back on it."
"Just say no!"

But Rafael knows it's not that simple. You can try to shake free from Trouble, but that doesn't mean Trouble will let go of you. He can tell you better than anybody how Trouble can even take a person's life, as it did his cousin and a neighbor. Staying alive is important to Rafael, because he knows his mother "would be crying all the time" if anything happened to him. Rafael stated, "I never want to look down from heaven and see my mom putting flowers on my grave."

You are receiving this letter because Rafael values his relationship with you. With one more chance to do right at Washington Elementary, he knows the stakes are high. Because you are someone Rafael has chosen to be on his team, along with God, Tia Maria, and his mother, we would be grateful for your help in continuing to provide whatever support is possible.

Thank you in advance. We will be in touch from time to time.
Sincerely,
Laurie Markham

Laurie's hope was that by sharing an equally true and virtuous account of Rafael's character, it might be possible to expand the number of people who stood with him united against Trouble. After receiving the letter, the principal called Rafael into her office to see how he was doing. Rafael told Mrs. Garrett that he was worried he might get into trouble again, especially during recess. He explained, "A lot of kids here know my family and say bad things about them." Eager to see him succeed, Mrs. Garrett told Rafael that if he was willing to do volunteer work, he could skip recess whenever he felt it was necessary. Rafael was grateful and had a hard time choosing between a job in the cafeteria or one in the office. The cafeteria had cookies, but in the office, he would have special privileges, like delivering hall passes and using the copy machine. He chose the latter and was taken under the wing of an administrative assistant, Jody, who had a strong heart of her own. At Rafael's request, she was given a copy of his letter, which she kept in her desk drawer. From time to time, when Jody guessed Rafael's vision for his life was clouding over and Trouble was looming, she pulled it out and reminded him of his hopes and dreams.

The Relational Composition of Identity

In no time, Rafael grew to love Jody, and the two looked out for each other. Rafael helped to lighten her workload, and she made sure he had whatever he needed, whether it was a pep talk, a hug, or supplies for class. Things started looking up as Rafael became a valued member of his school community and was even recognized with a service award (which Jody pinned on the office bulletin board, along with Rafael's school picture).

Despite these encouraging developments, Trouble persisted, refusing to let Rafael move on with his life. Whenever he was disrespected, Trouble filled his head with reasons for reprisal, and this created a real dilemma. A month after sending out the first letter, Laurie wrote to Rafael's allies again in an attempt to reinvigorate the story under development and keep the team apprised. Notice Laurie's efforts to locate Trouble and Rafael's response to it within a broader social and cultural frame.

To Rafael's School Team:

In our last letter, Rafael and I asked for your support in his efforts to get free of Trouble. You all graciously accepted the invitation to join his team and have been true partners. Each of you has reached out in a vital way. And Rafael has been moved by your interest and goodness. This week I asked Rafael how things were going and he told me: "I love my school. . . . I have the best teacher, and the best principal, and Jody and me are friends."

Still, as Rafael put it, "Trouble is like a hunter. It gets kids in its scope." He's been "dodging bullets" since he returned to school. Rafael knows that Trouble would like nothing better than "to see me put away for good." Trouble tempted him the other day when he walked into the restroom and found two boys throwing wet paper towels at the ceiling. Rafael thought about joining them before he realized "it wasn't worth it." He left quickly, facing down a second temptation: "They called me a punk as I was leaving, but I didn't let it get to me."

Unfortunately, escaping Trouble is not always as simple as finding a different restroom. As Rafael can tell you, there is danger everywhere—not just on TV, but right outside the front door. Just last week, he shared a story about a group of people coming over and standing on his lawn, demanding that his family pay up for something they had nothing to do with.

In spite of the danger that is all around, the love in his home is undeniable and can be seen in the way "everybody takes care of each other." It is this love that Rafael draws upon whenever he stands up to Trouble. According to Rafael, "My family knows how to love strong." Their love is so powerful that it sometimes brings tears to his eyes. One story always gets to him. It's the one about his Uncle Miguel risking his life by coming back to the neighborhood to see the family on Christmas. Out of all the nieces and nephews, Uncle Miguel gave Rafael "the biggest hug. It was the best present." Rafael loves this story because he loves his uncle almost as much as he loves the women in his family: "I've learned how to take care of people from the best, like my mom. She had it hard when she was my age, and she had to help take care of her younger brothers and sisters."

As you all know, Rafael loves his mother very much. And he's been listening to her these days, like when she sits him down and tells him if anything happens to her, he and his brothers will need to look out for each other. He feels the gravity of her words and accepts the responsibility that comes with it. This starts with looking out for his family's reputation, even when there is a cost. And so, in getting to know Rafael and what he carries, I've been weighing a difficult question:

If leaving Trouble behind is no small order, and the advice that might work for others has less relevance in Rafael's world, what will such a bold move require? Will it depend on community support? Creative thinking in the highest order? "Loving strong?"

Early on, it became clear that I was getting to know a very special young man, someone who carries many people in his heart. He is one of those rare individuals, who just might end up living—and sometimes fighting—for love. Whether it is possible to hold this commitment and avoid any plans Trouble may have for him is something we are still sorting out. Thank you again for standing with Rafael in his efforts to avoid Trouble. Your commitment to him has made a real difference. Rafael and I both believe that nothing is better than belonging to a community. We

really appreciate you being on his team along with Tia Maria, Uncle Miguel, his mother, and God.
Sincerely,
Laurie

Sadly, a month after this letter was circulated, Mrs. Garrett took a leave of absence and a new principal arrived. Although efforts were made to hold onto an image of Rafael according to the developing counterstory, he once again became associated with Trouble. When he threatened violence against a boy who bullied his brother, Frankie, the new principal took swift action, initiating a school transfer. It was at that time that Laurie's work with Rafael and his family came to an end. She thinks about him often and hopes that others, like Mrs. Garrett, Jody, and Mr. Potts, will see beyond the Trouble that surrounds him, and into his world and all the love in his heart.

Conclusion

Problems can be fierce and seem insurmountable, given how deeply they can nestle in the lives of young people, their families, and their communities. They often "prosper" within social and economic contexts of hardship where there is a scarcity of resources and an abundance of risk. It is incumbent upon us to respond communally. The customary pathologizing documents that fill official files can be met by counterdocuments meant to make young people and their loved ones known for their virtues and steadfast affiliations. Letters can begin to establish a public record of young people's hopes and dreams, and testify to their values, their heartfelt commitments, and their relational vows. Young people can feel well supported in preferred identities within communities as a result of the circulation of such documents. But, even then, it may not always be enough.

CHAPTER SEVEN

Weird Science

Imagination Lost

Is science delivering on its promise to unravel the mysteries of the universe, and to our ends, the secrets of childhood and the developing mind? We might conclude, given the excitement over recent advances in neuroscience, that we have reached the highest point yet, ever closer to the apex of scientific revelation. No longer will we depend on young people to provide us with clues. Soon, a master key will unlock the door, taking us through the inner passage to the sanctum sanctorum, exposing the deepest crags in young psyches—leaving nothing to the imagination. Crossing the threshold of skin and skull, and journeying inward through imaging, neuroscientists will code and decode the human brain. Psychiatry is primed and already pointing to "underlying neural substrates" associated with so-called childhood disorders, as if to confirm the existence of attention-deficit hyperactivity disorder, social anxiety, oppositional-defiant disorder, and so on (Happe & Frith, 2014). We have been made out as the beneficiaries of a kind of knowledge that has not yet arrived but is somehow presciently felt to be in our possession.

Amid the fanfare, the psychologist Kenneth Gergen strikes a cautionary note. He warns that before we trace the latest topographical lines in brain mapping and draw conclusions regarding diagnosis, we would do well to examine the evidence, or lack thereof. There may be the assertion of linkages between brain activity and human (pre)dispositions, but such claims rely more on conjecture than fact.

Though the brain may be showing us something that is common to a given group, the meaning attributed to such findings is anything but clear. There is a gap between the data collected and the conclusions reached. What fills the breach is more constructed meaning than discovered truth:

> The chief question . . . is whether brain scan devices enable us to solve this otherwise intractable problem of inference. . . . We are presented with a collection of expressions that we classify as symptoms of an underlying condition, but we have no access to the causal condition itself. In effect, we are forced to speculate that loss of appetite, lack of sleep, and feelings of hopelessness are symptoms of an underlying state of depression. We now observe the neural condition of the person we have shakily diagnosed as depressed. Indeed, we succeed in locating a pattern of neural activity unique to this population. Yet, we may ask, how can we determine that the observed state of the brain is in fact "depression"? Why is it not simply a neural correlate of sleeplessness, appetite loss, or feelings of helplessness? Or for that matter, how could we determine that the neural state is not one of "spiritual malaise," "anger," "withdrawal from oppressive conditions," or "cognitive integration and regrouping"? (Gergen, 2010, p. 801)

Undaunted by this divide, the course has been set. It is by means of psychiatric intervention that human subjects will be unveiled, their problems seen as little more than carbon copies of others just like them (Cortese et al., 2012; Pandya, Altinay, Malone, & Anand, 2012; Hemmings et al., 2008). Upon hearing that 10-year-old Paula is compelled to say her bedside prayer 10 times in a row without error in order to slumber safely, we are far more likely to suspect obsessive-compulsive disorder is at work than we are to imagine the Sleep Thief might be at play. Our ears are already tuned to the former term. It has a "scientific ring" while the latter seems to strike a false note and exist only in a young girl's imagination. But has psychology chosen well in hitching its wagon to psychiatry and evidence-based medicine, a well-established system among physicians, though not without controversy itself (Devisch & Murray, 2009; Goldenberg, 2006; Whitaker & Cosgrove, 2015)? Or has it gone astray, a victim of its own ambition to gain rank and reputation as a lieutenant in the scientific revolution?

We have been drawn in by science's prestige and soothed, at least momentarily, by its promise to answer life's pressing questions. Having secured the preeminent soapbox in the public square, Western psychiatry has sought to amplify its voice, calling across continents and oceans (Watters, 2010). There is a vernacular gaining passport and bringing a new language to the citizens of the world. With "the power to give names to our pain" (Greenberg, 2013, p. 7), psychiatry has consigned other possible characterizations of problems to secondary usage.

As its boundaries seem to be ever expanding, so, too, do the parameters for what constitutes mental illness: "Psychiatry takes increasing license, reaching into our everyday experience and treating temper, distractibility, sadness, and nervousness as signs of disorder" (Frances & Jones, 2013, p. 12). We find ourselves referring to our phobias and addictive personalities, drawn in by the language of pathology. We are equally prone, though not in the least amused, as we weigh the question of whether to have our children tested for OCD, ADHD, or mood disorders. It is psychiatry out in the lead, with the rest of the field and the world in tow.

Psychiatry: The New Faith and Fashion

When we observe young people struggling with problems of one kind or another, by necessity, we turn to culture to make sense of what has gone wrong. We catch sight of available explanations from among those that are presently in circulation. We operate within the bounds of the known and familiar, our collective perception inscribed with the most prominent concepts of the day. Psychiatry, in its evangelizing, has struck an outsized profile. Its visage is made all the more prominent by the promise of deliverance from suffering. Over the span of the Christian era, we searched for signs of sinfulness in our daughters and sons. But today, it is the threat of abnormality we fear (e.g., "Is it normal for her to cling to me?" "Should he be so fidgety?"). Until recently it was understood that "un-baptized children were so full of sins that they were supposed to be buried below the roof-gutter of a church to have the holy water wash them of their sins" (Demause, 2010, p. 180). Nowadays they are cleansed by chemical means in the hope of absolution, not of their sins, but of their symptoms. The doyen of science is the new Messiah we turn to for relief. Immersed in this new brand of baptism, it is not young people's souls but their brains that are awash in such healing tonics as dextroamphetamine, methylphenidate, quetiapine furamate, fluoxetine, bupropion, and others. We deliver our children into psychiatry's waters, putting our faith in their rejuvenating powers and the belief that they will offer salvation, not by means of transformation from sinner to saint, but rather from a state of aberrancy to one of normalcy.

Parents and professionals alike maintain a watchful eye for behaviors that might be seen as a violation of norms. Children must learn to respect authority, focus their attention, manage their anger, delay gratification, self-regulate, and play well with others. There is nothing wrong with these precepts, per se, and any young person may do well to adopt them. Rather, it is a question of who has the authority to make these determinations, the means by which they are enforced, and whose interests they serve.

Before proceeding, it is important to clarify that this chapter is by no means intended to criticize those who have turned to psychiatry for help, or to dispute any claim of value found in the use of psychotropic medication. It is simply meant to reveal the historical, economic, and political forces at work in making psychiatry's reputation as it exists today. We leave it to each individual, family, and community to determine the best use of psychiatry and its offerings.[1]

Magic Bullets and Young Targets

Psychiatry called us to its cause in 1952, delivering the first printing of the *Diagnostic and Statistical Manual*—a slender text of 130 pages that somehow managed to fit no less than 106 disorders inside its narrowly bound casing. From there it grew exponentially with each reissue, becoming more book than booklet. Its current edition, the *DSM-5*, with a near-endless procession of mental disorders—roughly three times the length of the original list—is the grandest offering yet, if size is what matters most. The now 947-page opus practically requires a crane to lift it to eye level. And with problems "wrapped in the cloak of medical diseases" (Whitaker & Cosgrove, 2015, p. 89) more tightly than ever, they have become the near exclusive property of psychiatry.

With support from the pharmaceutical industry, psychiatry has widened its lens to include children as a population worthy of greater focus. Over the past 30 years, new disorders have been devised, while at the same time, the criteria required to qualify for older syndromes have slackened (Frances, 2014), making it more likely that a child who is ushered into a psychiatrist's office will walk out with a diagnosis and directions to a local pharmacy. With respect to ADHD alone, "children here [in the U.S.] consume three times the quantity of stimulants consumed by the rest of the world's children combined" (Whitaker, 2010, p. 220). This is not to suggest that the rest of the West is not doing its part: "In the United Kingdom, prescriptions for stimulants have increased from about 6,000 prescriptions a year in 1994 to over 450,000 by 2004—a staggering 7,000+ percent rise in one decade" (Timimi, 2009, p. 10). Dr. Sami Timimi, a leader in the critical psychiatry movement, makes the startling point that these "rapid changes in practice in the area of children's mental health have not come about as a result of any major new scientific discovery" (p. 10). If the rapid acceleration of prescriptive intervention is not the result of breakthroughs in the field, then how are we to make sense of it?

In a consumer society with pitchmen on every proverbial corner, psychiatric diagnoses have become as marketable as any item on display at a shopping mall kiosk or available for purchase on Amazon.com. Consider the diagnosis of bipolar disorder, which saw no less than "a fortyfold increase from 1995 to 2003" (Whitaker, 2010, p. 233). The swell was due in large part to the research of the highly influential child psychiatrist Joseph Biederman, who published numerous professional papers during this period, calling for early detection of and intervention in childhood bipolar disorder. By virtue of his scholarly output, not to mention his association with Harvard University and Massachusetts General Hospital, Biederman paved the way to the "widespread acceptance of pediatric uses of antipsychotic medicines" (Harris, 2008), not least of which was the drug risperidone. It was only after he had altered professional and public perception that he was exposed for having been on the take. It turned out that between 2000 and 2007, he received $1.6 million in consulting fees from the drug company Johnson and Johnson, the maker of risperidone. This was the very drug, known more commonly by its trade name, Risperdal, that Biederman had been so keen to promote. But this was the least of it. Including his earlier advocacy for the diagnosis of ADHD in children, "Biederman received speakers fees, consulting fees, and research funding from more than 24 pharmaceutical companies" between 1996 and 2011 (Whitaker & Cosgrove, 2015, p. 92).

Big pharma, with its vast resources, would seem to have little trouble recruiting even highly esteemed medical professionals (Harris, Carey, & Roberts, 2007) to sell its wares. New initiatives are funded, and their agents entrusted, to search out abnormality in previously untapped communities that might prove gainful. A proposal informed by this pharmaceutical-psychiatric alliance includes "the plan Australia has, to embark on nationwide mental health testing for 3-year-olds" (Frances, 2012, p. 695). And with an unceasing ambition to pathologize and commoditize additional groups, there are efforts underway to penetrate women's reproductive organs for the purpose of diagnosing mental illness in utero (Eisenberg, 2010; Richardson, 2014).

This momentum coincides with multinational pharmaceutical companies, such as Eli Lilly, Pfizer, Johnson and Johnson, and GlaxoSmithKline being relieved of stringent advertising guidelines by the American Food and Drug Administration (FDA). Through lobbying efforts, they were permitted to advertise directly to consumers beginning in 1997 via popular media, including television. Drug companies devoted tens of billions of dollars each year to pitch their lines to an even broader consumer base. With a proven marketing campaign no different from that used to foster a desire for products ranging from automobiles to anti-aging creams, the end game was in sight. They "devised the successful strategy of aggressively selling psychiatric ills as the optimal way of peddling psychotropic pills" (Batstra & Frances, 2012b, p. 5). Like any successful campaign, "the advertising was aimed at stimulating demand" and in this case, it benefited from "the lack of objective tests and clear diagnostic boundaries in psychiatry" (Batstra & Frances, 2012a, p. 475). Add to that the compelling voice of the medical establishment and the general public stood little chance. With purported progress in science, the mental health discourse was there for the purchase. It was simply a question of time before an illness narrative took hold.

Even when drug companies are penalized for reckless behavior, there would seem to be little motivation to alter their course. To illustrate, in February 2004, after having given drug companies permission to reach into American homes through direct-to-consumer advertising, the FDA could no longer ignore growing concerns over increased risks to children's health. In outcomes pertaining to antidepressant drugs, no greater benefit was found for children who were medicated than for those taking placebos in at least 13 of the 15 studies (Healy, 2006). Alarmingly, there was a greater suicide risk for those on medication. Despite resistance from both psychiatry and big pharma, the FDA mandated that stronger warnings indicating possible dangers to minors accompany prescriptions for such drugs as Paxil, Effexor, and Zoloft. Considering that "worldwide pharmaceutical sales amount to more than US $700 billion a year, with North American sales constituting around half of this market" (Batstra & Frances, 2012a), it can be argued that profits more than principles have shaped "best practices."

The pharmaceutical industry has long been a driver of research, funding trials, and outcome studies that claim to support the efficacy of medications used to treat ADHD and mood disorders in children (Greenberg, 2013; Watters, 2010; Whitaker, 2010). And while reports of positive outcomes have been magnified, the potential hazards have been set in small print, or in the case of television commercials, delivered via surreal voice-over descriptions. In dull tones intended to anesthetize, we are told of all that could go terribly wrong before being offered a final image of the peace and happiness that await us with the ingestion of a daily pill. But the possible costs are worthy of more deliberate consideration (Appelbaum, 2011; Turner, 2013), not least of all on behalf of children. Additional research is needed with respect to risk levels for everything from the rare instances of sudden death, liver failure, suicide, and permanent aversive changes to the brain, to the more common effects, such as growth restriction, tics, seizures, headaches, dizziness, psychotic symptoms, and ocular disturbances (Graham et al., 2011; Richa & Yazbek, 2010).

The FDA has let the tiger out of its cage and is now attempting to tame it. In recent years, it has "cited every major ADHD drug, including the stimulants Adderall, Concerta, Focalin, and Vyvanse, for false and misleading advertising since 2000, some of them multiple times" (*New York Times* Editorial Board, 2013). One of a series of charges leveled at drug companies was described by *New York Times* reporters Katie Thomas and Michael Schmidt (2012): "In the largest settlement involving a pharmaceutical company, the British drugmaker GlaxoSmithKline agreed to plead guilty to criminal charges and pay $3 billion in fines. . . . The agreement also includes civil penalties for improper marketing of a half-dozen other drugs. In May, Abbott Laboratories settled for $1.6 billion over its marketing of the antiseizure drug Depakote." In 2013, the drug maker Johnson and Johnson pleaded guilty to criminal misdemeanor charges and was ordered to pay more than $2.2 billion for urging wide distribution and use of the antipsychotic drug Risperdal and having "recklessly put at risk the health of some of the most vulnerable members of our society—including young children, the elderly, and the disabled" (Thomas, 2013). These penalties may seem sizable enough to curb shameful enterprise, but their impact is muted by the vast profits realized from the selling of disease and its concomitant remedies.

Local Knowledge at Risk

As psychiatry continues to advance its position, culturally specific and situated forms of knowledge inevitably lose ground. Ancestral knowledges, family and community knowledges, and, not least of all, knowledges generated by young people are diminished. Instead of pursuing what young people know, "facts" are generated about them. In an atmosphere that supports professional wisdom, generalities about human behavior are made possible. The human species, including its young, has been caged—its spirit, motivation, will, and character laid bare.

Such ambitions might be justified if only the advent of ADHD (and other diagnoses) were more about liberation than annexation. But it is too often the case that "by naming things, we take possession of them" (Spurr, 1993, p. 32). Despite the initial relief that might be found in putting a name to one's pain, the unintended long-term effects of being subject to a label can be emotionally decentering: "Importantly, controlled research indicates that the negative stigmatization outweighs the impairments related to the various forms of mental disorder themselves" (Hinshaw & Stier, 2008, p. 369). The potential detrimental effects of psychiatric branding can be acutely felt by consumers of public mental health, whose access to programs and resources (e.g., housing and financial assistance), and even parents' custody rights, may be tied to their medication compliance (M'Carthy, 2014). The following story is meant to illustrate the possible dangers of professional hierarchies and the consequences of adopting an expert stance, while remaining impervious to the knowledges of the young people and families we serve. Bear in mind, the story is not intended to represent the totality of work that takes place in the public sector. It was selected for the specific purposes of this chapter.

The Singing Treatment

Mia was only 5 years old when a team of field-based workers determined that a 3-day hospitalization was necessary for the purposes of medical observation. She and her family had been referred to a county-funded agency due to Mia's disruptive behavior at school. At the time of the referral, she was living with her aunt, Vicki, who assumed custody after Mia's mother was hospitalized for a drug overdose 2 months earlier. When an outreach team arrived at the family's home, Vicki described having heard Mia talk to an "imaginary friend." She was disturbed by her niece's report that the voice told her to do "bad things . . . like kill me [Vicki]." After hearing both Vicki's and Mia's reports, the team inquired about the family's mental health history and Mia's possible exposure to trauma before they withdrew to the next room to confer privately.

"At that point, I knew something was up," Vicki later conveyed. "But poor Mia, she had no idea what was coming." Mia and especially her gray cat, Felix, appeared unfazed by the interview and treated the team's huddle as a chance to return to imaginative play. Pretending that Felix was a hungry lion, she dangled a string just beyond his reach, shouting, "Here's the meat. Here's the meat for the lion!" Felix, who was lounging on his side, absently pawed at the air. His half-hearted efforts were met with shrill screams of delight.

Just as Felix caught hold of the string, the team manager reemerged, looking grave. She took Vicki aside and told her of the team's decision to transport the family to the hospital. Seeing the shock on her face, the manager tried to explain their reasoning: "Vicki, your niece is psychotic. She's hearing a voice that is telling her to kill you. The violent nature of her auditory commands, coupled with her young age, make her a risk."

"A risk? A risk for what?" Vicki responded, stunned.

"A risk to herself. To you. There's no guarantee that she won't act on what this voice is telling her to do. Children this age easily confuse fantasy and reality. We just can't let something happen."

"Are you saying you're worried she'll kill me?"

"Yes. Or harm you in some way. She could also harm the cat, and if she goes to the hospital, you'll all be safe. And the staff will have a chance to conduct a thorough evaluation during a 72-hour hold."

"Seventy-two hours?! She's not going to hurt anyone. I know my niece. This is ridiculous."

"Vicki, we just want to make sure that you both stay safe and that Mia receives the appropriate level of care."

"Safe?" she sputtered. "Do you think I'm not doing something about this? We have a problem. I know we have a problem. That's why I let you come here! But putting a 5-year-old in the hospital? You can't separate us like this. We've just gotten settled." As Vicki persisted, the remaining team members stepped forward. "Oh good, you all need to hear this," Vicki stated, unbowed in the face of greater numbers. "You cannot let her hospitalize my niece. We just got together, and she's been through a lot." Vicki went on to explain how Mia's mother was unable to care for her due to recurring challenges with drugs and a boyfriend with "a violent streak." Vicki returned to Los Angeles from Fresno, where she had been living and working, when it was made clear that if she did not get involved, Mia would end up in foster care. Vicki loved her sister, in spite of her struggles, and had cared for Mia once before under similar circumstances. "I came back in a hurry, so that I could find a job. It's been 2 months now, and we're finally getting things figured out." The manager expressed appreciation for Vicki's efforts and her commitment to family but reiterated that hospitalization was nevertheless "the safest option."

Vicki continued to voice her objections. Still hoping to make a convincing case, she told the team about the steps she had taken to ensure their safety (e.g., watching over Mia at night, holding her, and talking with her about the voice). But the manager, perhaps feeling the burden of responsibility and/or the threat of liability, stood by the team's decision. Arrangements were made against Vicki's wishes, and the two were transported to the hospital.

Whether a psychiatric hold was warranted is debatable. What cannot be denied, however, were the effects of the hospitalization. From Vicki's point of view, it was a setback in helping her niece overcome multiple traumas, including the violence she likely witnessed, instability with respect to home and school, and the loss of family members. Within the past year, her grandmother and great-grandmother had passed away and she had been separated from her mother. But there was more to it than that. Upon hearing about the voice, the team stopped consulting the family. Authority was turned over to "the authorities" (Buckley & Decter, 2006). Although they had been living together for 2 months without incident, Vicki's ideas about the problem, and how best to address it, had little impact. The team had engaged in the construction of a new identity for Mia—that of a psychotic child. This would invariably lower expectations for what might be generated by Mia and Vicki and raise the prospects for what would be required of the professionals around them.

Though worldly wise, Vicki was new to the world of psychiatry. She later recalled feeling overwhelmed and powerless during Mia's evaluation and admission: "The doctor wouldn't let me stay with her. He insisted on meeting with her alone. How did I know I could trust him? Or what he would tell her?" Vicki reported that when they were reunited the next day, Mia appeared sluggish. When Vicki learned the staff had given her antipsychotic medication, she was alarmed: "I didn't know they were going to drug her! If I had known that, I would have found a way to take her right out of there!"

Mia's inpatient treatment consisted of being isolated from family, psychiatrically observed, assessed, and medicated—and that was just the first 24 hours. Two days later, the process culminated in a discharge plan that was presented to Vicki. The plan called for antipsychotic medication, individual therapy for Mia, and parent coaching for Vicki. The hospital therapist urged Vicki to contact the outreach team right away to schedule a first session, along with an appointment with the agency's psychiatrist. Vicki was also given Mia's official diagnosis: "psychotic disorder NOS [not otherwise specified]." Had Vicki been more vulnerable to psychiatry's claims, she might have asked herself, "How do I care for a mentally ill child? Do I possess the necessary skills?" Instead, she left the hospital incensed, throwing the psychiatrist's prescription in the trash on the way out. As she would later tell it, the family was no better off than they had been 72 hours earlier. Only now, they would have to contend with the effects of another separation and the impact of the hospitalization, not to mention an intense suspicion of professionals.

Insisting that Vicki come to terms with a medical reality put a significant wedge between the family and the team who had been assigned to help. As a result of Vicki's disaffection for the agency and those who had a hand in Mia's hospitalization, the family was referred, at Vicki's request, to a new agency. It was at that time that Laurie was made aware of the events that had unfolded and was assigned to meet with them. Despite what they had been put through, Vicki knew she had little choice but to allow Laurie into their home if she was to have any hope of keeping Mia with her. The following is an excerpt from a conversation with Vicki and Mia three days after they returned from the hospital.

> Vicki: This whole hospital ordeal was a mistake. No one would listen to me. (Stated indignantly.)
>
> LM: What is it they might have learned if they'd listened? (Wanting to get at Vicki's knowledge.)
>
> Vicki: That she's been through a lot and we're working it out together. (Vicki's relational response to the problem stands in stark contrast with the team's individualizing and medicalizing approach [Freedman & Combs, 2016]).
>
> Vicki: She tells me about the voice. It scares her. I told her that anytime she hears it she needs to come to me.
>
> LM: Is that right, Mia? Do you tell your aunt?
>
> Mia: Yes!
>
> LM: Why do you tell your aunt instead of keeping it to yourself and just listening to the Voice?
>
> Mia: Because I love her. I don't want to hurt her . . . or Felix! (Becoming teary.)
>
> LM: So what do you do when the Voice tells you to hurt them, but you don't want to hurt your aunt or Felix because you love them?

Mia: I tell her.

LM: And what does your aunt do? Or what do the two of you do together? (Attempting to better understand what their connection makes possible.)

Mia: She hugs me . . . and I lay with her . . . and we watch TV . . . or we pray.

Vicki: And I tell you not to listen to it!

Mia: And she tells me not to listen to it. And Vicki tells it to go away.

Vicki: You bet I do.

LM: And then what happens?

Mia: I just stay in her bed.

Vicki: I told her to jump into bed and that nothing can happen to her when I'm with her. (Mia climbs onto her aunt's lap and Vicki wraps her arms around her.) Mia knows that she can talk to me. We've always been close.

LM: Can you tell me about the ways that the two of you are close?

Mia: We're family!

Vicki: That's right, and nothing comes between us!

LM: (To Vicki) Do you suppose this closeness has helped Mia when the Voice comes around?

Vicki: I think so. (Beginning to relax.)

LM: Mia, is that right? Does hugging and talking with your aunt help when the Voice comes around? Does it help to stay connected to your love for her?

Mia: Yeah.

LM: And what if the Voice comes around again? Do you think it will try to come between you and your aunt? (Inviting Mia to take a position in relation to the problem.)

Mia: I don't know. I don't want it around!

Vicki: You don't know?! You'd better know!

Mia: I'll tell it to go away! (She suddenly asserts herself.)

Vicki: She just might. Mia's always had an attitude. She takes after her mom and me.

Mia: Nobody messes with Vicki! (She stands up.)

LM: Mia, is it true? Do you take after your mom and your aunt? (Attempting to connect to a family legacy.)

Mia: I'm going to tell it, "You better go away! You! You!" (She seems to be engaging the Voice directly, shouting at it, and then caught in the spirit of the moment, breaks into song: *"You can't do that! No, no, no! You can't do that, no, no, no!"* She also starts to dance. *"Baby, please, please baby, please."* Now she appears in full performance mode, choreography and all.)

LM: Wow! That knocked me out. That was really something. What just happened? (Laurie is dazzled and wonders what to make of such a demonstration.)

Mia: I'm practicing being a pop star!

LM: When you were singing, "You can't do that, you can't do that, no, no, no," I wondered, were you singing to the Voice?

Mia: (Enthusiastically) Yeah!

LM: Did it sing back? Did it argue with you or try to tell you what to do?

Mia: It can't because I'm onstage. (Mia appears to be enlisting her imagination to provide a fresh plot twist. Often the imaginary is so close it is only a matter of time before a threshold is crossed.)

Vicki: When she sings and really gives it attitude, she's in a different place.

LM: Mia, how did you get yourself to that different place? Was it by singing with attitude? And is it singing with attitude that will help protect you from the Voice?

Mia: (Thinking.)

Vicki: It takes that attitude of yours . . . that attitude that you're always showing me.

Mia: I don't have attitude! (Ironically, she says this with a good deal of attitude.)

Finding her voice through song and attitude and getting to a different place was not an intervention that had any basis in professional knowledge. Rather, it was grounded in the family's own repertoire and what could be harnessed to put against the problem. It involved Mia exercising authority over the Voice with her aunt's love and assistance—and in connection to her mother. It is worth noting that within a month after hospitalization, Mia reported that the Voice had gone away. It is hard to say whether it first appeared due to exposure to violence, loss of family, or for some other reason. (Over time, Mia would speak more openly about these events.) But being recast as mentally ill did not appear to benefit her in any way. Neither was it necessary that professionals strip her (and Vicki) of agency. With Vicki by her side, Mia proved herself a worthy match for the Voice, already embodying, at a very young age, the family legacy of "ladies with attitude."

Conclusion

Scanning devices would have young people lie still (and psychiatrists would have them sit still) as determinations are made with respect to their pathologies and (limited) potentials. Distinguished primarily by their diagnoses, young people and their problems are made indistinguishable. Given this unremarkable representation, there is little that can be expected beyond compliance, whether in regard to treatment protocols, medications, or behavioral objectives. We would never willfully leave young people at such a disadvantage, especially once problems have made an appearance and nothing less than a dynamic response will do. Besides, turning matters over to professionals alone sometimes produces little more than rationalizations for why problems persist. Though conventional wisdom would suggest otherwise, problems are not the least bit intimidated by professional diagnosticians. In fact, they often appreciate the attention they receive and the ways they are legitimized and awarded lofty titles. There is no substitute for young people as lead agents, though we can certainly supplement their efforts by taking active supporting roles.

As we proceed to Chapter 8, we find mothers similarly objectified, but absent the compassion shown to young people. The same empathy is past due to mothers, who labor under a critical gaze. The scrutiny reserved especially for them can be traced all the way back to the beginnings of our profession and antecedently.

CHAPTER EIGHT

It's All Mom's Fault!
A Figment of the Imagination

At first glance a chapter devoted to the defense of mothers would seem out of place in a book about children's imaginative know-how. But there is something to be reckoned with given the long-standing perception of the problems that enter young people's lives as stemming from mothers' injurious acts. All problems travel through "the motherland"—or so we've been taught. Mothers too, under the tutelage of professionals, have come to see themselves as potentially detrimental to the lives of their daughters and sons. This enduring view can inhibit our interest in children's imaginations and routinely focus our attention—therapists and parents alike, not to mention the general public—on what she is doing wrong. In order to safeguard our imaginations so that they might usher us down more equitable roads, we must first break stride with the interminable march against mothers.

When all is going well in the lives of their children, mothers can sometimes feel that it is more likely the result of their self-restraint than anything they are actively contributing. Conversely, when something has gone terribly wrong, they can be made to feel that it is, in fact, a direct consequence of their involvement. It is seemingly only a matter of time before their very presence will cause irreparable harm. Such a foreshadowed prospect can contribute to a mother's cheerless outlook and offer limited access to any lighthearted or imaginative impulse should a problem threaten to make an appearance. Tina, the mother of 11-year-old Ginger, described this predicament to DM:

> **Tina:** She's so amazing. We've got 7 years to go and I'm holding my breath. I'm just trying not to screw her up between now and the time she leaves home. (She smiles tightly.)
>
> **DM:** When you look at what's amazing about her, do you see the impact your mothering might have had? (DM wonders if Tina is subject to the conditions of mother blame that would deny her credit.)
>
> **Tina:** (Incredulous) God, no! She was born this way. There was something special about her pretty much from day one.
>
> **DM:** I see. I wonder if I just asked you a question that is off-limits to mothers?
>
> **Tina:** What do you mean?
>
> **DM:** Well, I think about whether mothers are allowed to entertain this question—the question of their positive impact on their children's lives.
>
> **Tina:** Yeah, that's not something I do a lot. (Seeming contemplative.)
>
> **DM:** Am I right in understanding that if a problem were to occur it would likely be traced to you, but whatever we might admire about Ginger would have little or even nothing to do with you?
>
> **Tina:** (Laughing) Yes, absolutely. (She responds to the absurdity of such a proposal.)
>
> **DM:** How is that?
>
> **Tina:** To be honest, I've never really thought about it, except for not wanting to do something to screw her up.
>
> **DM:** Is it just a one-sided case in which, if you have any impact at all on Ginger, it will be on the negative side?
>
> **Tina:** More or less. (She draws a heavy breath as if weighing the implications of such a predicament.) I've pictured her years from now, sitting in front of a therapist listing the things I did wrong. (She shifts nervously.)

DM: That's a haunting image. There does seem to be an all-too-common tradition of tracing people's struggles in a straight line right back to their mothers. (DM makes an attempt to expose the problem as something other than a private neurosis.)

Tina: It's a fear I live with. I just know something will come back to haunt me. (She looks distressed.)

DM: Is this a haunting that is showing you the future, as if it's already decided (Epston, 2008)? Is it less a question of *whether* Ginger will hold something against you and more a matter of *what* she will blame you for?

Tina: Right—I know she'll end up blaming me for something.

DM: So is this the bottom line for you and so many mothers, for that matter? (DM locates the problem in a broader social context, hoping to generate a sense of solidarity, Polanco, 2010.) You're of no consequence to Ginger's success, on the one hand, but on the other, you are a hazard to her future? (This is not the first time DM has heard of such a dilemma, and it will certainly not be the last.)

Tina: Yeah, that about sums it up.

Given the prevalence of blame, many mothers are made to live defensively, exhausted by efforts that in the end, never quite measure up. A steady stream of parenting guidelines intended to support mothers is regularly published and broadcast by (mine)fields of expertise. Daniel Siegel, a proponent of attachment theory, and coauthor, Mary Hartzell, urge new mothers to consider, among other things, "the sharing and coordination of nonverbal signals (eye contact, facial expression, tone of voice, gestures, bodily posture, timing, intensity of response)" for the purpose of improving interactions at the microlevel (Siegel & Hartzell, 2004, p. 117). The minutiae of everyday interplay between mothers and their young has been placed under surveillance. Mothers' imaginations have been made secondary to "high theory" (Halberstam, 2011). There is a resulting production of self-conscious mothers who watch their children closely, fearing their own liability in each frown, tear, and vacant look. The outcome is one in which they can be made to feel that the only possibility for success is by means of "their undivided attention, and by making themselves available as an unfailing source of love, comfort, and support" (Pollack, 1998, p. 82). This may seem advisable—putting the reality of other demands aside—but when wielded unrelentingly and accompanied by the prediction of damage to children who are denied such exquisite care, it is enough to turn motherhood into a hazardous enterprise—an 18-year-long high-wire act.

We can effortlessly conjure the image of a father dealing with competing pressures, who shares himself with the family as he is able. We allow for rival enterprises to carry him outside the home for days or longer. But the image of a mother with divided attention can elicit scorn. Developmental psychologist Erica Burman cautions, "Mothers have been portrayed as so central to, and absorbed within their children's development that any assertion of power or independence on their part appears to be at the expense of damaging children" (2008, p. 134). Unfortunately, the predilection to scrutinize mothers is nothing new. Psychology has had mothers in its sights for some time.

Psychotherapy's Penchant for Mother Blame

From its inception, psychotherapy has treated mothers with ambivalence at best and more often with suspicion. Freud's psychoanalytic "omnipotent phallic mother who must be castrated if the son is to survive" (Hartke, 1994, pp. 656–657) is but one haunting specter, more fiend than friend. Surely, no mother would ever conceive of so scathing an image. It was this portrayal of the mother-son relationship that marked the entrance of psychology into the family home, and with it, the professional gaze (Foucault, 1995).

Even prior to Freud, there had long been a popular, if not professional, movement meant to chastise "uneducated" mothers and secure their homebound devotion: "The prevalence of advice manuals in the second half of the nineteenth century indicates that although middle-class mothers held full responsibility for the upbringing of their children, they were considered ignorant, if not deliberately culpable" (Rosenberg, 2005, p. 493). Psychology enhanced its reputation by adding formal theory to this well-established sentiment. With the splash of behaviorism in the 1920s, the science of mothering won notice. John B. Watson warned in no uncertain terms: "Mother love is a dangerous instrument . . . which may inflict a never healing wound, a wound which may make infancy unhappy, adolescence a nightmare, an instrument which may wreck your adult son or daughter's vocational future and their chances for marital happiness" (1998, p. 475). While Watson distinguished himself from Freud by focusing on what was observable rather than unconscious, he was no more inclined to spare mothers. He forewarned them, in no uncertain terms, to guard against their loving impulse or risk their children's ruin.

Another diviner of doom, Bruno Bettelheim achieved popularity in the mid-20th century in the United States, less by virtue of his credentials than as a result of the mystique that came with a thick Austrian accent and a psychoanalytic bent. Bettelheim posited that "autistic children suffered from 'extreme situations' similar to being in the holocaust but caused by maternal deprivation" (Stace, 2010, p. 68). He decided this holocaust had its beginnings in troubles with breast-feeding (Bettelheim, 1967). Similarly, the image of the "refrigerator mother" gained currency at this time and was purported to cause autism as children were left no other option, due to a lack of warmth, than to turn inward and "seek comfort in solitude" (Kanner, 1949, p. 425).

The terms were set along a continuum of hot and cold at the extremes. Too much love or too little could spell disaster. It was the task of mothers, under psychological guidance, to hit the emotional bull's-eye. True aim in one instance was no guard against an errant shot in the next. Any number of problems revealed in her child's behavior exposed the breakdown in her efforts. She was implicated for everything from migraine headaches (Fromm-Reichmann, 1937) and schizophrenia (Bateson, Jackson, Haley, & Weakland, 1956) to homosexuality (Hornstra, 1967) and stuttering (Langevin, Packman, & Onslow, 2010).

The preponderance of mother blame inevitably contributed to compulsory self-blame. One mother bemoaned,

> I had a sense of disbelief, bewilderment if you will. I wondered, how did this happen? Why had this happened? Can I fix it? Will he be okay for school, etc.? I felt defensive and worried, there's nothing wrong just a little stutter, and then, what if it's not fixable? I also felt guilt; had I not read to him enough? Done the alphabet earlier? (Langevin et al., 2010, p. 416)

Mothers were even at fault, it was reasoned, for sexual abuse perpetrated by fathers. It was a mother's rejection of her husband and the forsaking of her role as wife and lover that put her daughter in harm's way (McLaren, 2013; McNamara, Tolliday, & Spangaro, 2012). It was by means of these sorts of psychological gymnastics that mothers were blamed for anything in the family's life that could be theorized. Mother blame served as a clarion call to a burgeoning profession as it sought to achieve legitimacy and fill out its expanding borders. Though feminist scholars would provide a much-needed rebuttal to claims of mothers' culpability for child abuse perpetrated by men (Stark & Flitcraft, 1988; Liebman-Jacobs, 1990), their critique functioned as but one point of resistance to an advancing brigade.

As the women's movement persisted with its critique of patriarchal domination through the 1960s and into the 1970s (Martinez, 2011), a question arose. Would the field eventually repent, or at least yield to fatigue in its Hundred Years' War against mothers? Paula Caplan and Ian Hall-McCorquodale investigated whether psychology had attempted any reconciliation with mothers and arrived at a more judicious understanding of their roles in family life. They culled notable professional journals and found little evidence that researchers had altered their views. In fact, it was quite the opposite case. They concluded, "The authors of the 125 articles read for this study attributed to mothers a total of 72 different kinds of psychopathology" (Caplan & Hall-McCorquodale, 1985, p. 347). Remarkably, "in no article was the mother's relationship with the child described as simply healthy, nor was she ever described only in positive terms" (p. 348). The energy devoted to mother-blaming theories covered a vast linguistic range beginning with the letter A and "absence of genitalia" and traveling through the alphabet to U and "ulcerative colitis." One might not have readily expected that mothers would be held to account for their children's medical ailments beyond expressions of emotional distress. Nevertheless, every symbol in between A and U, with the exception of J, O, and the ever-challenging Q, assisted in labeling mothers for their destructive impact in the lives of their children according to "the taxonomies of healing professionals" (Kleinman, 1995, p. 96).

Such is psychology's long and checkered past in its dealings with mothers, and not much has changed, other than mother-blame going viral. With the ink still drying on the pages of the latest crush of parenting articles, manuals, and books headed for actual and virtual bookstore shelves, mothers are reminded that there is more to do—more to read, more to learn, more to give, and more to get wrong.

Society in general has been deputized to do its part as collective agent of the civic interest in regulating mothers' movements. We take their measure as indulgent mothers, neglectful mothers, hovering mothers, preoccupied mothers, anxious mothers, guilty mothers, aborting mothers, and only occasionally, the right sort of rarefied mother—devoted, though not zealous. And in our eagerness to evaluate them, we no longer wait for the event of a child's birth. Pregnancy, once the private domain of mothers, midwives, and obstetricians, has become its own disciplinary site. As Heffernan, Nicolson, and Fox warn, "The more comfortable people become with policing pregnant women, the more pregnant women may experience public criticism, becoming 'public property' on which everyone is an 'expert'" (2011, p. 324).

Responding to Mother Blame

It is against this prejudicial backdrop that the wonderfulness interview introduced in Chapter 2 can be seen as activism as much as therapeutic practice. It is a demonstration of our resistance to those elements in psychology that continue to treat mothers dubiously. By asking mothers to relate what is wonderful about their children and, by extension, inviting consideration of their own invaluable contributions to their daughters' and sons' lives, we are implicitly confronting biased practices that have given near-exclusive attention to the harm they cause.

Externalizing conversations provide the same shelter for mothers as they do for young people (e.g., the problem is the problem; *she* is not the problem). They take us beyond the person with an eye toward culture and discourse. For example, we might contemplate why mothers more than fathers find themselves saddled with the disreputable moniker of nag. It is also their likely misfortune to grapple unduly with guilt. These unwelcome occurrences can arise from a lopsided arrangement in which the greater share of responsibility for daily family life falls on mothers' shoulders (Maume, 2016). Similarly, the predisposition to admonish mothers for either excessive caretaking or woeful neglect leaves them at further risk for evaluation (Walters & Harrison, 2014). We are disinclined to study mothers as private cases and instead are determined to appreciate their struggles within social frames of reference and fields of power (Sax, 1997). Externalizing creates an atmosphere in which there is more to consider beyond *her* personal failings.

Therapy with young people and their families should be a regrading (rather than degrading) experience for all, including mothers. This fulfills our ethical obligation, and it certainly makes the encounter more hospitable for future imaginative endeavors as mothers find relief and are able to speak less guardedly about their struggles. Sarah, the mother of 4-year-old Leah, is found in mid-conversation with DM, describing her relationship with Anger:

Sarah: Last night she [Leah] said she wanted her father [Lance] to read to her and not me. She actually told me to leave her room (Laughing). Now I can laugh, but last night . . . (She shakes her head, seeming caught in the memory.)

DM: (Giving her a moment) What is it you can laugh about sitting here now? (DM is interested in making room for what may be a preferred response, even if only in retrospect.)

Sarah: She loves her daddy and wants him to read to her. Why should I care or take it so personally? But I do. When she pointed at me and said, "Not you!" it was like—whew!

DM: When she said, "Not you!" and ordered you out of her room, what hit you? (Looking to name a problem.)

Sarah: It made me angry. I am so devoted to her, and the way she can just dismiss me out of hand—I know it's ridiculous. She's only 4.

DM: I can understand. I'm thinking of women who would resonate with your reaction. I've talked with mothers who have felt the effects of giving so freely . . .of devoting so much of their lives to their children. It's what we require of mothers, isn't it—to be selfless? (DM attempts to expose a patriarchal discourse that calls for "a caring mother's ready acceptance of suffering and self-sacrifice," David, 2011, p. 132). But I don't know . . . is it fair that they shouldn't tire of it, or sometimes encounter resentment? (DM posits this in the third person to provide Sarah some distance from which to reflect on the question and also to suggest that she is far from alone in her experience.)

Sarah: I know, but really, there's no excuse, even if she does behave badly. I mean, come on, I'm the adult here.

DM: Are you finding yourself in two different positions—one brought about by Anger, and then a second position? When you say, "Why should I take it personally" and "I'm the adult here," what might you be getting at? Is this a second perspective that interests you? (Externalizing Anger makes room to take notice of a possible moral position.)

Sarah: (Hesitating)

DM: Or, is it something like Guilt telling you how you should be reacting? (Offering further speculation as to what might be operating on Sarah.)

Sarah: I do feel guilty when I react so strongly.

DM: Does that mean the Anger is unwelcome? (She pauses.) Or is it speaking in one way or another to an interest or a concern? (DM is careful not to assume the Anger has no basis.)

Sarah: I'm not sure. The Anger can overwhelm me when she treats me badly. But at other times too. I've been talking with Lance about it and whether I need something more. It's tough on days when it's just the two of us from morning to night. But then I think, come on, Sarah. This is what you wanted. Enjoy it while it lasts.

DM: Is it easier said than done? Does Guilt give you, and lots of mothers for that matter, a hard time when you're not cherishing time with your children? (Once again, DM attempts to put Sarah in good company as he speculates about the problem's influence. His efforts reflect a discursive awareness.)

Sarah: Definitely.

DM: Can I go back to something you mentioned earlier?

Sarah: Sure.

DM: So there's something you, or you and Lance, are trying to figure out? Have you been talking it over?

Sarah: Yeah, we have. I feel like I've been out of the loop for so long, and it's made me a little crazy. I still plan on staying home with Leah for a few more years, but some days I miss my old life. Some days it looks pretty good to be Lance. (Sarah may be implicitly critiquing male privilege.)

DM: Are you speaking to a certain advantage that men enjoy?

Sarah: Lance has been nothing but supportive, but his life hasn't changed. I'm the one who has to give something up. And, bottom line, it's my problem to figure out. (In a patriarchal world, it is often women who are faced with the dilemma of having to choose between work and family.)

DM: And while you're in the process of figuring it out, does it make sense that Anger would show up? (DM is not looking to justify Anger but rather to acknowledge the conditions that might be contributing to it.)

Sarah: I'm afraid so. (She lets out a deep sigh. She may be finding some relief in the tone of the conversation.)

DM: It's not easy.

Sarah: No, and I think Lance understands that, or at least I hope he does. But, in any case, I don't want to take it out on Leah. (She indicates a possible moral stance.)

DM: Is that Guilt again, placing an unreasonable demand? (DM wants to make sure this is a conviction of Sarah's and not one imposed on her by the exacting standards of mother blame.)

Sarah: Guilt or no guilt, I don't want to take it out on her.

DM took care to see where Sarah might stand in relation to Anger and Guilt rather than knowing ahead of time where she ought to stand. If he had entertained ideas of right and wrong, independent of Sarah and the context of her life, or had turned a blind eye to the operations of cultural discourse, it would likely have been alienating and only contributed to an experience of personal blame. This is not to deny the fact that mothers, like anyone else, can behave problematically. But we are more interested in knowing who they might hope to be apart from problems than we are in policing them, however subtly. Of course, in instances of egregious offenses, we see to our responsibilities as mandated reporters, but even then, we do our best to team up with mothers, to whatever degree possible, rather than gang up on them.

Indebted Mothers

It is within an elaborate social web that motherhood is popularly conceived of as a blessing that delivers unparalleled rewards. All else, we are told, pales by comparison. America's royalty—television and movie stars—come into our living rooms by satellite and cable when promoting their latest projects. And with female stars at least, the conversation predictably turns to children as they are pressed to extoll the joys of motherhood. Just listen to these well-known actors being cajoled into devotional poses and the compulsory image of mother devotion that is invoked:

Sherry Sheppard: (Speaking with Sandra Bullock on the television show *The View*, Smith, & Santopadre, 2013) "You had so much going on before you had a child but then you look at your child and you go, 'What the hell was I doing before I had you? It doesn't matter.'"

Bullock: "I wasn't having fun. I wasn't connected. I had no idea what love was."

In an online interview for *Entertainment Weekly* (Scharf, 2015), Drew Barrymore is prompted to explain, "My daughter gets all my time, and if I get to sneak out and do some work, I feel really guilty that I'm not with her."

Despite their travels and triumphs, or perhaps as a result of their far-reaching success, powerful women in Hollywood are obliged to reassure viewers/readers by renouncing the outside world and returning to their "natural habitat." Imagine the risk to their reputations in a patriarchal culture as America's (white) sweethearts if they were to utter the unimaginable: "My child is of great interest to me, but she [or he] is far from my only interest." If a woman were to make such a statement in a public forum, it would undoubtedly stir controversy. These women survived the moment unscathed and were predictably rewarded by appreciative audiences for upholding the well-circulated image of a "self-sacrificing, saintly figure who performs the moral, caring work of society" (Crittenden, 2002, p. 7).

This is not meant to dismiss any woman's right to embrace motherhood or to dispute the greater value she may find in it—not in the least. Rather, our concern is with the endless stream of messages meant to carry women along, as if on a river current, delivering them to one inevitable source. It is the propagation of motherhood that would turn it from an idea into an ideal, a timeless truth, a naturalized ornament of history and even prehistory. Who has not encountered gendered references to the nature of the caveman and the domesticated cavewoman through "imaginative recreations of Stone Age life" (Dupré, 2001, p. 17)?

Within a culture that extols the idealized devotional mother, women can sometimes feel as if they are living an indebted existence. Their children fill in as creditors, having bestowed the gift of motherhood by virtue of their arrival. Mothers carry a moral mortgage that must be serviced with payments perpetually due. There is mounting pressure to double their efforts and provide growth opportunities for their daughters and sons at every turn. Even when they are having fun with their children, they are reminded that the job of fun must have its purpose (Ginsburg, 2007). Demands placed on children in this configuration are minimal, given that their mere existence promises endless returns. And there is little cultural support for the idea that the mother-child relationship is meant to be reciprocal. One would have to venture outside the mainstream and look to feminist writing to find a definition of motherhood that "does not involve selfless love" (Mullin, 2006, p. 197) or a conception of young people as "capable of genuine mutuality" (VanDeCarr, 2013).

This is not to say that women are powerless in determining the attitudes they bring to motherhood—not by any means—or that those who are at home full-time with their children are not living according to their own deliberate moral commitments. But whatever their preference may be, they must contend with a barrage of messages meant to reach them by endless routes of transmission. Like X-rays conducted invisibly across the currents of social discourse, images of devotional motherhood are recurrently delivered via "commentaries, correspondence, novels, biographies, treatises, rituals, artistic endeavors, prescriptive articles and manuals, television/film/theater scripts/performances, and so forth" (Griswold, 1994, p. 48). These various modes of programming permeate the social spaces that make up our everyday lives with the intention to influence not just women. Indeed, they are devised for mass appeal. It is through these converging and intersecting lines that mothers make their way, some more easily than others.

Reauthoring Motherhood: Daughters and Sons Doing Their Fair Share

With limited attention paid to the ways that children contribute to their mothers' lives, beyond the "gift" of their existence, we sometimes find them living free of obligation and untroubled by their own behavior, no matter how flagrant. This freedom can extend not only to the careless treatment of their mothers, but also to a haphazard approach to their own lives. In such instances, we resist the mother-blaming tradition that would have us hold her accountable and recommend such practices as consistency, structure, and limit setting. Here DM is found in conversation with Dalia, a divorced mother, and her 12-year-old son Jonah. The two appear caught in an arrangement in which any concern regarding the direction of Jonah's life appears to reside exclusively with Dalia, and any energy to preserve the quality of their relationship is likewise hers to expend:

> **Dalia:** I bother you, as you put it, because I want to make sure you're getting your work done, and getting showered before it gets too late, and getting to bed on time, and getting up on time. It's my job as your mother to make sure you're okay and that you're seeing to your responsibilities. (She smiles, attempting to convey this in a light tone.)
>
> **Jonah:** You're not helping me. You're just annoying me. (Perhaps Freud would interpret Jonah's behavior as illustrative of the son's inevitable repudiation of the mother, but DM has something else in mind. Guided by a feminist ethic, he wonders about a possible unequal distribution of responsibility between mother and son, with the vast preponderance resting with Dalia.)
>
> **DM:** What annoys you, Jonah?
>
> **Jonah:** She should worry about her own life and let me worry about mine. Why doesn't she worry about whether *she* showered? (Jonah responds contemptuously. DM has witnessed this

sort of attitude in young people from time to time. To his ear, it has the sound of privilege, fostered by a culturally mediated arrangement of nonreciprocity.)

DM: So you're advising your mother to stop worrying about you?

Jonah: Yes! I tell her all the time. Stop worrying about me! (He glares at her.)

DM: Dalia, is Worry something you or mothers you know, for that matter, can shrug off or sidestep? (DM means to acknowledge the plight of mothers who find themselves unavoidably burdened.)

Dalia: I wish! Although Jeff [Dalia's ex-husband and Jonah's father] tells me not to worry so much. It's easy for him, though. I'm still the one who has to see to every little detail—school projects, due dates, carpool.

DM: Jonah, I'm wondering about your idea that your mother should let you worry about your own life. Did I get that right? (DM wonders if there is a possible intention Jonah might make known—even to himself—to carry more of the responsibility for his life.)

Jonah: Yeah.

DM: Are you finding that you're worrying about your own life? No, wait—that's not the way to put it. Are you taking more interest in your life or facing responsibility yourself? What's the best way to put it?

Jonah: I don't know. (He seems disinterested.)

DM: Is it a matter of letting your life fall through the cracks so that no one's looking after it, or have you, or you and your dad, begun taking more care of your life? (DM tries again.)

Jonah: I do take care of things. She just doesn't see it. (Still petulant.)

DM: Would you be up for answering some questions about how you're taking care of things so that your mother *can* see it? (Jonah may very well hold concerns for his life, though still tentatively. DM owes it to him to help make his concerns evident.)

Jonah: I guess. (Somewhat engaged.)

DM: Dalia, would it be helpful to you to learn more about the ways Jonah may be taking care of his life?

Dalia: I'd love to hear it! (It is often a welcome relief to parents to discover that their daughters and sons are taking an active interest in the direction of their lives, and Dalia is no exception. Even if the past justifies skepticism, both Dalia and Jonah may very well benefit from any movement in this direction.)

DM: Where should we start, Jonah—school, homework, chores, relationships, or somewhere else entirely? Where have you begun to see your own interest in looking after your life?

Jonah: I don't know . . . (He flounders initially.)

DM: It's not an easy question. Feel free to take some time to think it over. You say you're caring for your life . . . (DM is prepared to stretch the question out to allow Jonah the time to shift into a reflective posture without the pressure that can come from a more sudden or condensed delivery.)

Jonah: I've been going to bed lately without her telling me. (He interjects.)

DM: No kidding?

Jonah: No!

DM: Is he kidding, Dalia? (Turning to Dalia.)

Dalia: Well, now let me think about it. Last night I had to tell him to get ready for bed, but he did go right up without a fight. (Though Jonah needed to be told, the fact that he went right up may represent a significant development.)

DM: Why are you getting to bed earlier some of the time? And why did you go right up when your mom asked you to rather than fighting for extra time?

Jonah: Because if I don't get enough sleep it's too hard to get up in the morning.

DM: But don't most kids fight it anyway and try to stay up as late as they can without thinking about how tired they'll be the

It's All Mom's Fault!

next day? (It is this kind of expression of concern for one's own life that can begin to redistribute responsibility.)

Jonah: I don't know.

DM: And what do you want to be awake for the next day? Why not just sleepwalk through the day? (DM utilizes the metaphor Jonah introduced to see if it will underwrite an emerging plotline.)

Jonah: I don't like to be tired during the day.

DM: By any chance, do you think you are waking up more to your life?

Jonah: I guess. (He looks at DM directly as he answers, a possible indication of his growing engagement.)

DM: If you are, Jonah, what's it about? Why might you want to be more awake to your life? Is there something you're noticing about your life that deserves more of your attention?

Jonah: I can handle things myself. . . . I don't need her reminding me to shower or get my work done. (This is said with less spite and with a measure of self-assurance, as if he is on his way to reaching a conclusion.)

DM: Dalia, what difference would it make to you if Jonah were to wake up to things himself rather than having to be woken up by you? (DM wonders what a more equitable arrangement, or at least one that is fairer than the current one, might mean to Dalia.)

Dalia: It would make a huge difference! (She seems enthused by the prospect.)

DM: (Turning back to Jonah) Would you be willing to answer more questions the next time we get together, about how you might be waking up to your own life? (He nods.) Let's see, what might I ask you? (Pausing to think.) How did you come to decide to concern yourself with your life rather than leaving it to others? And why now? Why is now the time you've chosen to wake up to your life? And is there something promising about your life that you really would not want to miss out on? (Jonah appears genuinely thoughtful.) I could e-mail these to you and give you a chance to look them over beforehand. Or would that be a bother?

Jonah: You don't have to send them because I already know the answers. (Confidently stated.)

DM: Fair enough, Jonah. I'll definitely look forward to catching up with you next time.

As promised, when they next met Jonah was ready with answers. After reviewing the questions from the previous meeting, he explained in simple terms: "I can do it. I'm older now and can do more for myself." DM wondered whether getting older might point to a different future with his mother. Jonah was modest in his prediction: "It will probably take a while," but over time he believed things would "slowly improve." For example, "I might not get so annoyed with her, or at least try not to show it." When reminded of the last question about whether there was something he would not want to miss out on, he said, "The whole thing. I don't want to miss any of my life." Dalia responded positively to the impact of Jonah's efforts, saying, "*I* might be able to have a life again."

Following this meeting, Jonah's father, Jeff, was invited to join them. With all three in attendance, Dalia pointed to the "imbalance" in how much she was relied upon "by the two of them, even when Jonah is at his father's house." Jonah seemed to enjoy watching his father struggle with the same questions he had entertained. At one point he even offered his father the following unsolicited advice: "Gee, Dad, maybe *you* could wake up a little more." This was delivered with the same glib aplomb he was well known for. Jeff explained good-naturedly, "I do what I can," averting any further expectation by plainly stating, "There are only so many hours in a day," to which Dalia provided the following well-considered response: "Welcome to my world."

During the very first meeting, Jonah had created the original opening, not just with the proposition that his mother should be doing less, but by implication, that he might have an interest in doing more. DM followed this implicit suggestion (Carey et al., 2009; White,

It's All Mom's Fault!

2000), and Jonah joined in, though tentatively at first. Over time, he grew more adept at moving into the lead. When DM asked him some time later, "What is the best thing about being awake to your own life?" Jonah replied frankly, "If you're asleep you'll miss everything."

Given the ever-present specter of mother blame and the resulting uneven distribution of responsibility, it is certainly understandable that a mother would need to see her son (and ex-husband) stepping up in order to take a step back. If mothers carelessly relinquished responsibility and no one (e.g., fathers, sons) was roused to pick up the slack, there's no telling where young people might end up.

The Benefits of Mutuality

In our work with economically stressed families, we sometimes see greater expressions of mutuality in mother-child relations. Whether by need or preference (or both), children are often held to the expectation that they, like the adults in the family, consider the greater good. It is well known that in single-parent families, children make important contributions, such as taking on a share of the housework and care for younger siblings. Their involvement can be vital to the welfare of the family (Anderson & Anderson, 2011). It may serve an especially important function when mothers are dealing with extenuating circumstances. Sharon, a single mother, describes the emotional support she received from her then-6-year-old son during a time of transition:

> Jamie used to be a real mama's boy. He was always looking out for me. When life got too hard for us in Tucson, and I knew we had to move out here [California]—for his sake and mine—I bought two bus tickets with all the money I had left. Jamie was real quiet the whole time. But it was like he knew what I was going through. Other kids would have complained—all that time on the bus! But Jamie, he was with me every mile. He didn't ask for much. . . . He understood that we have to be strong and pull

together. Sometimes it doesn't just take Mommy. It takes all of us being strong.

After hearing this description, Jamie, by then 13, spoke to his sense of pride at being able to return the love and understanding his mother had shown him throughout his young life: "She did everything for me, and it wasn't easy. . . . I like that I did something for her." One cannot help but wonder how this experience might have continued to shape Jamie's relationship to himself and others. Rather than imposing a middle-class value of mother devotion to the exclusion of mutuality, as if all families have equal access to a privileged existence, we give consideration to an ethic of exchange. An appreciation for reciprocity that might otherwise be muted is given attention and accorded value. After all, economic advantage, and what it makes possible in the way of ardent care, is in no way an indication of moral advantage.

Marginalized Mothers and Communal Care

The mother-blame apparatus can be especially denigrating of mothers who "fall short" of the mandate to do it all. Given the increasing emphasis on austerity in the current neoliberal age (Bockman, 2014), more is expected of nuclear families than ever. With cutbacks to various forms of social support, including childcare, nutrition, and public education, the added burden placed on families is masked by the laudatory image of an idealized self-sustaining unit guided by its own freedom of choice (Peck, 2012). Families are likened to entrepreneurial entities or private mini-corporations. The optimally functioning family handles everything "in house." Within this configuration, mothers are expected to exemplify self-reliance in parenting, seeing to their children's physical, social, and emotional well-being (Rose, 1999). Anything less (or less private) could be seen as a failure to satisfy the requirements of their job description and result in unsatisfactory performance reviews.

Contrary to the neoliberal model, many mothers benefit—and so do children—when extended family and/or community members take an active role. Listen in as Laurie prepares to meet with a family for the first time. The mother, Louise, has three children (ages 12, 10, and 8). The eldest, J.T., opens the door and shows Laurie inside, while Louise wraps up a telephone conversation. Laurie catches on that Louise has been discussing J.T. In a frustrated tone, she lists each of his recent offenses, including skipping school, talking back to a teacher, and smoking marijuana. Before hanging up, she tells the person on the other end, "Here! You talk some sense into your nephew!" and thrusts the phone in her son's direction. After J.T. hangs up, Laurie asks about the phone call. He complains that any time he does anything wrong, his mom calls everybody in the family and "spreads my business."

"That's right," she says. "And if you keep this up, I'm sending you to Uncle Kenny's. You think I won't? Keep pushing and see what happens." She turns to Laurie and explains, "My brother was just like J.T. when he was growing up. He thought he knew everything. Then he got into the military. That taught him real quick. And he's all military now. You hear that, J.T.? I'd like to see you pull these stunts with him."

Given the prominence of such notions as privacy and boundaries, a therapist could draw any number of hasty conclusions about Louise and her parenting (e.g., she should be handling things herself, she ought to show more discretion, she is negatively affecting his self-esteem, etc.). Instead of recognizing these assumptions as favoring individualism over collectivism, it is not uncommon for therapists to mistake such biases as applicable across cultures (Gergen, 2006). At the behest of the juvenile justice system, mothers of color whose children end up on trouble's path are typically referred for parenting classes (Schaffner, 1997). In many instances they are made "fit" (and made to fit in) by professionals whose interventions, by design, move them closer to inhabiting white middle-class, neoliberal values (Fox, Prilleltensky, & Austin, 2009).

But is parenting even the problem? Consider Louise, who turned to her brother, Kenny, for help. She described to Laurie the advantages in calling on extended family for assistance, as she reflected on her own experiences growing up.

Louise: You never knew who my mom was going to call. My

brother and I would try to guess based on what we'd done wrong. When we were caught doing something we shouldn't have, we'd be walking home from school, and Kenny would say to me, "Whose car is it going to be? Guess whose car, Lou." (Louise clearly finds pleasure in this recollection.)

LM: Meaning . . . ?

Louise: Guess whose car is going to be in the driveway. We'd know by the car exactly what was going to happen next. We'd approach the corner and say, "You look." "No! You look!" and push each other toward the house. (She delights in the memory, though at the time, it undoubtedly stirred a very different emotion.)

LM: And what happened when you got home?

Louise: That depended. If it was my grandma, we were fed. If it was my great-grandma, we were hugged and kissed and put to bed. If it was my aunt, we were talked to. You just had to sit there. Same with Cousin Dave. And if it was Uncle Vic, well, let's just say you'd better run and hide. (Louise shakes her head and laughs.)

LM: Oh gosh.

Louise: He was a lot of talk, but still, you didn't want to test him.

LM: And what was it like for you and Kenny to have to answer to the whole family?

Louise: (Laughing) I hated it then! But I get it now.

LM: What do you get? (Anticipating this might be a growth opportunity, less for Louise than for Laurie.)

Louise: It helped. It gave us more guidance. We couldn't get away with anything. But there's no guarantee they'll be safe, no matter what you do, or what you teach them. I have three sons, and I pray . . . (becoming tearful) . . . anything could happen to one of them.

LM: Is that why you called your brother?

Louise: That's right.

LM: And how might he help? What can you count on him for?

> (Laurie is opening herself up to the African American tradition of family ties [Boyd-Franklin, 2010; Taylor, Chatters, Woodward, & Brown, 2013] rather than giving license to professional knowledge. This requires a conscious effort on her part to separate from dominant cultural notions regarding parenting.)
>
> **Louise**: He knows how to get through to J.T. And I trust Kenny. I know he's a good influence.

Louise went on to describe her hope that Kenny might reach J.T. before "he ends up too far down a bad path." She also spoke to a fear of her son's life being cut short by violence at the hands of those who are appointed to serve and protect.[1] Turning to an "extended family kinship network" (Kane, 2000, p. 692) is exactly what a caring mother does when her children appear at risk, unless she is being measured by a neoliberal yardstick. Escaping the confines of dominant culture and entertaining alternative images of motherhood—in this case, as a communal concern—requires a readiness to suspend individualistic edicts and open oneself up to local, community, and cultural traditions.

Conclusion

From the inception of life and the handing over of freshly powdered babies, mothers have been met by a forewarning—a premonition of their latent capacity as "weapons of maternal destruction." Meanwhile, fatherhood has remained largely uninterrogated (Adamsons & Buehler, 2007), except for the amount of time fathers spend at home, with the implication that more is better (Mullins, 2011). Recent interest by researchers in the quality of fathers' participation is an encouraging development, although we would never advocate that fathers be subjected to the same professional scorn in the name of gender equality.

Of late, genetics would appear to be raising the banner of mother blame, pointing to "the fundamental way in which gene expression is determined by [early] experience" (Siegel, 2012, p. 112). Daniel

Siegel and coauthor Mary Hartzell warn that "[i]n the presence of an unhealthy genetic variant, lack of proper nurture can lead to its activation" (Siegel & Hartzell, 2004, p. 116). Does this leave mothers in the untenable position of defending against the inevitable? "Have I done the unthinkable? Have I flipped the dreaded genetic variant to the on position?" Neuroscience may serve to further heighten tensions, pointing to the cost of "failed mothering" in how "[t]he caregiving adult's mind and patterns of communication directly shape the organization of the developing child's brain" (Siegel, 2012, p. 103). Have we entered a new frontier, moving beyond mere theories about mothers as ruinous causal agents and into an evidential field—a scientific supreme court of sorts—in which every mother is a potential perpetrator who may be brought up on charges of genetic obstruction, brain injury, and even neuronal murder (Siegel, 2012)? Or might it be that these disciplines are using new technologies to perpetuate old biases, at least where mother blame is concerned, and holding mothers' already scorched feet to the flames?

It would seem the prosperous business of mother blame will continue to offer solid returns to the professional disciplines. Whether countertheories and counterpractices more hospitable to mothers will gain increasing traction, working their way into family therapy textbooks, conference curricula, workshops, clinical supervision settings, direct practice, and the culture at large, is a matter for hope and speculation.

As we move to the last section of the book the authors, each in turn, provide a longer account of a young protagonist's engagement with a seemingly intractable problem. Chapter 9 illustrates how, when freed from the strictures of blame, a mother might, in a more favorable atmosphere, find her way to playful and imaginative undertakings, even with a problem that is particularly foul.

CHAPTER NINE

Grow Me Up—Grow Me Down
Travails With Sneaky Poo and Sneaky Wee

In the following story, Shelley describes her efforts to help her eldest son, Billy, gain the advantage over Sneaky Poo and Sneaky Wee. With the assistance of DE and family allies, Shelley discovers that a little imagination can go a long way. Given the geographical distance between them, with Shelley, her partner, Jim, and their three young children living in the United Kingdom, and DE residing in New Zealand with his partner, Ann, the work proceeded through e-mail correspondence and with aid from the Growing-Up Fairy, who joined in by telephone. Shelley serves as the narrator in the unfolding drama that follows.

We were in a dire situation! Billy had just turned 5 and I had my two younger children, ages 3 and 1, to care for. I had been cleaning up urine and feces five times a day or more for the past 2 years. Billy would never say he needed the toilet and would only use it when I directed him there myself. This was indubitably against his will, but in case there was any remaining shred of doubt, he made his position entirely clear by screaming his lungs out whenever I tried to advise him on the matter. His school was on the verge of banning him as a health hazard and, by implication, sanctioning me as an unfit mother. As to my blameworthiness, I had to agree. After all, what kind of mother is unable to toilet train her child by the time he goes to school?

Billy and I had always cherished our close bond but now there was a great divide between us, making communication seemingly impossible. I tried to bridge the gap but whenever I brought toileting up, even to praise his efforts, I was met with resistance or worse. I oscillated between anger and despair, and most days were spent under a cloud that soiled the household atmosphere. I tried every potty-training trick in the book, and more.

Nothing ever worked for more than a day or so. I realized I was completely out of my depth and was referred to a health visitor who came to the house a couple of times before admitting she, too, was at a loss for what to do. I was devastated and felt completely alone. I fantasized about sneaking out in the middle of the night when no one would notice. But this was strictly a fantasy brought on by fatigue and desperation. I was linked to my children by an unbreakable bond, and so I turned to the Internet, hoping there might be an answer out there, somewhere.

Sneaky Poo, I See You

As I searched for anything that might help, I chanced upon a story, *Beating Sneaky Poo: Ideas for Faecal Soiling*, by Terry Heins and Karen Ritchie (1988), which I now realize was an adaptation of Michael White's seminal article, "Pseudo-encopresis: From avalanche to victory, from vicious to virtuous cycles" (1984). Reading through its pages, I began to feel inspired, and soon my anger toward Billy dissipated. I reread it and resolved to read it through with Billy to see how it might affect him. It turned out he loved the story, the same as me, and asked to have it read again and again. As a consequence, he started to gain a measure of confidence in his ability to tackle the problem. We immediately began to implement some of its suggestions, such as planning and timing routes to the toilet and making a poster of his favorite TV characters, *The Octonauts*, cheering him on to victory. He took the storybook along with him to school, tucked in his bag. I also confided in him, apologizing for thinking he was the problem when really it had been Sneaky Poo and Sneaky Wee all along. I admitted that until then I was unaware of such miscreants, and I was certainly glad I had found out about them. Billy started telling me when he needed the toilet and even had some days when he was completely clean and dry! This story seemed magical to me. Presto! It changed everything. I felt like my son had been restored to my love and care. My feelings of frustration were significantly reduced, since we were no longer at odds and were instead able to work as a team against a common foe. But, no sooner did my hopes rise than they sank again as the effects of the Sneaky Poo story began to wear thin.

I phoned my mother-in-law, who worked in special education in Auckland and told her about Sneaky Poo. The story rang a bell for her, and she went directly to her bookshelf and found *Playful Approaches to Serious Problems: Narrative Therapy With Children and Their Families* (Freeman et al., 1997). She read to me from a section named "You Stink and My Brother Doesn't." Remarkably, we discovered that David Epston lived in Auckland, the city to which we would be returning in a few months' time. I e-mailed him at once and was elated when he agreed to assist us. Our isolation was over. From my short-lived success with implementing the Sneaky Poo story, I knew we could not do this all on our own.

The following are abstracted from DE's email correspondence with us over the next few months. Here is what he wrote that told us he empathized with our struggle:

No doubt, young people, by 3 or 4 years of age, have become intensely aware of Sneaky Poo or Sneaky Wee, if they have been dogged by one or both of them since developing retrievable memory. And Sneaky Poo has undoubtedly dogged parents far more than their children, even though the Poo is in their daughter's/son's pants, not theirs. As we all know, we take pains to deliver the Poo to sewage plants and see to other sanitary measures in order to dispel the risk of infectious diseases, such as typhoid fever. Perhaps more than anything else, this risk has contributed to us considering feces to be malodorous, generally offensive, and threatening to our well-being. Not surprisingly, according to such cultural views, a young person's rapid toilet training is a matter of concern for everyone. However, the young person is sometimes the least concerned of all concerned parties (e.g., parents, siblings, grandparents, aunts and uncles, family friends, school teachers and principals, health professionals and the general public).

As everyone goes about attempting to assist the young person when the problem isn't rapidly resolved, what can inadvertently result are antagonistic relationships. Parents, and especially mothers, feel the weight, given the seriousness of the problem, to "put pressure" on the young person in the hope, often in vain, that s/he will in turn "put pressure" on her/himself. To spare themselves disappointment at their failure to rapidly achieve cleanness or dryness, young people often come to believe that their parents are the problem rather than Sneaky Poo or Wee. As a result, they handle the Sneaky Poo problem the only way they know how: first, by denying that the problem is a problem; second, by going to great lengths to conceal the consequences of it; and third, by becoming so habituated to it that what bothers others—filth and foulness—has little or no effect on them. The situation comes to be not just tolerable, but insignificant.

However, what cannot be made trivial are humiliations, chastisements, rebukes, and punishments. Once again, young people may take what they consider the only route available in "tuning out." This is usually demonstrated whenever the problem is brought to their attention. They can be seen putting their fingers in their ears, physically turning away from the conversation, and appearing to retreat to a space all their own. And I would suspect the more sensitive or concerned a young person is over the charged feelings of their parents, the more likely s/he is to leave the conversational field one way or another. Consequently, s/he becomes unavailable to parental counsel, which almost inevitably leads to feelings of resentment or bitterness all around.

The question is, how can we engage young people in a way of thinking and acting that allows for very different options for both them and their parents, so that everyone can evade this "misery-go-around"? Here we might favor a view of a young person putting pressure on her/himself to put pressure on the problem. This would relieve the parents of vain efforts and, in turn, relieve the young person of the negative effects of pressure imposed from the outside.

The Growing-Up Fairy: More Than a Wing and a Prayer

Given the burden and futility Jim and I felt in trying to more effectively manage our son, it came as a great relief that, rather than evaluate our management skills, DE had something very different in mind. We were delighted by his explanation:

"The Growing-Up Fairy Meets Sneaky Poo/Wee" approach allows parents to set themselves to one side, leaving the matter to the young person in consultation with none other than the Growing-Up Fairy (GUF). Of course, these dialogues are coached initially by the therapist and mediated by the parents, but slyly, rather than outwardly. Here the parents' desperation as well as the young person's futility, which have often led to deadly seriousness, can be rehabilitated and replaced by mischief making, something that has been sorely lost in the lengthy struggles over the child's bowel/bladder control or, more pointedly, the lack thereof. We can now enter the domain of tricksters, tricks, and countertricks, in support of a young person's desire to grow up, and in opposition to the problem's interest in growing her/him down.

From what you tell me, based on your discussion with Billy, he came to the conclusion that Sneaky Poo had effectively "grown him down to a 1-year-old," and my guess is, he was either unhappy or perhaps despairing about the loss of his claim to full-fledged status as a 5-year-old boy. I have yet to meet a 5-year-old who would relish such a demotion. In fact, I wonder if what you describe as "his disheartenment" might have arisen from his sense of being unable to do very much about his Poo sneaking out, despite his fervent desire that it should not happen. This is where the GUF comes into play.

So who exactly is the Growing-Up Fairy? This kindhearted being circles the globe looking out for young people who, for reasons such as misfortune, misadventure, mayhem, and the challenges of illness and disability, are not as grown up as they might otherwise be. She[1] aids those who may benefit greatly from a helping hand (or wing). Whenever the GUF is either informed of, or chances upon, a young child who is being grown down by an onerous problem of one kind or another, she offers assistance, because she cares and believes all children deserve a fair chance to grow up. The occupational class of a GUF is the same as that of the better-known Tooth Fairy who has the benevolent job description of repairing any pain or discomfort when a young person loses a milk tooth, either by chance or extraction. Perhaps the Tooth Fairy is far better known because she is so regularly called to action when children are between the ages of 7 and about 12. Over this 5-year span, one by one, 20 milk teeth are shed and replaced. And she is a generous fairy, though even fairies must keep an eye on their store of not just precious dust, but cash reserves in determining affordable rates of return per tooth. A recent survey in *Harper's* magazine reported the average payment per milk tooth in 2010 was $3.00 (U.S.) dropping to $2.60 in 2011, perhaps indicating that tooth fairies were no less subject to the Great Recession.

How do you introduce Billy to the GUF, you might wonder? It is highly unlikely that he has ever heard of the GUF, although he may have made the acquaintance of the Tooth Fairy or fairies in general from children's literature. Such fairies are generally regarded as child-friendly and child-supportive and probably haven't had any previous association with parents. Why? These fairies pretty much exist in a wonderland (or Neverland) of their own making, not unlike the one Alice enters by falling down the rabbit hole. We might find that as we match the malevolence of Sneaky Poo/Wee with the benevolent intentions of the GUF, Billy's imagination will awaken and offer him passage to new realms of possibility. We are creating relationships in which his comrade and his antagonist will vie for his allegiance, each to their respective cause: the GUF lending a hand up, as Sneaky Poo/Wee makes every effort to grow him down.

I expect that even though he is regarded as having the intellect of a 6- or 7-year-old, Billy cannot read adequately to be in correspondence of any kind with the GUF without you and Jim having to read her com-

Grow Me Up—Grow Me Down

munications to him. This means we will have to dream up some hijinks to engage Billy's interest. I propose you recruit a family member or friend to playact the role of the benevolent and kindly GUF and brief her on what might be expected. First of all, she will have to feel sympathy for Billy and respect for you, and second, have some idea of the significance of the role. In general, the best candidate should be well known for mischief making, take delight in storytelling, and possess a capacity for dramatic presentation, outrageousness, and good humor.

Inspired by DE's imagination and sensing the opportunity that might be found in a mischievous approach to the problem, I readily set the plan in motion. I had no trouble proposing such a project to Jim's sister, Clare, age 21, who lived in New Zealand. She could not have been better suited to play her part, given her previous casting in major roles in every drama at her high school. We let her in on Billy's problem, which to that point we had kept a secret from our Kiwi family. I explained this approach at some length with extracts from our correspondence with DE, in which he advised how we might dramatically heighten Billy's dilemma of whether to grow up or be grown down. Either he would be outwitted by Sneaky Poo or seek the counsel of his GUF to outwit the problem and claim his rightful status as a 5-year-old, perhaps even going beyond his chronological and intellectual age. Jim and I also accepted that it was up to us to provide Clare with a script or at least an outline, which we would regularly e-mail to her. She was to phone, and if we missed the call, to leave a message on our answering machine for Billy.

DE explained how this might work:

Here is a scenario that might permit a private conversation between the two of them. The phone rings and either of you can answer it. You talk loudly so that Billy cannot help overhearing you saying something of this sort: "Who is this? What do you want? You want to speak to my son, Billy? Would you mind repeating that? You are a Growing-Up Fairy? I thought that's what you said. You want to speak to my boy? Will you look after him and be a good friend of his? Okay, I will hand the phone over to him!"

I expect that Billy's curiosity will be piqued by overhearing such an unprecedented conversation. And I'm guessing he would have had very good associations with telephone calls from speaking to adoring grandparents, kindly aunts and uncles, and excited cousins from New Zealand before today. [DE was right. Jim came from an extremely close family of six siblings who were in constant contact with one another.]

Here the GUF will introduce herself reasonably succinctly. And then, like the White Rabbit from *Alice in Wonderland*, might say something to this effect: "Oh dear. I've got to go! I've got an urgent job. There is a boy who has a problem that is growing him down, and he is on the other phone. I have got to lend him a hand. But I want you to know, Billy, that I like you a lot. I have been watching you and I see that old sneak, Sneaky Poo, tricking you and growing you down. I don't like that about Sneaky Poo. That's why I called. By the way, I've heard, while flying over the UK, about your many wonderfulnesses, so I know you are a wonderful boy who wants to grow up to his age. Look, I really wish I could talk longer but I've just got to go. I will ring you back in a few days' time when I am not so busy helping other kids grow back to their age."

Not having met Billy in person, I cannot predict his response but he would be a very unusual boy if this did not arouse his interest as to who in the world the GUF is. Given that I suspect Billy will want to talk to you in order to seek clarification, I suggest you deny all knowledge of the GUF, except to say something of this sort: "I have never met a Growing-Up Fairy myself, but my mum and dad told me that I just grew up without much standing in the way or any problem trying to grow me down. So I guess I was lucky and never needed a Growing-Up Fairy. I am pretty sure I heard of them when I was your age, though, from my girlfriend, Martha, but when I think about it now, I can't really remember what she told me. What did the Growing-Up Fairy say to you? We couldn't hear a word."

From here on, you are going to have to play it by ear. But, you might wish to indicate to Billy that you are very interested in GUFs in general and if Billy insists, you will ask family and friends if they have any memories and stories about GUFs. If it turns out they do, why not propose to

Billy that he phone his aunties and uncles in New Zealand to learn what they know about such fairies? Had they or their friends ever been lent a helping hand by a GUF when they were his age? Once again, you might have to coach family with what this is all about and what stories they might tell. I also suggest that for the time being they avoid any Sneaky Poo stories to steer clear of possible embarrassment.

DE helped us with the kind of dialogue we might write for the GUF. He provided examples at first, and then we wrote our own and ran them past him. We felt we would be communicating with Billy in the most entrancing way. Here is the guidance DE offered:

Just think of all the ways children Billy's age grow up. Then, come up with a story about a child who might have required assistance from the GUF. No matter how you go about the specifics of this introduction to the GUF, it should obviously be embroidered with a kind of charm that would have everyone pass through the looking glass to the other side, which we might refer to as a "counterworld." It is in such realms that the GUF can inspire undergrown young people to get their own back against sneaky problems. You might expect that sooner or later a dialogue will be established between Sneaky Poo and Billy. However, in the early stages of this conversation, Sneaky Poo might best be sidelined. Instead, the Growing-Up Fairy should spend a great deal of time teaming up with Billy by getting to know him through his wonderfulnesses, which she would have observed while floating above him at school, at home, on the playground, with grandparents, etc.

DE elicited from us Billy's wonderfulnesses, which was a welcome request after having been so captured by a problematic view for so long, and we responded with pleasure. Without Sneaky Poo, Billy would have been about 98% wonderful to us. DE suggested:

Here's how you might think up these wonderfulnesses. Jim, could you interview Shelley with a pen and pad by your side? Ask Shelley the following: "What do you consider the most wonderful and heartwarming things Billy does that, if Sneaky Poo knew full well about, it would undoubtedly think twice before continuing to try to grow a boy like Billy down?"

Next line of inquiry is: "Shelley, can you tell me a story about what you refer to as his 'imagination'?"

Next line of inquiry: "Who do you think he gets his 'imagination' most from? Anybody on your side of the family?"

Then reverse this and, Shelley, you take notes and interview Jim. It might be good to convey who, between you, is the source of a given wonderfulness so that in any conversation with Billy, the GUF can say, "I heard your dad tell your mum (or your mum tell your dad) about your 'sharing with your brother' wonderfulness, etc."

DE then suggested how we might get the show on the road, and we couldn't wait.

How about for the next five phone calls from the GUF, with two or three days in between each call, she says something like this:

"Billy, *look*, sorry for not ringing you but I am *so* busy helping good kids grow back to their age. But look, I have heard about a wonderfulness of yours. As I was floating by your house, I think I overheard your mom call it "Billy's imagination." Do you know what that is? Well I don't blame you if you don't because it is a pretty big word for a 5-year-old. Do you want to hear the story she told your dad about you? Is my voice loud enough? Ready. Here goes. Well, last week when you were ... " Make sure the length of the story is about right for his comprehension and attention span, even though it is highly likely his attention will be at its "full span" to hear a wonderfulness story. At the end of the story, have the GUF ask Billy, "Hey Billy! Do you want me to lend you a hand to out-trick my old enemy, Sneaky Poo?"

When Billy agrees, once again the GUF should suddenly receive another urgent call and, in the same style as the White Rabbit, shout, "Got to go! Got to go! An urgent call! Need to lend a hand to a 7-year-old boy who is a really good kid but got grown down by a problem. I will phone you as soon as I have time. But don't worry, this 7-year-old boy is playing a trick on Sneaky Poo so maybe when he wins, he will also lend you a hand. Don't worry, Billy! You can count on me even if I am very busy helping so many young boys and girls grow up. After all, that is why I am called the Growing-Up Fairy and not the Tooth Fairy!"

DE's coaching had us thinking back to those few times when Billy had responded best to the expectation that he train himself to use the toilet. These had involved some sort of game or other that we imagined into existence. So when DE told us about the GUF and how she helped so many other kids, I anticipated Billy would be enthralled by her. I could only imagine that Jim and I and our other children would be equally beguiled. We were well overdue for a visit from a fairy of any kind since Jim and I had never really promoted her cousin, the Tooth Fairy. Already, it was a considerable relief to be freed from the responsibility to put pressure on Billy as that had clearly failed in every possible way. Most troubling had been our growing mutual detachment. Released from the burden to pressure him, we were able to migrate to an imaginative space, where Billy and the GUF could conspire to take control of the problem.

With the Planning Done, It's Time for Fun

The moment for action had arrived. The first call came through. Jim answered and, having sought some clarification from the caller, eventually handed the telephone to Billy. After, recovering from his confusion, Billy concluded disappointedly, "The Fairy is a Kiwi because she has a Kiwi accent." It seemed, after all the hours spent viewing animated films, he simply would not countenance a Kiwi fairy. This meant that Clare would need to adopt an American accent. After a bit of rehearsal she rang me on the phone for a tryout. She offered a passable version of a Disney-trained actor and proved herself worthy of her casting as we prepared to advance the plan.

Billy was somewhat unsure about the events that had transpired and mentioned after the first call, in addition to being thrown off by her accent, he suspected the Growing-Up Fairy "was really you, Mum." I was relieved that we had been in the room when the call came through, as I was able to counter this: "It couldn't possibly have been me talking to you on the phone. I was sitting right here beside you and Daddy the whole time!" Billy had to admit this was so, which increased his bewilderment. It was hard not to bombard Billy with questions, given our own excitement. Jim and I were even more engaged by this new plotline than he was—a GUF of his very own!

As the calls continued, Billy and the GUF became companionable, talking about anything and everything. On occasion, we were concerned that the GUF could not get a word in edgewise, though Billy did come around to listening. He especially enjoyed hearing descriptions of his wonderfulnesses and marveled at how much the GUF knew about the day-to-day events of his life. He reached the conclusion, "She loves me!" Knowing only too well how much his Aunt Clare adored him, we couldn't help but agree.

What happened next indicated an extraordinary paradigm shift. When the GUF offered to lend him a hand with Sneaky Poo and Wee, Billy assured her and us that he could defeat them on his own. What a turnaround! He was no longer hiding himself away, but rather looking straight into the eyes of his tormentor. Was it possible that momentum had finally arrived and might stick around and replace complacency? My faith in my son was renewed, even if tentatively, along with my newly acquired belief in the power of fairies. Not having made the acquaintance of a GUF myself as a young girl, I asked Billy to tell me about her. He happily informed me about the noise her wings make when she flies, that "she is pink," and how "she comes out at night and not much at all during the day."

Then we found the coin. It was an extremely shiny five pence coin and I wondered, as it was so shiny, whether it had been left for him by his GUF. Billy told me it was shiny because of the sun, but nevertheless, he was absolutely confident that she had purposely left it for him. My curiosity made me ask Billy if it was a magical coin. Billy thought that it probably was and we speculated that, being magical, it would most likely return to its owner if it were ever spent or lost. We hurried home to try it out. Billy arranged to buy one of my cupcakes for his brother, Andy, handing the magic coin over to me as payment. Sure enough, as soon as Andy ate his cupcake, the coin began to tingle in my hand and then tug as if being attracted to a magnet of the opposite pole. I tried really hard to hang onto it, but no matter how tightly I held it, its force pulled my hand, arm, and whole body toward Billy. I stumbled forward, trying to keep my hand closed over the coin only to have it forced wide open. Much to Billy's delight and wonderment, the coin was inescapably returned to his possession. Later that evening, we were discussing how this magic had transpired. Billy happily let us in on the secret: "The fairy waves her wand and then it comes back to me." And he provided us with a fuller description of the GUF: "Her wand is gold too, and she has a crown!" Under closer inspection, I realized that the coin was covered in "fairy dust" (which looked remarkably like my natural collection bronzing pearls).

The next day the Growing-Up Fairy called and left the following message on our answering machine: "Hi, Billy. It's your Growing-Up Fairy. I am so pleased you found the coin I left for you. I sprinkled it with fairy dust so when I wave my wand it will come back to you. I saw that you used it when you got home. You are such a good sharer, Billy. I wasn't surprised one bit that you bought a cake for Andy, too. That's why I wanted you to have the coin. I really hope to help you soon. I'm so busy helping other kids right now, but don't give up on me. I am your Growing-Up Fairy, too."

One Good Trick Deserves Another

We were all really enjoying ourselves, not least of all Billy, who, we came to realize, had a particular talent for trickery. It was only fair, he felt, and we agreed, that the problem deserved some of its own medicine. He made up his mind to trick Sneaky Poo and Wee. They would think they were coming out in his pants but Billy would rush into the bathroom and be on the toilet before they had a chance to escape. When they realized it would be too late, according to Billy, they would shout, "Ahhhhhhhhhh!!" and "Nooooooooo!!" as they went down into the sewer, and we would laugh and shout, "Take that, Sneaky Poo and Wee!" Finally we were getting our own back. Billy also informed us that Sneaky Poo would rot on the journey to the sewage plant. My son the trickster did not stop there. He decided he would trick me. He put a toy down his pants and confessed he had pooed. On closer inspection, it turned out to be a toy! We laughed and laughed about that trick. It had been quite a while since we laughed so easily together, and I was delighted to have his good humor back in our family.

As time went on, it became difficult to tell when Billy had soiled and when he was tricking me. One day I thought he was playacting, and I reacted theatrically, "Oh no, not another poo to clean up!" As I went to check I saw his expression fall and quickly realized that it was not a trick. Thinking fast, I cried with equal melodrama, "You double-tricked me! I thought it was a trick but it wasn't; you double-tricked me!" and we laughed about his trickiness. The double trick was born, and it grew into the "double-triple-quadruple-gazillion-gillion-trick." He seemed to savor any conversations about his mischief making and trickiness.

However, he was not the only trickster in the family. Jim and I decided that it was high time we got into the game. We took some mini Mars bars out of their wrappers and laid them on his bed. I ran to Billy with mock seriousness, exclaiming, "Billy, Billy, there is a poo on your bed! Did you do a poo on the bed?" He was confused and rushed there, perhaps to disconfirm my allegation. When we inspected the offending article closely, we discovered it was chocolate! We were all completely mystified as to how it got there. The next day I sneaked a mini Mars into Billy's lunch box, along with a note from the GUF reading, "Did you like my trick?" I could hardly wait for him to comment when I picked him up after school. So I asked him how his day had gone, who he sat next to at lunch, and so on. He told me he couldn't remember. By now I was dying for him to tell me about the trick, and my questions were getting me nowhere. I decided I needed to be a little more direct and asked if his sandwiches were nice. He said he had a mini Mars bar in his lunch box. At last! "A Mars bar?" I exclaimed. "I can't remember putting a Mars bar in your lunch box!" Billy produced the fairy note with a flourish: "It came with this! It says, 'Did you like my trick?'" Well, to say I was flabbergasted would be an understatement. "Your fairy!" I cried. "She must have left it!" Billy wasn't sure what the note meant. We talked more and I had a thought: "Do you think she meant to play the same trick on you that she played on me with the Mars bars in your bed?" "Oh yeah!" Billy cried aloud as if he had solved a riddle that had perplexed him all day. We laughed and laughed and wondered if she would leave any more chocolate candies around.

As we walked we looked for more fairy things. We found a feather from a fairy wing and a tennis ball. Billy saw that it had come from the tennis court and was sure his GUF had been playing tennis there that day. We found some bottle tops and a pink strap with stars on it, and Billy went on what he referred to as "the fairy rollercoaster," which involved running up and down hills at his top speed.

Our lives had become enchanted. Billy insisted he could feel the motion of fairy wings in the air, and he decided that his GUF would get Sneaky Poo and Wee with thunder and lightning, and that she would come down in hail. Billy said he only had one small accident that day and that the sun had dried it up. He decided that the Growing-Up Fairy had taken Sneaky Poo's and Wee's sun hats and sun cream and every other sun protection, including helmets with holes in them, so they would get sunburned. I was glad they'd got all dried up. Billy said the rain could also help by drowning them. He no longer had any trouble expressing his anger by way of his antagonism toward the problem that had beset him for too much of his young life. Doing so gave him a great deal of satisfaction, which I could now share in. Billy was able, at long last, to engage his frustration, rather than simply suffer it.

He had been aided in shifting into a narrative very different from one of personal failure compounded by humiliation. From his present location, "those sneaks" that had been beyond his reach and uncontested could now be confronted. He could now entertain the possibility of evening up the score, which had for so long been heavily tallied against him. Jim and I wanted to do our part to add to the momentum without usurping Billy's lead role. Knowing how much he loved reading books, Jim had the idea to make a comic. He searched for images on the Internet and created a storybook in which the GUF and Super Kids vanquish Sneaky Poo and Wee after some struggle and several clashes.

Soon after, the GUF called to say she was sending a gift via fairy post. We waited until he was bubbling over with curiosity, then left it on the doorstep for him to find when he returned from school. Billy opened the package in a flurry, tossing the string and wrapping aside, but not before making sure it was addressed to him and noticing (with a little help) that it was stamped "F-AIR-Y MAIL" with the F and Y having been added as neatly as possible by hand. He loved the comic instantly and read it over and over. Pretty soon he was playing Super Kids with his younger brother, Andy; they would shoot at Sneaky Poo and Wee, tricking them at will. When he went on a school trip, he put invisible Super Kid clothes over his uniform to help combat those sneaks, who would surely attack and try to ruin his trip with an embarrassing accident.

Jim and I were having far too much fun to stop there. Billy got more fairy posts. The next was a parcel. He was at home when I quietly snuck out the back door, bending low as I passed under the den window, creeping as quietly as I could around the side of our house. After tiptoeing back in, and again concealing myself, I called Billy and asked if he'd like to play outside. Despite throwing a ball close to the parcel, Billy did not discover it until finally, I felt compelled to draw his attention to it. The parcel contained a CD. On it was a magical fairy rhyme to help him beat those sneaks. Billy was very excited and wanted to listen to it straight away. We also played it at his bedtime, and he would fall asleep listening to the GUF rhyme. Here is what he heard:

> Sneaky Wee and Sneaky Poo
> Like kids best at 1 and 2
> But when we're 3, and then turn 4
> They know much less, and we know more
> They try their best to grow us down
> And turn our smile into a frown
> But fairies who are good and true

> Can help us outsmart Wee and Poo
> And when we flush them down the pot
> We'll be in charge, and they will not

Jim and I were rediscovering the value of play and were having as much fun as Billy and his brothers. Our family had passed from a most disenchanting time to a time of utter enchantment.

And it turned out it wasn't just Billy who was on the receiving end of surprises. While we were out in the garden, he came over to ask if I could see him when he was behind the bush. I told him I wasn't sure, so he went and stood behind the bush and yelled out, "Can you see me, Mum?" "No, I can't see you!" I assured him. I have to confess that I could see him a little. He then came back over to me and said that I mustn't watch him. I replied that I was far too busy looking after his baby brother, Paul, to be watching him. He asked again, "You won't watch me, will you, Mum?" "No," I said. "I can't possibly watch you. I am far too busy." Then, out of the corner of my eye, I saw him go behind the bush and put Sneaky Wee right where he wanted it to go. I was oblivious when he came out from behind the bush, and ever so busy with Paul. He repeated this process three or four times, and each time I was far too busy to watch him. It wasn't long before he clued me into the trick. Billy was very excited about using the garden, and in the future decided to report "I need the garden" instead of "I need the toilet." He was proud of himself and believed this would grow him up to age 10, and as an added bonus, Sneaky Wee was very likely to get pricked on the thorns of the bush. It was clear to both Jim and me that Billy was now able to confront his problem.

One day Billy came running into the kitchen and asked me to come and look at something. He took me to the shed where there was a small poo on the floor and confessed that he had done it. I told him, "Don't worry! We'll clean it up together." Billy paused and replied, "I'm sorry, Mum!" I said, "It's okay. Sneaky Poo should be sorry, not you!" Then we talked about how dastardly Sneaky Poo and Wee were, doing this to him. It struck me what a difference it made, not just bringing the GUF into our lives, but identifying Sneaky Poo and Wee as culpable. Distinguishing Billy from the problem freed him to find his own initiative and take responsibility. When Billy was the problem, he would hide his poo and refuse to admit to even the most obvious accidents. Here he was seeking me out and facing it directly.

Billy was also now able to voice his anguish. He came to me very upset one day, declaring, "Sneaky Poo and Wee made me 1 year old!" I commiserated with him: "That is really unfair!" I gave him a cuddle and asked what we should do to them. He said he had a plan and laughed like a mad scientist: "We should grow them down." I was interested to know what age he would grow them down to. "Younger than me," he replied. "Zero!" "They won't be able to do anything!" I exclaimed with glee. "Not even crawl!"

One day Billy was getting particularly annoyed about being asked to go to the toilet. He had a position he adopted on all fours when he soiled. We named it the "pooing position." He also had a "playing position," which was very similar. Billy was getting angry, because we thought he was in his pooing position when in fact he was playing. Jim asked him, "How will I know if it's a playing or pooing position?" Billy answered, "You don't say anything, and I will tell you. I know the difference because I can feel the signals. I am the only one who can feel the signals, so I am the only one who can do something about it." This blew us away. He was stridently taking charge, when not so long ago he would have done anything to avoid it. He now had confidence in his ability to tackle the problem, and it was his problem to confront, not anyone else's. This was liberating for all three of us.

Conclusion

The journey to being clean and dry proved to be one that would require long-term commitment and stamina. Though vastly improved, it would be 2 years before we saw the last of Sneaky Poo and Sneaky Wee. Prior to learning of the GUF, the short-term solutions we tried, much like fad diets, all ended the same way—with a predictable return to the status quo. But to our surprise, the wonderment that the GUF brought into our home not only improved the soiling problem, but also wove its way through many other areas of our lives as a family. One by one, the usual squabbles over eating vegetables, brushing teeth, and getting to bed on time lost their potency, as if rinsed of their rancor.

For so long, Billy being clean and dry was the hope I had come to desperately cling to. Now the journey itself became our guiding light. The end goal, though far from insignificant, seemed to dim among the bright colors of a newly discovered dream world. My washing pile reduced substantially, yet for me, the GUF's greatest achievement was not reducing Billy's accidents, but revitalizing all of our imaginations. The Growing-Up Fairy left an indelible mark on our family, and we are all the better for it. Although her whereabouts are unknown, she can always be found in our hearts. When we hold hands and close our eyes tightly, we can envision her circling the globe, keeping watch over the world's children.

CHAPTER TEN

"Somebody Needs to Pay!"
A Young Man's Coming of Age in a Culture of Male Domination and Entitlement

The following story about "Joel" is based on a range of conversations I (LM) had with boys who threatened or perpetrated violence. At the time, I was working in an intensive services department for a county-funded agency. Most of the boys referred to the program had histories of school suspensions, involvement with the juvenile courts, or frequent hospitalizations for aggressive ideation and behavior. While Joel is not a real person, he is emblematic of many boys, not only from the program but also in the broader culture. There is a foreboding fusion of inadequacy and conceit that can proliferate in boys. And while conceit alone can fuel fantasies of grandeur, the inadequacy that is its doppelgänger can turn combustible. Joel's story emerged, not through the examination of a single account, but rather from a body of work. It reflects a collective truth, woven together from many meetings with boys over a span of 15 months.

In his essay "How to Tell a True War Story," author Tim O'Brien appreciates the reader's investment in the events of a story being authentic. He acknowledges, "You'd feel cheated if it never happened. Without the grounding reality, it's just a trite bit of puffery, pure Hollywood" (1990, p. 79). But he challenges the reader to move beyond a literal interpretation of truth: "A thing may happen and be a total lie; another thing may not happen and be truer than the truth" (p. 80). It is my hope that in offering this composite, I will more aptly represent the cultural forces that can seize upon boys' imaginations and result in one of the most tragic outcomes in contemporary times. It was my interactions with real boys that brought these conditions more clearly into view and inspired my experimentation with the practices illustrated here. Although the story you are about to read is not a war story, it is about a young man drawn to war and the promise of glory that awaits him, not on foreign shores, but right here at home among members of his own community.

Meeting Joel

When I first encountered 11-year-old Joel, he was in a world of trouble. Given recent events, his mother, June, doubted that any school would risk opening its doors to him. She held her breath as the telephone rang and could hardly believe her ears as the principal on the other end informed her that Joel had, in fact, been admitted. In stark contrast to June's immense relief, Joel felt cheated. Although he "never liked the old school," he "finally got used to it." Perhaps not unreasonably, he anticipated that "being new and not knowing anyone would be way harder." To make matters worse, he soon learned that his new school was 30 miles away. He dreaded the long bus ride. Even with his smartphone in hand, he would surely be "bored to death."

But there was no going back. District expulsions were rarely overturned, and in Joel's case, there was no denying his wrongdoing. At the expulsion hearing, the board reviewed screen shots of his older cousin's social media page, where Joel had posted threats to "bomb the school" and "blow people's heads off" with his cousin's hunting rifle. Equally troubling incidents had preceded these. Two weeks earlier, Joel had simulated a "sniper attack" during art class. Crouching in the corner of the room, he fashioned his hand into a makeshift gun, taking aim at unsuspecting students and "shooting" invisible bullets from his fingertip. And a month prior, he had arrived at school wearing a trench coat, which, by his own account, was intended to "scare people." When administrators confronted him, he refused to remove it, calling their request "a violation of my rights."

After reading the full account of his expulsion, Joel's new principal declared his admission conditional upon the family's willingness to participate in a field-based therapy program. June was only too happy to comply. She welcomed "the extra support," fearing that without it, a residential placement would not be far off.

As I approached their front steps for the first time, June was there to greet me. She smiled and led me inside to their warmly appointed living room. Photographs of family, past and present, lined the walls, and hand-sewn doilies decorated antique tabletops. "Help yourself," she said, pointing to a tin of cookies as I took a seat. Before I could reach for one, I was startled. What was that noise? First there was the sound of gunfire, then an explosion. Radio static, then more gunfire. A cry for help. An automatic weapon unloading. I looked up, searching for the source. Seeming embarrassed, June escorted me to a room a few feet away. Joel was propped up on his knees facing a big screen, his back turned to us. He was a thinly framed boy, surprisingly meek in appearance.

Beyond the edge of Joel's silhouette, I spied a futuristic landscape littered with smoldering military hardware. Joel's arms gave an occasional jerk as he guided his avatar through the smoking wreckage. "Joel, will you come and join us?" June pleaded.

"Later," he mumbled, glancing up at me indifferently.

"I try to limit his time, but you know how kids are . . . " her voice trailed off. I nodded, hoping to convey sympathy.

"Maybe I'll just introduce myself for now," I said tentatively.

"Sure," she agreed, as we stood in the doorway.

"Hi," he responded, his eyes fixed on the game. "Want to watch me play?"

"Okay, but do you think you could spare a few minutes for me?"

"When I'm finished," he shot back.

"Great," I said, deciding it best to take him at his word. I wondered how his imagination was being enlisted and deployed in this virtual space. Perhaps the game would offer a portal into Joel's world. But as I stared at the television, my stomach dropped. More machine than man, Joel's avatar crossed a scorched battlefield in quaking strides. "What's the story line?" I asked. He eagerly explained an elaborate plot in which a lone mercenary embarks on a dangerous mission to save humanity from imminent destruction at the hands of an alien combatant.

"Here," he said. "Take a look." Joel slid a book across the carpet. It stopped at my feet.

"Nice shot," I said, picking up the guidebook and flipping through it. The primary section was an encyclopedia of arms. Each weapon was shown in remarkable detail and accompanied by instructions meant to pique the player's interest in the technology of warfare. Eventually, Joel granted me a few minutes of his time but was soon drawn back to the action unfolding on screen.

Returning to the living room, I attempted to assure June that I was there to offer whatever support I could and not to execute a forensic assessment. I asked her to tell me about Joel according to his wonderfulnesses, ahead of any concerns, though I also made clear that we would get to the problem soon enough. June spoke about "the loving things Joel says" and "the help he offers around the house." Because of chronic health issues including arthritis and asthma, June moved with difficulty and tired quickly. "I can usually count on Joel to stop what he's doing and help me when I need him. I don't know what I would do without him. . . . "

"Like when I bring in the groceries," Joel shouted proudly from the other room. "That's true, but sometimes you disappear as soon as you find the Cheetos," June smiled, as if recalling a joke between the two of them.

"Cheetos? Did someone say Hot Cheetos?" Joel came to attention, hitting the pause button on his video game. He assumed the position of a sprinter ready to bolt at the sound of a starting gun (or crinkling cellophane bag). It was my first opportunity to see Joel acting apart from his avatar—in a playful spirit. His performance, which I guessed was part of a well-known routine, clearly endeared him to June.

"See that? That's what people don't realize. Joel is a good boy. He's sweet and funny. He makes me laugh. I see that side of him."

Then her mood darkened, as if the ghost of an evaluation past had come back to haunt her. "The last social worker thought he'd be better off in a facility and that he was too much for me to handle. But she didn't see the good parts or how hard he tries. I do. I'm his mother. The kids at school have never accepted him. Still, that's no reason to want to go out and shoot people. That, I will never understand."

As we were wrapping up, I made sure to get Joel's consent for my return. On the way out, I noticed a DVD case sticking out of an unzipped, camouflage backpack near the front door. I recognized the title, *Diary of a Wimpy Kid* (Kinney & Freudenthal, 2010), though I had not seen the film or read the books. "Hey Joel," I called, making one last effort to engage him.

"Yeah?" He responded.

"This DVD in the backpack, is it yours?" I asked.

"It's from the library."

"Did you watch it?"

"He was supposed to read the book—" June interjected.

"It's really funny. He does everything wrong," Joel laughed.

"Would you recommend it to me?"

"Yeah, maybe."

As I drove away, I wondered what might be drawing Joel toward violence, and what, if anything, might call him down a different road. That night, as I downloaded *Diary of a Wimpy Kid*, I crossed my fingers and hoped the film might offer a less brutal entry point for connection.

A Story of American Boyhood: Specialness as a Birthright

In the film and book series *Diary of a Wimpy Kid*, Greg Heffley is a middle-class, male protagonist starting his first year of middle school. Perhaps like many American boys, Greg dreams of making it big someday. "I always figured they'd make a movie about my life," he muses. In his daydreams, Greg indulges images of celebrity as ostentatious as those of any A-lister. His face is everywhere—on billboards, buildings, and magazine covers—followed by the tagline, "Greg Heffley Rules!" The city itself seems to pulsate to the beat of his name. Paparazzi and fans flock to him, vying for his attention. "Were you always this rich and handsome?" a reporter asks. Greg scoffs. Don't they know? He has "better things to do than answer people's stupid questions all day."

Even in his everyday life, Greg looks down his nose at others. He perceives incompetence in his parents, especially when they deny him what he wants. And he frequently criticizes his best friend, Rowley, for not being cool enough. While looking through his older brother's yearbook, Greg points to the mock elections and tells Rowley, "See this? This is where a person like me needs to be: Class Favorites. They're the best in their class. These people aren't nobodies. They're famous." For Greg, stardom appears to be more providence than pipe dream.

According to the sociologist Michael Kimmel (2013), privilege teaches white males that anything they want can and should be theirs. It is a fantasy perpetuated by a particular rendering of American history, and it creates "an ethos of insularity and entitlement" (Schiele & Stewart, 2001), deeply ingrained in boys' experience long before peach fuzz turns to stubble. Such privilege encourages not only a preoccupation with personal gain, but also a consequent disregard for the interests of others (Schiele & Stewart, 2001). In Greg's case, it fosters a desire to rise to the top and take his place among the rich and famous. It also produces a powerfully felt "truth" that it is his "God-given right" (Kimmel, 2013, p. 18) to expect such a reward. My mind flashed on Joel. Did he share Greg's ambition? After all, both boys were making their way in a culture where male specialness starts with make-believe but ends with a mandate.

The male specialness discourse can pierce a boy's psyche with minimal pain at first and, if nothing else, yield new and intoxicating material for fantasy. But over time, it is less a pinprick and more a poison-tipped arrow, releasing a mind-altering toxin that orients him to a newly framed reality. The world no longer welcomes him as he is. He must stand out. Ironically, the pursuit of greatness involves conforming to a singular vision of manhood. This vision is continuously reworked as the main plotline in popular American media. A white male born to humble beginnings is overlooked or demeaned only to discover a secret lineage or otherworldly power that sets him apart from others. With this awareness comes grave responsibility as he prepares for a mission of epic proportion. Eventually, he proves all those who doubted him wrong. As he emerges victorious, he is met by a grateful nation and accepts his prize, the requisite heart of a beautiful young ingénue.

Iconic heroes like Superman and Spiderman overcome one obstacle after another with courage, strength, and will. So do the less likely, though no less valorous, Ender Wiggins and Harry Potter. Then there is Emmet from *The Lego Movie*. Emmet could not be more interchangeable until he is singled out as "the Special"—the one who will save the [Lego] universe from a permanent freeze. He performs so valiantly that even duly acclaimed heroes are left awestruck. A humbled Batman admits to his girlfriend, "He's [Emmet's] the hero you deserve." Even when male specialness is realized outside of violence (e.g., Flint Lockwood's scientific genius in *Cloudy With a Chance of Meatballs*), the stakes are just as high. A city teeters on the brink, and a reluctant champion steps forward.

As similar stories came to mind, I wondered what role male entitlement and the call to greatness might have played in Joel's turn to violence. What options did a boy have when the world dismissed him as unremarkable? When he possessed no special talent? No secret lineage? When there was no epic quest laid out before him? Was there an example in our culture of a boy's safe and dignified passage into ordinary life? I held my breath, hoping that Greg Heffley might show us the way.

"It's Payback Time": When Dreams of Greatness Turn to Fantasies of Revenge

And show us the way he did. Alarmingly, it was the road to revenge. On his first day of sixth grade, Greg is devastated to discover that others appear oblivious to his specialness, treating him as common or worse. In a matter of hours, he is terrorized by his brother, rejected by classmates, and taunted by older peers. Greg is more than defeated. His sense of order has been violated. Things are not as they should be. After being ridiculed by an older boy named Quentin, Greg writes in his journal, "Right now, I have to take abuse from these morons. But in 20 years, Quentin will be working for me." He envisions a grungy adult version of Quentin, wearing a faded uniform and standing on the manicured lawn of a vast estate. Quentin begs Greg not to fire him: "I really need my measly pathetic job scooping your dog's poop." Greg, now a muscular paragon, appears impassive. Lying on a chaise lounge with a stack of dollar bills and a butler at his disposal, he is the epitome of American male success. Just then, a scantily clad blond-haired woman dressed as a French maid brings him an ice cream sundae. He stares at it indignantly before reprimanding her: "Vanilla on the bottom, chocolate on the top. I can't eat this."

When I returned to Joel's house for a second meeting, I brought a picture of this scene, along with several others from the movie, which I had printed from the Internet. I hoped, if nothing else, they might provide incentive for Joel to wrench himself from the video screen. The following conversation unfolded in his living room.

> **LM**: Do you remember the scene where Greg imagines he's rich and famous? (Pulling out the picture of Greg's imagined future.)
>
> **Joel**: (Coming closer and examining it) Yeah, but he looks kind of gay.
>
> **LM**: Oh, that's right. Boys and men are at risk of being seen as not man enough, aren't they? Or at risk of being seen as the "wrong" kind of boy . . . (I make an attempt to gently point to the discourse of heteronormative, hegemonic masculinity. This is no small task and not one to be undertaken at any single boy's expense. I try to think of Joel's attitude not simply as a reflection of individual prejudice but rather as the reproduction of a broader social and institutional malady. Joel shrugs.)
>
> **LM**: What about Greg's dream of becoming famous? Remember

this scene? (I pull out a second image, this one of the "Greg Rules!" billboard.)

Joel: (He looks on approvingly) Yeah, but nobody gets *that* famous.

LM: That's true. His chances might be slim, but that doesn't stop him from dreaming about it or from feeling like it just has to happen. (Making a first attempt to render visible an effect of privilege.)

Joel: I'm going to join the Marines when I'm older. Those guys are badass. (Talking about Greg's aspirations seems to have sparked Joel's interest in describing his own.)

LM: How long have you wanted to join the Marines?

Joel: I don't know.

June: (Coming out from the kitchen) I think it was after you heard about Teddy. (To Laurie) Joel has a cousin—

Joel: You can join when you're 18.

June: That's why I've told you, you can't keep getting in trouble . . . all those suspensions and now an expulsion. (Shaking her head.)

Joel: That doesn't matter. I'm going to be a Marine. (Joel proudly displays a set of replica dog tags from underneath his shirt.)

June: You also have a mental health history that could disqualify you if you don't turn things around.

Joel: You can get rejected and still get in. Captain America did it. People do it. Real people, I mean. (Looking sheepish.)

LM: What happened with Captain America?

Joel: He was weak, but he kept on trying, and this guy finally lets him in. And then he's part of an experiment that makes him a super soldier.

LM: And he becomes a war hero? A superhero?

Joel: Yeah.

LM: Joel, is this the kind of dream that would be like a dream come true for you?

Joel: If you love your country, and you have the guts. It's what you do. (Joel seems to shift into a state of reverie.)

LM: So you plan to enlist?

Joel: It's not a plan. It's my destiny. (Stated in a dramatic tone.)

LM: Wow. What's it like having a destiny, and knowing that it's yours, but not being able to realize it, at least not for a while? (Highlighting what may be a real dilemma for boys who might be impatiently awaiting their casting as leading men.)

Joel: I don't know.

LM: The movie got me thinking about this, and it seems kind of tough to me. I started wondering . . . (Joel appears restless.) Can you hang in there for a few more minutes, or have you had enough for today?

Joel: No, it's okay. (He settles back in.)

LM: I'm just wondering, what does a boy do if, according to his destiny, he's so special that he shouldn't have to put up with anything he doesn't like? And what if people, like the kids at school, keep treating him like he's average or just part of the crowd? (Returning to the difficulty that Greg faces in the film and still wondering whether Joel might relate.)

Joel: You just have to show them who you are.

LM: Show the kids—

Joel: (Interrupting) Show everybody. Captain America fights this guy twice his size, just because. He's like . . . (Joel comes to his feet and acts out the part of a fighter throwing slow-motion punches.)

LM: Let me see if I've got it. Destiny or specialness says to boys, "Hey, there's no way you're average or ordinary!" (Joel nods.) "You've got to show the world!"

Joel: You've got to show them you're somebody they shouldn't mess with. (Boys can feel pressure, or perhaps a calling to prove they are somebody. What this will mean for Joel, or how it might have contributed to his expulsion from school, is still unknown.)

Perhaps like Joel, Greg decides there is no time to waste in proving himself a somebody. On the eve of his second day at school, Greg declares, "I can't be the guy who eats his lunch off his lap in the cafeteria. I should be at the top of the food chain by now. Something's got to change fast!" Following the advice of his father, he pursues sports, a traditional proving ground for males, as a means of improving his rank in the pecking order. But at his first wrestling practice, Greg suffers two defeats. He is easily pinned by the nerdiest boy at school and then, of all things, by a long-standing female adversary.

Joel and I continued reviewing images from the film, mostly of Greg's attempts to fit the masculine norm. According to Debby Phillips (2005), American boys are typically offered only one of two subject positions: popular kid or outcast, the former being contingent on a boy's flawless execution of a masculine ideal (i.e., physically strong, heterosexual, powerful, in control). According to such stringently defined criteria, middle and high school boys are perpetually at risk of exclusion based on inadequate gender performance—or not "sizing up" (Earp et al., 2013; Kalish & Kimmel, 2010; Kimmel, 2013; Phillips, 2005). Perhaps having internalized this norm, instead of empathizing with Greg, Joel belittled him. But when we arrived at a picture of Greg's teenage brother, Rodrick, the conversation took a turn.

> **Joel**: (Looking at the picture) He's so mean.
>
> **LM**: His brother bullies him, doesn't he?
>
> **Joel**: Yeah, he's bigger, so it's not fair. He locks him in his room so he can't pee, except later Greg pees all over him (smiling). But he gets in trouble for it.
>
> **LM**: Gosh, what is it that can turn a kid mean? (Attempting to name a problem.)
>
> **Joel**: Guys punk each other all the time.
>
> **LM**: You've seen or experienced it too? (By connecting with what Greg has suffered, there may be room to inquire about Joel's experiences of being bullied.)

Joel: Yeah, but Greg asks for it.

LM: What do you mean?

Joel: His best friend is a loser.

LM: You mean Rowley? (Pulling out a picture of Rowley and handing it to Joel.)

Joel: Yeah, that's not good.

LM: How come?

Joel: I don't know. (I sense that Joel may have an answer, but with the discourse of hegemonic masculinity not sufficiently externalized, fear of judgment might prevent him from sharing.)

LM: Are there rules about not just how a boy should look and act but who he can hang out with? (Alluding to the discourse.)

Joel: Kind of.

LM: Or a "code" [Pollack, 1998] of some kind, like boys are supposed to be tough, athletic—

Joel: You don't have to play sports. (Said defensively.)

LM: But be tough? (Joel nods solemnly.) And the Code says you should have friends who are, I don't know. . . .

Joel: Big but not fat. The fat kid always gets it. (Snickering.)

LM: And what's it like for boys to deal with the Code . . . a Code that says you've got to look big but not fat, and have friends who are the right kind of guys? (Attempting to map the problem's effects.)

Joel: I don't know. (Joel appears absorbed in thought. Perhaps he is considering the restrictions imposed by the Code, even if he is not speaking to them just yet.)

LM: And does the Code get boys picking on other boys for not being big or tough enough?

Joel: (Puffing himself up in a quasi-aggressive posture) You just can't take it. I've never started a fight, but I've finished every one. (Said pretentiously. Joel suddenly realigns with the Code.)

LM: Is that what the Code requires of boys, or requires of you?

Joel: A man's gotta do what a man's gotta do! (Said with bravado.

This is a popular quote by John Wayne, an American actor and the embodiment of rugged individualism.)

LM: I see. And if the Code gets him into trouble? If it costs him? (I am aware that Joel's threats of violence and other aggressive acts have been met with consequences, especially in his school life.)

Joel: It doesn't matter.

LM: Is the Code showing him the way? Here's the way to greatness . . . to respect and self-respect. Or is it promising greatness but delivering something different?

Joel: No.

LM: I see. So the Code says, "Follow me. Never mind the price." (Thinking aloud.)

Joel: There's no price. Just respect. (Joel pulls himself up in his chair, indicating he is pleased with what he has just come up with. Given that he is speaking "in Code," I decide to let things rest for the time being.)

Despite Rowley being the wrong kind of friend, Greg's life only gets worse after their association comes to an end. When he tries out for the school play, the drama teacher decides his voice is too high for any of the male leads in *The Wizard of Oz*. Relegated to the role of an apple tree, Greg waddles awkwardly onstage only to endure further humiliation when the girl who plays Dorothy exposes him for missing his cue. Although the audience finds it funny, it is no laughing matter to Greg. Mortification turns to rage, as he writes in his journal that night, "This entire year has been terrible, and nobody even cares. My family, my best friend. Well, I'm sick of it! *Somebody needs to pay!*"

Payback in the Form of Violence

Who would pay and in what currency were questions that weighed on my mind. In American culture, there are far too many examples of young men who have felt victimized and sought reprisal for what they were due and what was seen to be overdue in the way of respect and restitution. Watching the film that first night, I was haunted by images of Joel in his trench coat. What enticements lured him away from the respite he might otherwise find in life? And what drew him toward a gruesome plotline so often replicated that the phrase "pull a Columbine" had made its way into the American lexicon (Kimmel, 2013)? If the Code won out in the end, it would be by means of fostering:

- A sense of entitlement (i.e., "The world owes me")
- The necessity of popularity, specialness, or greatness (e.g., "I have to be somebody, or I am a nobody.")
- A singular account of male success (e.g., domination, power, control, aggression; Earp et al., 2013)

In American culture, these forces have paved the way to a particular brand of "heroism" that promises to be worth killing and dying for. On an April morning in 1999, Eric Harris and Dylan Klebold—two former nobodies—entered their high school and opened fire, murdering 13 people and wounding more than 20 before turning their guns on themselves. The night prior to the rampage, Harris and Klebold video recorded a statement that located their act of retaliatory violence within the tradition of American vigilante justice: "We've always wanted to do this. This is payback. We've dreamed of doing this for years. This is for all the shit you put us through. This is what you deserve" (as cited in Kimmel, 2013, p. 69).

For years, Harris and Klebold were "targeted, bullied, beaten up, gay baited, and worse" (Kimmel, 2013, p. 81) at a school where traditional codes of masculinity (e.g., toughness, athleticism, size, and strength) were enforced and revered by the community at large. Kimmel identifies Columbine, along with other school shooting sites such as Virgina Tech, as "jockocracies"—places where athletes are valorized to the extent that any expression of difference in boys (e.g., shyness, bookishness, creativity, smallness) is punished by students and adults alike (Kimmel, 2013, pp. 91, 95; Kalish & Kimmel, 2010, p. 455). Although the vast majority of school-aged males who are bullied do not retaliate with murderous intent, Kimmel argues that "aggrieved entitlement" is an experience common to many:

> So many boys feel aggrieved, and many also feel that sense of aggrieved entitlement that might legitimate revenge—whether in fantasies of blowing up the galaxy or in being superheroes and taking vengeance against all who have wronged them, or in actually becoming bullies themselves and enacting on others what they, themselves, have endured. (2013, p. 82)

He describes the phenomenon as "a fusion of that humiliating loss of manhood and the moral obligation and entitlement to get it back" (Kalish & Kimmel, 2010, p. 454). Aggrieved entitlement begins with a male's experience of being wronged by a system that is "cruel or demeaning" (p. 454). With the resulting injury, the cult of American manhood encourages the use of violence as a means of reasserting himself. A boy can be convinced it is his right to get even and to make others suffer as he has (Earp et al., 2013; Kalish & Kimmel, 2010; Kimmel 2013). "Going out in a blaze of glory" (Kimmel, 2013, p. 73) may seem to cost him everything, but there is something gained. Though he is certain to be decried in the 24-hour news cycle, his masculinity, which had been sorely compromised, is newly restored. And he is guaranteed celebrity, however grisly and brief.

Throughout the film, Greg and Rowley are repeatedly taunted, not just by older males, but also by those in their cohort. When they are caught wearing similar outfits, the whole class sings a rendition of "Greg and Rowley sitting in a tree, K-I-S-S-I-N-G." As their only defense, Greg teaches Rowley how to look more macho while walking and carrying his backpack. As they practice together, he tells Rowley, "One strap is cool. You know what has one strap? Machine guns." Like so many boys, Greg and Rowley put on a front to protect themselves from further ridicule. Jackson Katz observes, "It doesn't matter how unnatural, complicated, or ridiculous the role is, boys are expected to learn their lines and master the 'tough guise,' or else risk being shamed as less than a man" (Earp et al., 2013). Boys are one misstep away from being called out as "pussies, punks, fags, and an endless list of other sexist and homophobic putdowns" (Earp et al.,

2013). Any deviation can be costly to their reputations and sense of safety.

Despite having learned to walk "tough," Greg and Rowley face further derision from three boys on Halloween night. Initially they take cover in Greg's grandmother's garage, but moments later, reemerge with smoke rising and electric yard tools blazing. In the dark evening hour, Rowley's leaf blower is mistaken for a chainsaw. Although they let their teenage assailants escape physically unharmed, Greg puts a large gash in their truck's side panel when he loses control of a weed whacker. It is an act of violence that affirms his masculinity, at least momentarily.

"Gandhi, but Without All the Fanfare": Putting Joel's Imagination to New Use

Perhaps it is no surprise that by age 11, Joel had already pledged his allegiance to a code of morality that regards violence as restorative (Kalish & Kimmel, 2010; Kimmel, 2013). He was, after all, subject to a discourse that promotes violence as a legitimate means of "settling scores and expressing manhood" (Earp et al., 2013). At his new school, however, Joel was greeted by a subculture with an unexpected code of ethics.

In our dialogues that followed, I focused on tracking his responses closely with an ear for expressions of alternative preferences, rather than staking out moral claims ahead of him. When therapists attempt to instill values, despite any hoped-for results, they may regrettably create "an adversarial context that either produces passive accommodation or perhaps protest, but with little ethical realization and behavior change" (Jenkins, 2009). It would also be hypocritical, not to mention coercive, to govern boys according to a higher sense of right and wrong, while at the same time attempting to critique the practice of exerting power over others (Jenkins, 2009). Besides, it can be further emasculating and potentially dangerous to exert control over boys in therapy when they are already on the verge of responding violently to the effects of domination. I had a responsibil-

"Somebody Needs to Pay!" 235

ity to Joel's new community, and anyone who might cross his path, to negotiate power carefully.

During my next visit, I found Joel playing a video game on his X-Box in the living room. June and I sat together on the couch.

> June: (Sounding heartened) Everything's better over there.
>
> LM: Is your mom, right, Joel? Are things better at your new school?
>
> Joel: Yeah, kind of.
>
> LM: In what way?
>
> Joel: (Talking over his shoulder) The kids are nicer.
>
> June: They aren't picking on each other. Those boys at his old school could be so cruel. His teachers let a lot slide. It used to make my blood boil, but not at the new school.
>
> LM: Is that right, Joel? The teachers don't put up with the Code?
>
> Joel: Yeah (Appearing distracted but perhaps still listening).
>
> LM: What's it like?
>
> Joel: It's boring. If anyone freaks out, the teachers stop it right away. Ahh! Darn it! (Responding to what is happening on screen.)
>
> LM: I'll give you some time to finish your game. Let me know if you're up for a little conversation.
>
> Joel: (Sighing, then pausing his game and turning to face us) Go ahead.
>
> LM: Great, thanks for taking the time to talk, Joel. So let me get this straight. Is it the staff rather than the Code running the school?
>
> Joel: Yeah, nothing ever happens.
>
> LM: How is it being at a school where nothing ever happens?
>
> Joel: It's good.
>
> LM: Yeah? What's good about it?
>
> Joel: An eye for an eye and the world would go blind. (Joel seems to have a penchant for well-known adages. Still, I am caught off guard.)

LM: What?

Joel: It's what Gandhi said.

LM: (Incredulously) Gandhi! Where in the world did he come from? (Wanting to understand why Joel may have suddenly changed his tune.)

Joel: India?

LM: (Smiling and impressed) Oh right! But I was actually wondering how in the world Gandhi entered our conversation or came to your mind.

Joel: I don't know, but it's true.

LM: How so?

Joel: If everybody in the world got revenge, there would be no one left and nothing good. Gandhi believed in love and peace. (Although Joel's air is somewhat performative, I decide there is no harm in taking him seriously. Besides, there would have to be some alternative identity position for Joel to step into in order to consider leaving the current one behind.)

LM: And why bring up love and peace? Are these ideas or values that speak to you in some way? (Attempting to move the conversation closer to home.)

Joel: I don't want to end up locked away somewhere.

LM: How come, Joel? I've known the Code to convince boys, and men for that matter, that it's better to have gotten the last word, the last punch, or the last laugh, than to have backed down, even if it means getting locked away or ending their own lives.

Joel: That's stupid.

LM: (Taken aback) When you think about your own life, is standing for peace a better fit?

Joel: Gandhi stood for peace and millions of people followed him. (Joel's answer might still be grounded in grandeur.)

LM: I see. But with that many people, that many admirers, with a nation behind him, is it easier for a man to stand for peace under those conditions? (This is not meant to diminish Gand-

"Somebody Needs to Pay!" 237

> hi's moral resolve or achievement. Rather, it is intended as an opportunity for Joel to reflect on the stamina of his own commitment.)
>
> Joel: It's not hard. (Joel might have interpreted the question as a challenge to his masculinity and responded accordingly. Nonetheless, I am curious to find out if his response reveals something more.)
>
> LM: It's not?
>
> Joel: You don't need all that . . . all that. . . . (He searches for a word.)
>
> June: Worship? Fanfare?
>
> Joel: (Excitedly) Yeah, I'm going to be like Gandhi but without all the fanfare!
>
> LM: What appeals to you about standing for peace, even if it comes without all the fanfare?
>
> Joel: It still has rewards and bonuses. You think you're winning when you get revenge, but you're not. (Joel turns his attention back to the video game.)

After bargaining for more time I asked him about the tactics of Revenge, as well as the rewards and bonuses that come with standing for peace. Joel explained, "You think you'll feel good when you get revenge, but it's not as good as the feeling of living at home." He attributed this "good feeling" to the love he shared with his mother. When I inquired about whether peace was a value that suited Joel, or one he imagined he might grow more accustomed to over time, he hesitated initially but eventually replied, "I'll know after I've tried being like Gandhi." Although I was eager to find out more about his new initiative (e.g., what might have prepared him for it, how he came up with it, who else knew about it, what it had been like so far), Joel answered most of my questions with a version of the same sentiment: "I just like my new school, so I'm doing what I have to."

It seemed, for now at least, we might have found a new direction. I would make every effort to continue to earn my way to an understanding of Joel as a boy on a path to peace. The next morning, I was able to meet with Joel again—this time at his new school with a behavioral aide, Mr. Caruso (Mr. C), who had been assigned to stick with Joel at all times. I started by interviewing Mr. C about any wonderfulnesses he had noticed in Joel. He talked about Joel's politeness and sense of humor, which he had experienced firsthand. When I asked Mr. C what he appreciated about being on the receiving end of such practices, he described his pleasure at being able to relate to Joel "as a friend and not a cop." I wondered whether soliciting these reflections would lend further support for Joel's interest in Gandhi. After becoming reacquainted with him through Mr. C's eyes, I read aloud the notes from our last meeting while Joel listened approvingly, perhaps savoring his own words of wisdom. Mr. C was ardent in his reaction.

> Mr. C: I like everything I heard.
>
> LM: What do you like about it?
>
> Mr. C: It makes my job easier. (Smiling.) And it makes things easier for everyone here . . . the staff, the students.
>
> LM: Have you ever heard of a boy drawing inspiration from Gandhi and standing for peace, though it goes unrecognized and without any fanfare? (Recruiting Mr. C as a witness to the developing counterstory.)
>
> Mr. C: I don't know, but it makes me think of something I saw him do yesterday.
>
> LM: What was that?
>
> Mr. C: Well, there was a student who got knocked down in PE [physical education class].
>
> Joel: Oh yeah, that kid got nailed in the head—
>
> Mr. C: Joel went over and helped him up.
>
> LM: And what did you make of it?
>
> Mr. C: I thought it was a nice thing to do. The boy was across the yard, but Joel walked all the way over.
>
> LM: Joel, can I ask, why did you walk all the way over?

Joel: I knew he was probably embarrassed, because it happened in front of everybody. (Joel seems to have separated from the Code in his expression of empathy.)

As I continued interviewing Joel about his moral action, as well as the thinking behind it, he expressed a budding interest in helping others. He also resonated with Mr. C's description of it as "an act of compassion." When I asked both Joel and Mr. C about how such an act might impact the school community, they agreed that it could help other students feel safe. Joel also relished the idea that he might have "made a friend." To document the developing counterstory, I wrote Joel a letter summarizing these moral developments and posing the following questions:

1. When denied a life of glory, and having experienced bullying, many boys can find themselves captured by ideas of war and revenge (i.e., making others pay). How is it, Joel, that you've managed to develop a wish to help others, despite what you've been through? Is it a fleeting wish, or is it one you hope to hang onto?
2. If helping others is not the sort of deed that wins a war, saves a nation, or earns the admiration of millions (or even achieves much recognition), why bother? Why care about things like "peace," "compassion," and "friendship"? After all, these are not the things that boys are taught to dream of.
3. In a world where boys learn that greatness is what matters most, and not just any kind of greatness, but greatness that takes place on the battlefield, in a faraway galaxy, in the Wild West, and so on, what might it take to be satisfied with a more humble life? Imagination? A modest heart? Something else?

At my next meeting with Joel and June we read the letter together. In response to my first two questions, Joel described bullying as causing "pain in my mind" but added with seeming conviction, "I want to take the pain and twist it around and turn it into something positive." He also alluded to "keeping goodness locked away," as if he was afraid of losing it. Tracing the history of how Joel managed to keep it safe all these years, we discovered that it was his affection for a former friend, Bobby, and his love for his mother that provided the inspiration. Bobby was a boy he met in kindergarten, and though their friendship ended 6 months later when Bobby and his family moved away, Joel never forgot him. Even still, when I asked Joel how friendship measured up against other things boys are taught to value, such as glory and greatness, he admitted, "That stuff still comes first. A friend is just a nice bonus." I meditated on Joel's response, considering the cultural context in which boys are given little space to entertain a broader range of values.

A few days later, I received a report from Joel's teacher, Ms. Clark, complaining of his "preoccupation with war games." During break times, he reenacted intergalactic warfare and largely ignored his classmates' objections to being unwillingly cast as enemy combatants and wounded comrades. In one instance, his fantasy play provoked a conflict that turned physical, though it was stopped by Mr. C's swift action and followed by Joel's unsolicited apology to those involved. And in math class, Joel was worse than "spaced out." He was in outer space when he suddenly threw himself on a plasma grenade at Ms. Clark's feet, "saving her life" at a necessary cost to his own. Although this act of mock heroism was outwardly prosocial, Ms. Clark did not appreciate the disruption, to say the least, or her casting as a "helpless female."

For Joel it seemed a stretch once again to connect with an identity other than hero or menace. For this reason, I decided we needed something that was both original and deeply appealing. Joel deserved more time to consider his nascent interest in modesty, not because it is morally nobler in any objective sense, but because he had indicated it might be of interest to him. Given the prominence of the Code and its relentless recruitment of a "brotherhood of men," young and old, I figured he might appreciate a brother, not in arms, but in peace.

Captain Ordinary: The Untold Story of Steve Rogers

"Do you want to see something that I can guarantee you've never seen before?" I said in a hushed, conspiratorial tone. Joel gave me a strange look, perhaps doubting what I had just told him about Steve Rogers, a.k.a. Captain America. After waking up from a 70-year slumber, and prior to joining the Avengers, Steve lived for a short time as a nobody in New York City. That part, everyone knew. But because this period of his life received little attention, no one really knew all that he went through—that is, until now.

> **Joel:** (With curiosity) How do *you* know what happened?
>
> **LM:** I have a friend who's a comic book collector, and he gets his hands on some pretty interesting stuff.
>
> **Joel:** What kinds of stuff?
>
> **LM:** Documents . . . objects . . . (Deliberately coy.)
>
> **Joel:** What are some examples, I mean?
>
> **LM:** Oh, there are lots of examples. (Continuing to be vague to cultivate suspense.)
>
> **Joel:** Like what? (Growing impatient.)
>
> **LM:** Well, he doesn't share much with me, but when I told him that I know a boy who shares his interest in Captain America, he let this one slip.
>
> **Joel:** What is it?
>
> **LM:** I don't have the original. He wouldn't let that out of his sight, of course. It's too precious. (Rambling.) He would never even think of letting me touch it. But, he did give me a copy—
>
> **Joel:** (Bursting with curiosity) What are you talking about?!
>
> **LM:** Do you really want to know?
>
> **Joel:** (With enthusiasm) Yes!
>
> **LM:** Well . . . (Building up to the moment.)
>
> **Joel:** (Insistent) Just tell me!

LM: Can I trust you to keep a secret?

Joel: (Bordering annoyance) Yes!

LM: All right. It's a page from a diary that Captain America wrote while he was living in New York. He wrote it a few days after waking up, but before Fury started training him for his next mission. My understanding is only a handful of collectors know about his diary entries. But my friend got his hands on a copy.

Joel: (Sounding doubtful) Where does your friend live?

LM: I can't tell you that.

Joel: Where is it? (I pulled out a scroll wrapped in red, white, and blue ribbon and handed it over to Joel. Unsure of what I was up to, and in spite of his skepticism, Joel carefully accepted it, as if it was something treasurable. He gently unrolled the yellowed paper and began reading.)

Entry #3

Nothing in this world makes sense. People walk past me as if I don't exist, as if they don't know who I am, or don't care. I want to scream, "I'm Captain America! I saved the world!" I've never felt so invisible.

At least before the war, I had Bucky. He was a true friend. I miss him more than words can express. And Peggy is gone. I never got that dance with her. I hope she had a happy life.

I thought being a hero meant everything and that all that mattered was being courageous and strong. Sure it was thrilling—all the attention, the cheering crowds, a grateful nation, the adrenaline rush. But sitting here now, it seems to have cost me everything . . . my family, my friends . . . so much of my life.

I fear my heart can only grow cold under these conditions. Fury tells me that soon, I will be offered another mission. Of course I will accept it. It's what I do. But what I wouldn't give for one true friend, someone to talk to. . . . (At the bottom of the entry is the insignia of Captain America's shield.)

Joel: (Smiling) You wrote this, didn't you?

LM: (Keeping a straight face) I told you. I got it from a friend.

Joel: Who's your friend? (Clearly suspicious.)

LM: I can't tell you that.

Joel: Why not?

LM: (Still straight-faced) If I told you . . .

Joel: You'd have to kill me? (We both burst out laughing. I take pleasure in having passed through to Wonderland where this kind of play is de rigueur. There was a time when such a joke would have been considered off-limits due to the deadly seriousness of his violent threats and behavior at school.)

LM: You can imagine that if word got out, anyone who owned one of the diary entries would be in danger. People go wild over this stuff.

Joel: That's true. (Perhaps a little more swayed.)

LM: What do you make of it?

Joel: I don't know.

LM: Any reaction to his wish for an average life? It certainly caught me off guard.

Joel: Yeah, right! He's not even real, but if he was, come on, he's a superhero! (Pausing) But I get it.

LM: What do you get?

Joel: Everybody needs someone.

Joel and I further considered the idea that everybody needs someone. He came to see it as more than a cliché, attributing value to it, not just for others but for himself as well. Captain America's diary entry gave him a chance to consider how trying to be somebody might get in the way of finding and preserving friendship.

Over time, Joel's relationship with Mr. C proved invaluable in helping him try out new ways of relating to others. I often solicited Mr. C's firsthand accounts of Joel's efforts along these lines. Together, with the love of his mother, the support of Mr. C and other staff members, and a steady line of narrative questions, Joel found his way into a counterworld, at least for the time being, where companionship and peace offered themselves as values to live by.

Conclusion

Near the end of *Diary of a Wimpy Kid*, just as Greg appears to have reached his breaking point, the plot takes a predictable turn. He narrowly escapes the indignity of being placed on the lowest rung of the social ladder. Upon reuniting with Rowley, the two boys win the "best friends" mock election. The award secures their popularity for eternity, and the film ends with a snapshot of the two appearing on one of the most "sacred" pages of their yearbook.

Joel's fate, however, is undoubtedly less secure. When I first met him, he was living within the bounds of American boyhood, his imagination filled with images of glory. He is certainly not the only boy to have been found in such a dream state, and who, one day, will very likely grapple with a reality that falls short. Too often, the promotion of violent revenge in a dominant hegemonic masculine culture wins out. It commonly manifests in the worst possible way. In the United States alone, there was an average of more than one mass shooting per day in 2015 "that left four or more people wounded or dead" (LaFraniere, Cohen, & Oppel, 2015). Contrary to the popular belief that young men who threaten or perpetrate mass violence are deviants, sociologists argue the opposite is the case (Earp et al., 2013; Kalish & Kimmel, 2010; Kimmel, 2013). Mass shooters are in fact "over-conforming to our norms and ideals of manhood" (Earp et al., 2013).

It is undeniably easier for a boy to stand for values such as compassion and peace in a community that cultivates these same interests and where adults are there to intervene whenever the Code beckons. Joel, his mother, Mr. C, and I may have found our way to an alternative realm where trench coats and weaponry have been traded in for peace-keeping adornments. But whether he will linger in that province and eventually call it home or, like Captain America, answer the call to battle once again, is anyone's guess.

CHAPTER ELEVEN

Making Progress Toward Progress

As I (DM) mulled over what to include as a last representation of my work, I decided on what follows as a fitting coda, not because it stands out as an exemplary illustration of my skills, but precisely for the opposite reason. It can be tempting, especially when writing in indelible ink, to put one's best foot forward, leaving any evidence of missteps off the record or locked away in a bottom desk drawer. But that would fail to acknowledge the realities of our work, or at least mine. This story is meant to speak to the ups and downs in a therapist's life and the doubt that can sometimes visit. It is a story I wrote up about 4 years ago, shortly after a second round of meetings with then 11-year-old Colin and his father. As luck would have it, after a less than impressive beginning, the family was kind enough to offer me a second chance. Despite faring somewhat better in the end, I remain humbled by the experience and by the limits of my own imagination. By my calculations, Colin would have reached his 15th birthday by now.

Almost 6 years ago, an old classmate, whom I had not seen or heard from in more than 20 years, contacted me out of the blue on behalf of a family member, Jackie, who was seeking help. Jackie and her husband, Phil, had two young children, the oldest of whom, Colin, was 9 at the time. I learned that he had been "wreaking havoc" at home. Over the telephone, Jackie explained that living with Colin had them all "walking on eggshells." Whenever someone disagreed with him, or denied him something he wanted, he was angered. At such times he could make life unpleasant for the rest of the family. Even when Colin was in good spirits, he was prone to "whipping his sister [Liza] into a frenzy." He readily confessed this himself, stating, "Sometimes it's fun getting a rise out of people."

In our first meeting, it took no time at all for Colin to make his presence felt. As Jackie and Phil attempted to speak to their son's virtues, Colin nonchalantly interjected, "I'm a genius." In fact, in our time together he gave me little reason to dispute this claim and plenty of cause to believe him to be exceptional. His vocabulary alone impressed, with his use of such words as "truculent" and "abasement." His memory and recall, his eye for detail, and his storytelling skills were each enumerated. In addition, Jackie described him as science minded and explained that, among other things, "he likes to think about infinity." These talents did not appear out of nowhere. Jackie and Phil pursued advanced degrees and were no slouches themselves, though they valued modesty, a tenet they hoped Colin would cultivate.

From the outset, Colin's interest in friendship and "compassion" were also made evident. Jackie spoke sympathetically about a classmate of Colin's who was "easily provoked." She described how Colin "befriended Joey early on and looked out for him." Still, for most of the hour, Colin appeared largely unimpressed. Perhaps he was wary, and understandably so, given that he would have to make up his mind about me. And I had not yet proven myself useful. I would make a first attempt:

Jackie: His friend Joey has a great deal of difficulty with his reading and writing, and Colin is very supportive and understanding if he has a tantrum or a meltdown. That seems unusual for a kid his age.

DM: (Turning to Colin) Are you seeing Temper or Frustration get the better of your good friend? Have you begun to figure something out about Temper? Are you seeing something about it or how it can operate on Joey? (I wonder if Colin might have a better vantage point from which to spy on Temper in the context of his friend's struggles rather than his own. Sometimes we can be "too in" something to see it [Bird, 2004a]).

Colin: It's a horrible parasite and can eat away at your kindness.

DM: Oh my gosh . . . wait just a minute. You had me going there. Was that serious or was it just a joke? (I quickly gather that he is being comical and perhaps having a little fun with me. Still, I will see if there is something to tease out.)

Colin: It was sort of both.

DM: It was both? So is there something to what you said?

Jackie: I haven't heard it before. I will say it's a new one for me.

DM: Should I disregard it or should I write it down? (I need confirmation in order to treat it as anything more than a wisecrack.)

Jackie: That wasn't planned.

Colin: Yes, yes, yes. Wait. Everybody quiet for a second!

DM: Yes, go ahead. The floor is yours. (Anxious to hear what he might say next.)

Colin: My dad ate a mealworm on a cookie. (Though his comment may be irreverent, it easily fits within a tradition of mischief.)

DM: That is not what I expected. (Said in the spirit of fun.)

Colin: (Turning to his father) No, at the bug fair, at the bug fair you did!

DM: Okay, before we wrap up for tonight, I've just got to know. Was what you said about Temper just a joke? Do you mind me asking? (Sometimes what is said in fun is found to hold significance only upon subsequent reflection.)

Colin: That was 75% a joke and 25% real. (This provides important guidance. I can now move forward, awarding the comment a certain value.)

DM: Can I ask you, if it's 75% a joke, what's the 25%?

Colin: Twenty-five percent was true, but the way I said it was a joke. (He may be generating fresh meaning.)

DM: So the way you said it was a joke, but you're saying that you put 25% truth into it?

Colin: I mean the words I said, the actual words I said, that's 25% truth, but if I said it with different words that were more serious, it would probably be a much bigger percentage. (Without the sort of reassurance Colin offered, it would be difficult to extend any inquiry about Temper without centering my values instead of his.)

Our first meeting ended with high hopes on my part and a sense of much to be gained. The following is excerpted from a longer e-mail I sent to Colin via his parents.

Dear Colin,

It was good to meet you and your mom and dad today. I've been mulling our discussion over and wanted to put my thoughts down and send them to you for your review. Let me start with a thought or two about a comment you made that I found the most striking of all. Can you guess which one it was? Speaking about Temper, you announced, "It's a horrible parasite and it eats away at your kindness." When I asked you about the "25% real," you explained, "If I said it with different words it would be even more true." How many more points would you give it if you said it with different words? What words would be best?

Too bad it was the end of our time. I'm sure I could have spent a while talking this over with you. Were you as interested as I was to figure out what was "true" about such a declaration? Don't be surprised if I have a dozen questions about Temper, the Horrible Parasite, the next time I see you. By the way, don't you think that would be the perfect name for a spooky Halloween movie? "Opening this weekend at a theater near you! TEMPER! THE HORRIBLE PARASITE!" What would Temper look like if it dressed up as a trick-or-treater? Of course, it wouldn't be interested in treats. Only tricks, don't you think?

According to your dad, you have all the skills for taming Temper [Epston, 2008; Freeman et al., 1997]. As your dad sees it, you

- Like "to solve problems" (Have you begun to put your problem-solving skills to work with Temper?)
- Like "to look at things"
- Are "into observation"
- Have "a keen eye for detail"

If you combined your observation skills with your keen eye, would you expose Temper for the parasite it is? Would it have the ability to hide in the shadows and sneak up on you and take over, or would you see it coming? Have you ever caught it red-handed before it caught hold of you?

Maybe I'm getting a little ahead of myself. I should probably ask you first how you feel about being a host to Temper the parasite. People usually want to get rid of parasites, but I don't want to make any assumptions. Are you happy to give it a home, or do you feel differently? I suppose I'll get to know the answers to these questions and more over time.

Looking forward to seeing you soon.
Yours truly,
David

At our next meeting, Colin's compassion was on further display in a story that centered on forgiveness.[1] I wondered, as we began to talk about forgiveness, if it would serve as a counterweight to Temper. It is by means of such opportunities, as in the following sample, that young people can engage in moral deliberation and establish the conditions by which they come to know themselves apart from problems.

> Colin: At school we do this thing called Artwork for Education, where you decide on a theme, and last year, it was Christmas and Hanukkah, and we were brainstorming stuff we could draw and I said, "Hanukkah Harry," because I thought that it was a real tradition, but then everyone looked at me like I was crazy. (His dad told him about Harry Hanukkah, but it was not clear to Colin that Harry was not a culturally established symbol.)

Jackie: Yeah. (She offers a sympathetic look.)

DM: Did you come back to your dad and say, "Why did you do that to me?" (I want to understand whether Temper had him take aim at his father.)

Colin: I forgave him.

DM: You did?

Colin: Because I knew that he wouldn't do something like that.

DM: Like what?

Colin: He wouldn't embarrass me on purpose.

DM: Are you forgiving? Do you believe in forgiveness? (I take interest here because this may offer a window into another account of Colin—one that Temper would have little interest in supporting.)

Colin: Sometimes I stay mad at people for a long time and sometimes I'll forgive them automatically. Sometimes I partly forgive them but still think about how I'm upset with them. (These are three variations with respect to forgiveness, each warranting further exploration.)

DM: Are these all different ways of forgiving? Well, sometimes not forgiving, too, right?

Colin: Yes.

DM: Can we take this in parts? First of all, why do you sometimes automatically forgive someone? (I inquire about this first because it may represent the most dramatic contrast to any disposition Temper would saddle him with.)

Colin: If they didn't mean it or if they did something wrong by accident.

DM: But still, can't something hurt your feelings, or get Temper going, even if it was a mistake or an accident? (I'm giving him a chance to either rethink his stance or further establish it.)

Colin: Yeah, but if it's a mistake then I don't want to get mad.

DM: How do you manage that? (I'm genuinely interested to know.)

Colin: I just do. (If he has not been previously inclined to give this question much thought, he may now come to consider it more deliberately.)

DM: Are you pleased you can forgive automatically? Is this something you're proud of? (I invite Colin to take a moral stance.)

Colin: I guess.

DM: And you also partly forgive sometimes? (Here again, something is indicated about Colin's character that may deserve attention.)

Colin: Yeah.

DM: Why have you taken an interest in different forms of forgiveness, Colin? Are you thinking about different ways to take onto your shoulders what other people your age, or any age, could easily refuse to carry?

Colin: I don't know. (Perhaps the question could have been put more simply.)

DM: How do you pull that off? (I am attempting to give him ample opportunity to consider forgiveness as a value.)

Colin: Well, for example, my grandma. I was really mad at her, because when I was 2, she had this cat . . .

Colin went on to tell a story about his grandmother having to "put her cat down." He only heard about it many years later but found it disturbing nonetheless. He had since repeatedly voiced his disapproval, never having reconciled his own views on euthanasia with those of the family. With the benefit of the story, I was eager to understand more about Colin's forgiving ways. He explained how in spite of being "really mad" about his grandmother's fateful decision, he loved her and "didn't want to hold it against her." Colin could be obstinate in his opposition and already knew himself, and was well known to others, in this mode and tone. I therefore persisted in focusing on his ideas regarding forgiveness. I gathered that he had been given to less contemplation over this sort of practice, but perhaps not for lack of interest.

The Best-Laid Plans . . .

To this point it seemed we were on a promising path, having identified Temper and a possible counterstory guided by compassion and forgiveness. Our next meeting, however, took an unexpected turn, or, more precisely, a U-turn. Rather than picking up where we left off, we were stymied—at least I was. I found it difficult to engage Colin. In spite of my efforts, I was outwitted, not by Colin so much as by the usual suspects (i.e., boredom, fatigue, tomfoolery) who, like the Cat in the Hat, delight in making mayhem. What follows is a small sample of what took place at our third meeting, which Liza, Colin's sister, also attended.

> Colin: Liza, sit on top. (Colin is lying on the floor, beckoning his younger sister to come and sit on top of him.)
>
> Jackie: No, no.
>
> DM: Colin, Colin, the other thing . . .
>
> Jackie: But I don't really feel like I . . .
>
> Liza: No! No! No! (Having gotten hold of Liza and wrapped his arms tightly around her waist, he is rocking her from side to side.)
>
> DM: Colin—
>
> Jackie: Okay, Colin, you know what, can you focus? (Jackie physically separates them, attempting to bring about a degree of order, for which I am grateful.)
>
> DM: Now when he . . .
>
> Colin: That's why I wanted to bring my toys last time!
>
> DM: Can I, can I . . . (Clumsily overlapping.)
>
> Jackie: Okay, next time we'll bring your toys, okay? (Trying to reassure him.)
>
> DM: Now, can I ask . . . (I am persistent, but not authoritative. I am hopeful that striking a less insistent tone will pay off in the long run—that by not usurping authority, I will contribute to a

sense of shared agency and an increased atmosphere of cooperation. This is not, however, to be confused with any interest in reverse hierarchy, which would leave me entirely at Colin's whim.)

Jackie: Liza!

DM: So . . .

Jackie: Yeah, just quietly, okay? And please be gentle, okay, Colin? (He darts around the room and jumps up on the couch next to Liza. Jackie attempts to preempt any trouble that might ensue.)

DM: But the thing I want to try to sort out, is . . .

Phil: Don't break that chair. (Colin is off the couch again, having deposited himself in my desk chair, and is spinning around and around. Then he pushes against the desk with both feet and goes rolling backward.)

Jackie: Don't push the chair. (He's out of the chair now and heading back in the direction of his sister.)

DM: Were you telling another story about how when he was . . . (Liza is squealing in either delight or horror. No one is sure which.)

Jackie: Okay, Colin, we can't talk when you're sitting on top of her. (Having returned to the couch, he is leaning against Liza, now lying on top of her.)

Phil: Well, we've only got . . .

DM: Yeah, actually you'll be on your way in a couple minutes.

Jackie: Yeah, okay, Colin, it's almost over.

Everyone was frustrated by hour's end—myself included, but mainly by my own futility. I hoped that I would be more helpful in our next meeting and find Colin in a disposition to talk and reflect. When a conversation goes well, I always feel a degree of luck. Young people certainly have an inclination, from early in life, to make up their own minds about whether to cooperate with adult initiatives. (Just picture any 1-year-old who has no intention of being placed in a stroller or car seat.) While I make earnest and repeated attempts to arouse young people's interest, the decision is ultimately theirs to make. Anything more could very well constitute a misuse of power. And besides, endeavoring to exact cooperation is no more effective with a young person than it is with an adult. Lucky for me, Colin entered the next session seeming of a mind to talk things over.

I learned in our fourth meeting that Colin's interest in forgiveness was more decided with his father than his mother. Where his mother was concerned, he was inclined to view and treat her with a critical eye and sharp tongue.

> **Jackie**: Sometimes it seems like it's getting worse, and I can't seem to gain their cooperation. Our house just feels chaotic all the time.
>
> **Colin**: My mom goes hysterical. (He seems to have it in mind to expose her.)
>
> **Jackie**: Well . . .
>
> **Colin**: You were crying.
>
> **Jackie**: Anyway, he's really into Legos and he has tons of them, and they get thrown all around and I've been trying to slowly set them up on the shelf, but anyway, it seems like since this summer, our living room . . .
>
> **Colin**: Yeah. (Appearing to mock her.)
>
> **Jackie**: The living room where you walk into the house, it's like I don't have a place where it's just clear.
>
> **DM**: Uh-huh.
>
> **Jackie**: And sometimes I put blinders on, but I finally organized all of the pieces and put them aside in a box at the edge of the living room. Well, yesterday he wanted to work with those, so he just dumped everything out that I've organized. So last night, I was awake and started picking them all up and doing it again. (Colin chuckles, finding something funny in his mother's description.)
>
> **DM**: There's something familiar to me about this story.
>
> **Jackie**: Uh-huh.
>
> **DM**: That kids somehow get, or something gets them, used to

having Mom around or used to taking Mom for granted. Or even having a little fun at her expense. (Working my way up to exposing a possible discourse centered on privilege or entitlement.)

Jackie: Mm-hmm.

DM: Do you find yourself thinking of your mom as . . . ?

Colin: As a personal robot! (Stated with apparent amusement.)

Jackie: Yeah, that's clear. The other day, he actually went "chop chop."

DM: When you make a comment like . . .

Jackie: A put-down.

DM: I don't think I've ever heard you say something like that about your dad.

Jackie: Right.

DM: Is it more something that can get you going with your mom?

Colin: It's because I think my dad is more logical.

Sons in particular can feel a kind of authority over and a right to critically evaluate their mothers (Höpfl, 2000). I do not view this kind of attitude as a product of an individual boy's private labors or of a family dynamic that operates independently from broader social arrangements. Perhaps it was Phil's paycheck and work outside the house, as well as his gender, that accorded him greater worth in his son's eyes, at least in comparison to Jackie and her "invisible labor" (Crittenden, 2002). The ready bestowal of support for men's viewpoints and actions, along with inattention to women's ideas and experiences, is also built into the culture that Colin was a part of (Ferrucci, Schoenberger, & Schauster, 2014). In any case, this is not to suggest that Phil was beyond (Colin's) reproach. Certainly his father was not so commanding a figure in his son's eyes as to unequivocally merit his respect. And once Colin was possessed by Temper and dispossessed of such virtues as compassion and forgiveness, he could not be loosened from its grip very easily, no matter who was doing the prying.

Temper sometimes appeared to justify itself on the grounds of Colin's superior intelligence or specialness. We arrived at a tentative understanding of Colin's "Sharp Mind" as having convinced him he was peerless. What follows was a first attempt to externalize and characterize his Sharp Mind, both as something to be proud of and as something that could, at times, be found to sponsor adversarial relationships with others.

>**Jackie**: If I make a mistake, Colin will say, "You're lying, you're lying."
>
>**DM**: (Turning to Colin) "You're lying?" Do you ever get going like that?
>
>**Colin**: Sometimes.
>
>**DM**: I wonder if, in a way, it's a little bit tricky having a Sharp Mind. Like your mind can end up . . .
>
>**Colin**: I only do it . . . (He pauses for a moment.) I don't do it when the idea somebody else has is really super.
>
>**DM**: If it's really super, you open your mind to other people? (I wonder if, given the chance to consider it, Colin might be drawn to a practice of open-mindedness.)
>
>**Colin**: Sometimes.
>
>**DM**: Sometimes you open your mind, and other times it only lets you listen to yourself? (Mapping the problem.)
>
>**Colin**: Except the thing is, most of the time, even when what someone is talking about is good . . . (He is forming a thought.)
>
>**DM**: Yeah.
>
>**Colin**: I am able to find a reason why they're wrong instead of listening to them.

I e-mailed Colin that evening, believing that we might have come to an important understanding.

Dear Colin,
   Just a short note. I was most interested in what it's like to live with a Sharp Mind and whether your Sharp Mind ever tries to make you too big for your britches. (Do you know this saying?) You described some of the ways your Sharp Mind can get you into trouble, including:

- Making everything and everyone seem boring
- Discouraging you from listening
- Convincing you that other people's ideas are dumb

Although you did explain that sometimes you treat other people's ideas with respect. Colin, is there something that has to be figured out about living with a Sharp Mind? Do you have to train it to follow your instructions?

I hope you enjoy the weekend. See you soon.
DM

In the remainder of meetings that followed before summer arrived, Phil reported, "Things aren't really much different." I attempted another conversation with Colin about his Sharp Mind, but he quickly lost patience and conveyed to me, in no uncertain terms, "I'm tired of talking about my Sharp Mind." More and more, he seemed to act as if he was wise to me and his interest waned. Everyone seemed stressed, and I was not exempt. Whatever momentum we had achieved appeared lost.

For some time thereafter, I entertained (and was entertained by) doubt. What did I miss? I felt I let the family down. Had our conversations lacked a consistent theme and ended up less a story line than a patchwork of ideas? And what must my old classmate think of me? She had turned to me on Jackie's behalf, and I let her down, too.

It would be 2 years before they called again. When Phil contacted me, I was glad to hear from him and also anxious to know how they had fared in the interim. He told me that things were largely unchanged and that they wanted to come back and give therapy another try. I was truly sorry to hear about their ongoing difficulty but heartened by their interest in returning, and we set up a time to meet.

The Second Time Around

We began meeting again, just the three of us, Phil, Colin, and me. With Jackie's approval, we wondered whether we might, as a male trio, take the problem on and help to alleviate some of her stress. She remained hampered by her status and reputation in her son's eyes, and I was curious to see if we might find a way to address this inequity and perhaps counter the possible effects of male privilege.

Instead of beginning with a focus on the family, though, Colin wanted to talk about school and friends. He noted, "I've always been nice to other kids in more ways than one." But lately, he found himself on the outside looking in, socially. He speculated about whether this reflected a shortcoming of his. In one instance on campus, he noticed, "I was trying too hard." In another he admitted to "a little superiority," explaining, "Sometimes I get angry" and "I always have to be right." He was more open than in our earlier meetings. Phil and I readily recalled the unevenness of our own school experiences and the social pains we suffered as boys. We were more inclined to stand in solidarity (Polanco, 2010) than to offer suggestions, which are only too easy to come by. Besides, the answers Colin sought might have already been within his grasp. He seemed to have come to an implicit intention to show greater care in relationships.

Soon enough, his attention turned to life at home and to a view of progress. When asked about his old habit of "whipping people into a frenzy," he said, "Now it's a lot less, but I still enjoy it sometimes." He described it as "a little bit of teasing" and advocated for "everything in moderation." In revisiting Temper, he acknowledged that it could still use his Sharp Mind to incite an attitude of self-importance. I embodied Temper (Roth & Epston, 1996) and melodramatically posed the following question:

> **Temper**: How dare she [Jackie] ignore you? She's disrespecting you! You're important and what you have to say is important! (This question is meant to expose Temper and where it would lead in order to see if Colin is along for the ride, or if he might have a different direction in mind.)
>
> **Colin**: I think there's more self-regard in walking away.

Colin opposed self-importance, at least in the abstract, and any ready justification for Temper. He admitted, though, that it was an ongoing struggle. Each week he came to meetings in a frame of mind to think things over. He spoke to growing concerns for his life, not least of which involved his relationship with his mother and the conflict that could so easily reignite.

At one point, as he advocated for more peace, I asked, "Where's the fun or satisfaction in peace?" I wondered if he would be giving up too much and whether there was more thrill in chaos and the drama it can deliver. In response, he alluded to the Han dynasty, a culture he had been studying in class lately. He was drawn to what was possible in an era of peace. He described two long centuries, during which unprecedented advances occurred in areas of technology, medicine, and science, including the following:

- The invention of paper
- The development of the crossbow and sword
- Practices in acupuncture
- Identification of a solar eclipse
- Theories on blood flow
- The concept of reflected light
- Moxibustion (I had to look this one up)

Phil remained mostly unimpressed. He conceded that Colin might be thinking about things differently, but their home life, he reported, was largely unaltered, particularly in regard to Colin's relationship with his mother. Phil stated decidedly, "He is disrespectful to Jackie and her stuff [i.e., her computer, piano, and home office]." Colin still held out that something was happening, even if, upon further reflection, he acknowledged that things were not all that different. He put it thusly: "I think I'm making progress toward progress." He expressed a desire to see change in his conduct but described an irresistible "feeling of having to be right."

Colin was not the only one enamored with his own ideas. His dilemma struck a chord with me. It just so happened, I was presently attempting to sort out a problem of a similar kind. Either by circumstance or perhaps as a consequence of my privileged location in the world as a middle-class, heterosexual, white male, I could feel a certain entitlement to have my opinions treated with reverence. Was it our shared positioning in the culture that granted us this "right"? I realized I was in need of assistance and decided it might be helpful to confide in Colin. I also wondered whether enlisting him in the role of consultant might give him a leg up in dealing with his own struggle (Epston & White, 1992; Marsten et al., 2011).

At our next meeting, I opened up about a predicament involving a work project with a colleague. I feared that my own prerogative to know best might be getting the better of me. I was already feeling inclined to pull out of the venture if things did not go my way. I had a telephone conversation scheduled for that very evening and was feeling real concern about what I might say or do. After I disclosed my own dilemma, Colin expressed eagerness to help. He shared many insights, which I carefully noted, and then summarized in an e-mail I sent to him a few days later.

Hi Colin,
I finally had a brief conversation with my colleague yesterday. Coincidentally, I'll be speaking with her again tonight directly after our meeting. I carried your advice into our first conversation and it went better than expected. I'm not sure at this point if it was the attitude I took or if I caught her (or myself) in a good mood. But I do know I was dialing her number with your advice in mind:

1. Don't be ungrateful.
2. If I pull out of the project I'd better have a good excuse. (Did you mean this as a reminder to be kind to her, whatever I decide? Or that I should be keeping an eye on that thing that can take hold of both of us—"the feeling of having to be right"?)
3. Be honest. (What if it would hurt her feelings?)
4. Talk it over and compromise. (This is what seems to be happening, although I will have a better sense after we speak again tonight.)
5. Just deal with it. (Did you mean this as a reminder not to

take myself too seriously or to think of my ideas as too precious?)
6. It may just be a personality trait that has me thinking I'm always right. (Okay, but when I'm in the heat of the moment, what do I do if my personality trait tries to take over?)

You can see I still need a little help. It will be good to see you tonight and talk it over if you're up for it.
   Hope things are going well with you,
David

I hoped that, in addition to the guidance he offered me, Colin might be moved to see the wisdom in his own words and, upon reflection, determine whether it was applicable to his life. In the weeks that followed, there were promising developments. Colin continued to challenge himself to "think about why I don't want to get angry" and to "think about it before I act." In a subsequent meeting he reported, "A week ago we had very, very, very few fights." When I asked him how he accounted for it, he said it was "part luck, part good mood, which is kind of lucky, and part, not just progress toward progress, but actual progress." He conceded, "I don't think my mom and I will ever not get into arguments, but we talk more and are able to have normal conversations." He alluded to a number of changes he saw in his conduct—"not interrupting as much, not having to be right, not yelling as much"—but still found it "difficult to back down." Phil agreed, saying, "Though there's still about the same amount of arguing, there's a lot less fighting and a lot more talking."

Conclusion

As plans were under way for summer, the family decided to take another break. This one turned out to be longer than the last—it has extended to this very day. I had hoped to invite Jackie back after the guys spent some time carrying the concern for family harmony. I was interested to find out what she might have noticed in the way of progress, or lack thereof. But life has a way of taking over, and where summer plans are concerned, psychotherapy does not always make the to-do list—understandably so.

When I think about Colin these days, I am drawn to an image of a boy and family with no shortage of love but, at times, a scarcity of peace. I am reminded to look and listen for possibilities but never to fix my gaze on a distant goal or the necessity of a perfect outcome. People contend with difficult problems (e.g., Temper, Privilege/Entitlement, Nervousness, Temptation, Unfairness, Disrespect, Worry), and liberation from problems is not the only result that will do, though it certainly would be nice. Sometimes it is more a matter of living with problems and making progress where one can. At the very least, Colin seemed to have developed a more detailed view of Temper, and on his better days, the means by which to stick to his own values.

I give thought, not so much to what I may have contributed to their lives in some small way, but more to what I gained, in the time Colin, Jackie, Phil, and Liza visited me. I was distressed when the work seemed to run aground, and I failed to detect or inspire imaginative know-how. The memory of my own shortcomings continues to counsel me as I find myself in a variety of roles, including practitioner, supervisor, and teacher (not to mention husband, brother, son, and friend). Like Colin, I can still feel the urge to know best. But I would like to believe that even if I have not transcended the same old impulse (or the effects of privilege), at least, I am making progress toward progress, and on my better days, actual progress.

EPILOGUE

Imagination Revived

Imagination is an ideal traveling companion as young people make their way to new worlds. Without concern for modes of transportation or letters of transit, they traverse royal empires, vast deserts, battlefields, and secret gardens. Undaunted by the impracticality of their schemes, they "journey through the unplanned, the unexpected, the improvised, and the surprising" (Halberstam, 2011, pp. 15–16). Perhaps there is no more appealing example than our childhood idol, Peter Pan, who effortlessly travels between the real and the imaginary, seeking adventure and inviting other young people to join him. By contrast, if adults were attempting to locate Neverland, their first impulse would be to check GPS devices for directions. Having already said goodbye to her own childhood, Mrs. Darling carries the burden of practical concerns, her imagination too freighted to take flight:

> **Mrs. Darling**: (Shivering every time Wendy pursues him in the air) Where are you to live, Peter?
> **Peter**: In the house we built for Wendy. The fairies are to put it high up among the treetops where they sleep at night.
> **Wendy**: (Rapturously) To think of it.
> **Mrs. Darling**: I thought all the fairies were dead.

Mrs. Darling had long since arrived at an age at which any sighting of fairy dust would only lend itself to the assiduous polishing of tabletops. The world she inhabits prides itself on orderliness. It is a world in which adults head to offices to work each day, some of them the very places where children are brought to receive their diagnoses and medications. But this is not the world we seek in our partnership with young people and their families.

A final brief vignette reminds us of the provinces young people are capable of visiting. In conversation with a father and daughter, DM spoke with 7-year-old Jira about her love of the outdoors. She alighted on a recent memory of a classroom outing and was off and running with her description of the world around her, both real and enchanted.

> **Jira**: We picked a bunch of nature and flowers and leaves . . . and found tons of stuff, and it was really fun. We got honeysuckles and those jacaranda flowers. We used a lot of science, because we squirted out the honeysuckles. We realized they could be a good drink for the fairies, and squirted out the bottom. We called it fairy milk of the purple jacaranda things, because it's this white liquid that comes out and it's edible and it's really sour and they could use it for the fairies.
>
> **DM**: Jira, we were talking earlier about your imagination and how good it's gotten, especially over this past year. Is this a really great example of what your imagination is capable of imagining?
>
> **Dad**: I'm really impressed!
>
> **Jira**: Yep! Except I don't think the fairies are imagination. I think they're real.
>
> **DM**: Right. That's right. My mistake. (DM's momentary blunder had him making a misguided distinction between what is real and what is not. Thankfully, Jira set him straight.)

Childhood is that time in life before young people are fully indoctrinated into adult culture and drawn in by the indisputable order of things. They can amend reality and readily engage with storybook characters, pixies, and fairies and dive headlong into counterworlds. We follow them there as best we can and place our imaginations at their service. Any question regarding the authenticity of fairies is superfluous. It is simply best to remember that they sure do come in handy when needed.

NOTES

Introduction

1. We use the terms *children* and *young people* interchangeably. We find advantage in the term *children* for its familiarity, but we appreciate the designation *young people* for its nonpejorative and less categorizing qualities. *Children* and *childhood* as discursive categories come loaded with meaning and can be associated with notions of incapacity and vulnerability. Nevertheless, we have settled on the uneasy solution of using both terms.

2. *Wonderfulness* is a neologism created by David Epston to refer to a young person's skills and moral virtues.

3. Following Michel Foucault and Michael White, we refer to knowledges in the plural to dispute the notion that knowledge, at least in the realm of human relationships, can ever be reduced to a stable and single form or understanding.

Chapter 1

1. In view of the fact that two of the authors are named David, they will henceforth be referred to by their initials, for the sake of clarity, rather than by the given name they have in common.

2. It should be noted that in pursuing Maureen as a striking figure we do not mean to make her out as so individually gifted as to leave her unaffiliated. When we refer to her gifts we are implicitly alluding to skills that are traceable through family lines, community, and ancestry. Ultimately, it is up to Maureen to determine which values she will choose to receive as gifts and carry forward as part of a legacy, and which she may distance herself from or leave behind. In the same vein,

we avoid references to young people's strengths and resources that would promote a view of private reserves to be mined. This would have us "treating [a] strength as if it were a preexisting treasure just waiting to be dug up inside a skin-bound body" (Combs & Freedman, 2016).

Chapter 4

1. The idea for a Fear Fighters society is inspired by the work of Jennifer Freedman, David Epston, and Dean Lobovits and their creation of the Temper Tamer's Club of America.

Chapter 7

1. It should be noted that there are psychiatrists, such as Gene Combs, SueEllen Hamkins, and others (Bracken & Thomas, 2005; Bradley, 2011; Combs & Freedman, 2002; Hamkins, 2014), who have achieved distinction for their strong interest in narrative theory and practice and relational approaches to psychiatric care.

Chapter 8

1. Louise's fear can be situated in "deep-seated racial disparities in the U.S. criminal justice system" (Lee, 2016). In 2015, "Young black men were nine times more likely than other Americans to be killed by police officers" (Swaine, Laughland, Lartey, & McCarthy, 2015).

Chapter 9

1. We refer to the Growing-Up Fairy in the feminine only because it was a female family member who was recruited to play the part.

Chapter 11

1. We do not believe that forgiveness is in any way a requirement. We are equally open to the possibility that unforgiveness may provide a way forward. It is only when someone expresses an interest in forgiveness or finds the concept appealing that we take interest. Still, we remain alert to the possibility that any expression of interest in forgiveness might be

more a result of internalized cultural discourse and what has been granted elevated status. Too often, we find ourselves sitting across from someone who has been wronged, or whose basic human rights have been violated, and who now shoulders the additional burden of "needing to forgive."

REFERENCES

Adamsons, K., & Buehler, C. (2007). Mothering versus fathering versus parenting: Measurement equivalence in parenting measures. *Parenting: Science and Practice, 7*(3), 271–303.

Adichie, C. (2009, October). The danger of a single story. Retrieved from http://www.ted.com/talks/lang/en/chimamanda_adichie_the_danger_of_a_single_story.html

Almond, D. (1998). *Skellig*. New York: Yearling Books.

American Psychiatric Association. (2013). *Diagnostic and statistical manual of mental disorders* (5th ed.). Washington, DC: Author.

Anderson, C., & Anderson, M. (2011). Single-parent families: Strengths, vulnerabilities, and interventions. In M. McGoldrick, B. Carter, & N. Garcia-Preto (Eds.), *The expanded family life cycle: Individual, family, and social perspectives* (4th ed., pp. 317–347). Boston: Allyn and Bacon.

Appelbaum, P. (2011). SSRIs, suicide, and liability for failure to warn of medication risk. *Law and Psychiatry, 62*(4), 347–349.

Bakhtin, M. (1981). *The dialogic imagination*. Austin: University of Texas Press.

Barrie, J. M. (2005). *Peter Pan*. New York: Barnes and Noble. (Original work published as *Peter and Wendy* in 1911)

Bateson, G., Jackson, D., Haley, J., & Weakland, J. (1956). Toward a theory of schizophrenia. *Behavioral Science, 1*(4), 251–264.

Batstra, L., & Frances, A. (2012a). Diagnostic inflation: Causes and a suggested cure. *Journal of Nervous and Mental Disease, 200*(6), 474–479.

Batstra, L., & Frances, A. (2012b). Holding the line against diagnostic inflation in psychiatry. *Psychotherapy and Psychosomatics, 81*(5), 5–10.

Bauman, Z. (2001). *The individualized society.* Cambridge, UK: Polity.

Bettelheim, B. (1967). *The empty fortress: Infantile autism and the birth of the self.* New York: Free Press.

Bird, J. (2004a). *Practicing super-vision, extra-vision, extending-vision* [CD]. Presented at the Supervision Conference. Auckland, Australia: Edge Press.

Bird, J. (2004b). *Talk that sings: Therapy in a new linguistic key.* Auckland, Australia: Edge Press.

Bockman, J. (2014). Neoliberalism. *Contexts, 12*(3), 14–15.

Bourdieu, P. (1988). *Homo academicus.* Cambridge, UK: Polity.

Boyd-Franklin, N. (2010). Incorporating spirituality and religion into the treatment of African American clients. *Counseling Psychologist, 38*(7), 976–1000.

Bracken, P., & Thomas, P. (2005). *Postpsychiatry: Mental health in a postmodern world.* New York: Oxford University Press.

Bradley, L. (2011). *Narrative psychiatry: How stories can shape clinical practice.* Baltimore: The Johns Hopkins University Press.

Bruner, J. (1986). *Actual minds, possible worlds.* Cambridge, MA: Harvard University Press.

Bruner, J. (1996). A narrative model of self construction. *Psyke and Logos, 17*, 154–170.

Bruner, J. (2004). Narrative as life. *Social Research, 71*(3), 691–710.

Buckley, E., & Decter, P. (2006). From isolation to community: Collaborating with children and families in times of crisis. *International Journal of Narrative Therapy and Community Work, 2*, 3–12.

Burman, E. (2008). *Deconstructing developmental psychology.* London: Routledge.

Caplan, P., & Hall-McCorquodale, I. (1985). Mother-blaming in major clinical journals. *American Journal of Orthopsychiatry, 55*(3), 345–353.

Carey, M., Walther, S., & Russell, S. (2009). The absent but implicit: A map to support therapeutic enquiry. *Family Process, 48*(3), 319–331.

Caro, M., & Jeunet, J. P. (Directors). (1995). *La cité des enfants perdus* [Motion picture]. France: Club d'Investissement Media.

Carr, D. (1986). Narrative and the real world: An argument for continuity. *History and Theory, 25*(2), 117–131.

Carroll, L. (2000). *Alice's adventures in wonderland.* San Francisco: Chronicle. (Original work published 1865)

Chaudry-Fryer, M. (1995). Power-play: Games in Joyce's *Dubliners. Studies in Short Fiction, 32*(3), 319–327.

Cloke, P., & Jones, O. (2005). "Unclaimed territory": Childhood and disordered space(s). *Social and Cultural Geography, 6*(3), 311–333.

Combs, G., & Freedman, J. (2002). Relationships, not boundaries. *Theoretical Medicine and Bioethics: Philosophy of Medical Research and Pracice, 23*(3), 203–217.

Cortese, S., Kelly, C., Chabernaud, C., Proal, E., Di Martino, A., Milham, M., & Castellanos, F. (2012). Toward systems neuroscience of ADHD: A meta-analysis of 55 fMRI studies. *American Journal of Psychiatry, 169*(10), 1038–1055.

Crittenden, A. (2002). *The price of motherhood: Why the most important job in the world is still the least valued.* New York: Henry Holt.

Dahl, R. (1988). *Matilda.* New York: Puffin.

del Toro, G. (Director). (2006). *El laberinto del fauno* [Motion picture]. Spain: Esperanto Films.

Davis, R. (2011). Mother–child relations and the discourse of maternity. *Ethics and Education, 6*(2), 125-139.

Demause, L. (2010). Bipolar Christianity: How torturing "sinful children" produced holy wars. *Journal of Psychohistory, 37*(3), 172–206.

Denborough, D. (2014). *Retelling the stories of our lives: Everyday narrative therapy to draw inspiration and transform experience.* New York: Norton.

Denzin, N. (2003). *Performance ethnography: Critical pedagogy and the politics of culture.* Thousand Oaks, CA: Sage.

Devisch, I., & Murray, S. (2009). "We hold these truths to be self-evident": Deconstructing "evidence-based" medical practice. *Journal of Evaluation in Clinical Practice, 15*(6), 950–954.

Dr. Seuss [Geisel, T. S.]. (1985). *The cat in the hat.* New York: Random House. (Original work published 1957)

Dr. Seuss [Geisel, T. S.]. (1991). *Hop on pop.* New York: Random House. (Original work published in 1963)

Dupré, J. (2001). Evolution and gender. *Women: A Cultural Review, 12*(1), 9–18.

Earp, J., Katz, J., Young, J. T., Jhally, S., Rabinovitz, D., & Media Education Foundation. (2013). *Tough guise 2: Violence, manhood and American culture.* Northampton, MA: Media Education Foundation.

Editorial Board. (2013, December 18). An epidemic of attention deficit disorder. *New York Times.* Retrieved from http://www.nytimes.com/2013/12/19/opinion/an-epidemic-of-attention-deficit-disorder.html

Eisenberg, Z. (2010). Clear and pregnant danger: The making of prenatal psychology, in mid-twentieth-century America. *Journal of Women's History, 22*(3), 112–135.

Epston, D. (1989). *Collected papers.* Adelaide, Australia: Dulwich Centre.

Epston, D. (1998). *Catching up with David Epston: A collection of narrative practice-based papers.* Adelaide, Australia: Dulwich Centre. (Free copies available for download at: www.narrativeapproaches.com)

Epston, D. (2008). *Down under and up over: Travels with narrative therapy.* Warrington, Australia: AFT.

Epston, D., & Marsten, D. (2010). "What doesn't the problem know about your son or daughter?" Providing the conditions for the restoration of a family's dignity. *International Journal of Narrative Therapy and Community Work, 1,* 30–36.

Epston, D., & White, M. (1992). *Experience contradiction narrative and imagination.* Adelaide, Australia: Dulwich Centre.

Faris, W. (2004). *Ordinary enchantments: Magical realism and the remystification of narrative.* Nashville, TN: Vanderbilt University Press.

Ferrucci, P., Shoenberger, H., & Schauster, E. (2014). It's a mad, mad, mad, ad world: A feminist critique of Mad Men. *Women's Studies International Forum, 47*(A), 93–101.

Finley, S. (2012). Critical constructions of childhood: Globalized homelessness and poverty. *International Journal of Qualitative Studies in Education, 25*(2), 131–133.

Foucault, M. (1971). Polemic: Monstrosities in criticism. *Diacritics, 1*(1), 57–60.

Foucault, M. (1995). *Discipline and punish: The birth of the prison* (2nd ed.). New York: Vintage. (Original work published 1978)

Fox, D., Prilleltensky, I., & Austin, S. (Eds.). (2009). *Critical psychology: An introduction* (2nd ed.). London: Sage.

Frances, A. (2012). Better safe than sorry. *Australian and New Zealand Journal of Psychiatry, 46*(8), 695–696.

Frances, A. (2014). DSM, psychotherapy, counseling and the medicalization of mental illness: A commentary from Allen Frances. *The Professional Counselor, 4*(3), 282–284.

Frances, A., & Jones, K. D. (2013). Should social workers use *Diagnostic and Statistical Manual of Mental Disorders-5*? *Research on Social Work Practice, 24*(1), 11–12.

Frank, A. (2010). *Letting stories breathe: A socio-narratology.* Chicago: University of Chicago Press.

Freedman, J., & Combs, G. (1996). *Narrative therapy: The social construction of preferred realities.* New York: Norton.

Freeman, J., Epston, D., & Lobovits, D. (1997). *Playful approaches to serious problems: Narrative therapy with children and their families.* New York: Norton.

Freud, S. (1962). *Civilization and its discontents.* New York: Norton. (Original work published 1930)

Fromm-Reichmann, F. (1937). Contribution to the psychogenesis of migraine. *Psychoanalytic Review, 24A*, 26–33.

Fuentes, C. (2011). *Destiny and desire.* New York: Random House.

Geertz, C. (1973). *The interpretation of cultures.* New York: Basic Books.

Gergen, K. (1994). *Realities and relationships: Soundings in social construction.* Cambridge, MA: Harvard University Press.

Gergen, K. (2006). *Therapeutic realities: Collaboration, oppression and relational flow.* Chagrin Falls, NM: Taos Institute.

Gergen, K. (2010). The acculturated brain. *Theory and Psychology, 20*(6), 795–816.

Ginsburg, K. (2007). The importance of play in promoting healthy child development and maintaining strong parent-child bonds. *Pediatrics, 119*(1), 182–191.

Goldenberg, M. (2006). On evidence and evidence-based medicine: Lessons from the philosophy of science. *Social Science and Medicine, 62*(11), 2621–2632.

Graham, J., Banaschewski, T., Buitelaar, J., Coghill, D., Danckaerts, M., Dittmann, R. W., . . . Taylor, E. (2011). European guidelines on managing adverse effects of medication for ADHD. *European Child and Adolescent Psychiatry, 20*(1), 17–37.

Greenberg, G. (2013). *The book of woe: The DSM and the unmaking of psychiatry*. New York: Blue Rider.
Griswold, W. (1994). *Cultures and societies in a changing world*. Thousand Oaks, CA: Pine Forge.
Halberstam, J. (2011). *The queer art of failure*. Durham, NC: Duke University Press.
Hanson, B. (2011). *Peter Pan on stage and screen: 1904–2010*. Jefferson, NC: McFarland.
Happe, F., & Frith, U. (2014). Annual research review: Towards a developmental neuroscience of atypical social cognition. *Journal of Child Psychology and Psychiatry, 55*(6), 553–577.
Harris, G. (2008, November 25). Research center tied to drug company. *New York Times*, p. A22.
Harris, G., Carey, B., & Roberts, J. (2007, May 10). Psychiatrists, children and drug industry's role. *New York Times*. Retrieved from http://www.nytimes.com/2007/05/10/health/10psyche.html
Hartke, J. (1994). Castrating the phallic mother: The influence of Freud's repressed developmental experiences on the conceptualization of the castration complex. *Psychoanalytic Review, 81*(4), 641–657.
Hawkins, S. (2014). *The art of narrative psychiatry*. New York: Oxford University Press.
Healy, D. (2006). Manufacturing consensus. *Culture, Medicine and Psychiatry, 30*(2), 135–156.
Hedtke, L., & Winslade, J. (2004). *Re-membering lives: Conversations with the dying and the bereaved*. Amityville, NY: Baywood.
Heffernan, K., Nicolson, P., & Fox, R. (2011). The next generation of pregnant women: More freedom in the public sphere or just an illusion? *Journal of Gender Studies, 20*(4), 321–332.
Heins, T., & Ritchie, K. (1988). *Beating sneaky poo: Ideas for faecal soiling* (2nd ed.). Adelaide, Australia: Dulwich Centre.
Hemmings, S., Kinnear, C., Van Der Merwe, L., Lochner, C., Corfield, V., Moolman-Smook, J., & Stein, D. (2008). Investigating the role of the brain-derived neurotrophic factor (BDNF) val66met variant in obsessive-compulsive disorder (OCD). *World Journal of Biological Psychiatry, 9*(2), 126–134.
Hinshaw, S., & Stier, A. (2008). Stigma as related to mental disorders. *Annual Review of Clinical Psychology, 4*, 367–393.
Höpfl, H. (2000). The suffering mother and the miserable son: Organiz-

ing women and organizing women's writing. *Gender, Work and Organization*, 7(2), 98–105.

Hornstra, L. (1967). Homosexuality. *International Journal of Psychoanalysis*, 48(3), 394–402.

Hoy, M. (1992). Bakhtin and popular culture. *New Literary History*, 23(3), 765–782.

Hyde, L. (1998). *Trickster makes this world: Mischief, myth, and art*. New York: Farrar, Straus and Giroux.

Imagination. (1992). *Collins Concise English Dictionary* (3rd ed.). Glasgow: HarperCollins.

Jenkins, A. (2009). *Becoming ethical: A parallel, political journey with men who have abused*. Dorset, UK: Russell House.

Joyce, J. (1986). *Ulysses*. New York: Vintage. (Originally published 1922)

Kalish, R., & Kimmel, M. (2010). Suicide by mass murder: Masculinity, aggrieved entitlement, and rampage school shootings. *Health Sociology Review*, 19(4), 451–464.

Kane, C. (2000). African American family dynamics as perceived by family members. *Journal of Black Studies*, 30(5), 691–702.

Kanner, L. (1949). Problems of nosology and psychodynamics of early infantile autism. *American Journal of Orthopsychiatry*, 19(3), 416–426.

Kimmel, M. (2013). *Angry white men: American masculinity at the end of an era*. New York: Nation.

Kinney, J. (Producer), & Freudenthal, T. (Director). (2010). *Diary of a wimpy kid* [Motion picture]. United States: Twentieth Century Fox.

Kleinman, A. (1995). *Writing in the margins: Discourse between anthropology and medicine*. Berkeley: University of California Press.

LaFraniere, S., Cohen, S., & Oppel, R. (2015). How often do mass shootings occur? On average, every day, records show. *New York Times*. Retrieved from http://www.nytimes.com/2015/12/03/us/how-often-do-mass-shootings-occur-on-average-every-day-records-show.html?_r=0

Langevin, M., Packman, A., & Onslow, M. (2010). Parent perceptions of the impact of stuttering on their preschoolers and themselves. *Journal of Communication Disorders*, 43(5), 407–423.

Lee, C. (2016, July 7). Obama says police killings of two black men should trouble all Americans. *The Wall Street Journal*. Retrieved from http://www.wsj.com/articles/two-police-killings-of-black-men-part-of-pattern-of-racial-disparity-obama-says-1467919272.

Liebman-Jacobs, J. (1990). Reassessing mother blame in incest. *Journal of Women in Culture and Society, 15*(3), 500–514.

Lindemann, H. (2014). *Holding and letting go: The social practice of personal identities.* New York: Oxford University Press.

Lindemann Nelson, H. (2001). *Damaged identities: Narrative repair.* Ithaca, NY: Cornell University Press.

Madigan, S. (1992). The application of Michel Foucault's philosophy in the problem externalizing discourse of Michael White. *Journal of Family Therapy, 14*, 265–279.

Madigan, S. (2011). *Narrative therapy.* Washington, DC: American Psychological Association.

Madsen, W. (2007). *Collaborative therapy with multi-stressed families* (2nd ed.). New York: Guilford.

Madsen, W., & Gillespie, K. (2014). *Collaborative helping: A strengths framework for home-based services.* New Jersey: John Wiley and Sons.

Martinez, P. (2011). Feminism and violence: The hegemonic second wave's encounter with rape and domestic abuse in USA (1970–1985). *Cultural Dynamics, 23*(3), 147–172.

Marsten, D., Epston, D., & Johnson, L. (2011). Consulting your consultants, revisited. *International Journal of Narrative Therapy and Community Work, 3*, 57–71.

Marsten, D., Epston, D., & Johnson, L. (2012). The corner: One good story deserves another. *Journal of Systemic Therapies, 30*(2), 71–88.

Mattingly, C. (1998). *Healing dramas and clinical plots: The narrative structure of experience.* Cambridge: Cambridge University Press.

Mattingly, C. (2010). *The paradox of hope: Journeys through a clinical borderland.* Berkeley: University of California Press.

Maume, D. (2016). Can men make time for family? Paid work, care work, work-family reconciliation policies, and gender equality. *Social Currents, 3*(1), 43–63.

M'Carthy, M. (2014). Community treatment orders and the experiences of ethnic minority individuals diagnosed with serious mental illness in the Canadian mental health system. *International Journal for Equity in Health, 13*(1), 1–10.

McKenzie, J. (2005). Bums, poos and wees: Carnivalesque spaces in the picture books of early childhood. Or, has literature gone to the dogs? *English Teaching: Practice and Critique, 4*(1), 81–94.

McLaren, H. (2013). (Un-)Blaming mothers whose partners sexually abuse children: In view of heteronormative myths, pressures and authorities. *Child and Family Social Work, 18*(4), 439–448.

McLeod, K. (2014). *Pranksters: Making mischief in the modern world.* New York: New York University Press.

McNamara, L., Tolliday, D., & Spangaro, J. (2012). Are mothers still to blame for child sexual abuse? *The Australian and New Zealand Journal of Psychiatry, 46*(6), 582–583.

Meier, K. (1980). An affair of flutes: An appreciation of play. *Journal of Philosophy of Sport, 7,* 24–45.

Morson, G. (1994). *Narrative and freedom: The shadow of time.* New Haven, CT: Yale University Press.

Mullin, A. (2006). Parents and children: An alternative to selfless and unconditional love. *Hypatia, 21*(1), 181–200.

Mullins, D. (2011). Linkages between children's behavior and nonresident father involvement: A comparison of African American, Anglo, and Latino families. *Journal of African American Studies, 15*(1), 1–21.

New Yorker. (1990). *The New Yorker book of cat cartoons.* New York: Knopf.

New Yorker. (1992). *The New Yorker book of dog cartoons.* New York: Knopf.

O'Brien, T. (1990). *The things they carried.* New York: Houghton Mifflin.

Ochs, E., & Capps, L. (2001). *Living narrative: Creating lives in everyday storytelling.* Cambridge, MA: Harvard University Press.

O'Keefe, D. (2003). *Readers in wonderland: The liberating worlds of fantasy fiction.* New York: Continuum.

O'Reilly, M. (2006). Should children be seen and not heard? An examination of how children's interruptions are treated in family therapy. *Discourse Studies, 8*(4), 549–566.

O'Reilly, M. (2008). What value is there in children's talk? Investigating family therapists' interruptions of parents and children during the therapeutic process. *Journal of Pragmatics, 40*(3), 507–524.

Pandya, M., Altinay, M., Malone Jr., D., & Anand, A. (2012). Where in the brain is depression? *Current Psychiatry Reports, 14*(6), 634–642.

Peck, J. (2012). Austerity urbanism: American cities under extreme economy. *City, 16*(6), 626–655.

Phillips, D. (2005). Reproducing normative and marginalized masculinities: Adolescent male popularity and the outcast. *Nursing Inquiry, 12*(3), 219–230.

Polanco, M. (2010). Rethinking narrative therapy: An examination of bilingualism and magical realism. *Journal of Systemic Therapies, 29*(2), 1–14.

Pollack, W. (1998). *Real boys: Rescuing our sons from the myth of boyhood.* New York: Henry Holt.

Richa, S., & Yazbek, J. (2010). Ocular adverse effects of common psychotropic agents. *CNS Drugs, 24*(6), 501–526.

Richardson, S. (2014). Don't blame the mothers. *Nature, 512*(7513), 131–132.

Rieber, L. P. (1996). Seriously considering play: Designing interactive learning environments based on the blending of microworlds, simulations, and games. *Educational Technology Research and Development, 44*(2), 43–58.

Rose, N. (1999). *Governing the soul: The shaping of the private self* (2nd ed.). London, England: Free Association.

Rosenberg, T. (2005). A challenge to Victorian motherhood: Mona Caird and Gertrude Atherton. *Women's Writing, 12*(3), 485–504.

Roth, S., & Epston, D. (1996). Developing externalizing conversations: An exercise. *Journal of Systemic Therapies, 15*(1), 5–12.

Salazar, M. (1991). Young laborers in Bogotá: Breaking authoritarian ramparts. In O. Fals-Borda & M. A. Rahman (Eds.), *Action and knowledge: Breaking the monopoly with participatory action-research* (pp. 55–63). New York: Apex.

Sax, P. (1997). Narrative therapy and family support: Strengthening the mother's voice in working with families with infants and toddlers. In C. Smith & D. Nylund (Eds.), *Narrative therapies with children and adolescents* (pp. 111–146). New York: Guilford.

Sax, P. (2006). Developing preferred stories of identity as reflective practitioners. *Journal of Systemic Therapies, 25*(4), 59–72.

Schaffner, L. (1997). Families on probation: Court ordered parenting skills classes for parents of juvenile offenders. *Crime and Delinquency, 43*(4), 412–437.

Scharf, L. (2015, January 17). *Drew Barrymore on her new fashion gig, motherhood, and reteaming with Adam Sandler—EXCLUSIVE*. Retrieved from http://www.ew.com/article/2014/01/09/drew-barrymore-on-her-new-fashion-gig-motherhood-and-reteaming-with-adam-sandler-exclusive

Schechner, R. (1981). Performers and spectators transported and transformed. *Kenyon Review, New Series, 3*(4), 83–113.

Schiele, J., & Stewart, R. (2001). When white boys kill: An Afrocentric analysis. *Journal of Human Behavior in the Social Environment, 4*(4), 253–273.

Siegel, D., & Hartzell, M. (2004). *Parenting from the inside out: How a deeper self-understanding can help you raise children who thrive*. New York: Jeremy P. Tarcher/Penguin.

Siegel, D. (2012). *The developing mind: How relationships and the brain interact to shape who we are* (2nd ed.). New York: Guilford.

Singer, R. (2003). Are we having fun yet? In P. B. Pufall & R. P. Unsworth (Eds.), *Rethinking childhood* (pp. 207–228). New Brunswick, NJ: Rutgers University Press.

Smith, A., & Santopadre, F. (Writers), Gentile, M. (Director). (October 11, 2013). *The View* [Television series]. In B. Walters & Bill Geddie (Producers). New York: ABC Studios.

Snicket, L. (2002). *A series of unfortunate events, book the ninth: The carnivorous carnival*. New York: HarperCollins Children's Books.

Spurr, D. (1993). *The rhetoric of empire: Colonial discourse in journalism, travel writing, and imperial administration*. Durham, NC: Duke University Press.

Stace, H. (2010). Mother blaming; or autism, gender and science. *Women's Studies Journal, 24*(2), 66–70.

Stark, E., & Flitcraft, A. H. (1988). Women and children at risk: A feminist perspective on child abuse. *International Journal of Health Services, 18*(1), 97–118.

Swaine, J., Laughland, O., Lartey, J., & McCarthy, C. (2015, Dec. 31). Young black men killed by US police at highest rate in year of 1,134 deaths. *The Guardian*. Retrieved from http://www.theguardian.com/us-news/2015/dec/31/the-counted-police-killings-2015-young-black-men.

Tarpley, N. (1998). *I love my hair!* Boston: Little, Brown.

Taylor, R., Chatters, L., Woodward, A., & Brown, E. (2013). Racial and ethnic differences in extended family, friendship, fictive kin, and congregational informal support networks. *Family Relations, 62*(4), 609–624.

Thomas, K. (2013, November 4). J.&J. to pay $2.2 billion in Risperdal settlement. *New York Times*. Retrieved from http://www.nytimes.com/2013/11/05/business/johnson-johnson-to-settle-risperdal-improper-marketing-case.html

Thomas, K., & Schmidt, M. (2012, July 2). Glaxo agrees to pay $3 billion in fraud settlement. *New York Times*. Retrieved from http://www.nytimes.com/2012/07/03/business/glaxosmithkline-agrees-to-pay-3-billion-in-fraud-settlement.html

Timimi, S. (2009). The commercialization of children's mental health in the era of globalization. *International Journal of Mental Health, 38*(3), 5–27.

Tomm, K. (1989). Externalizing the problem and internalizing personal agency. *Journal of Strategic and Systemic Therapies, 8*(1), 16–22.

Turner, E. (2013). Publication bias, with a focus on psychiatry: Causes and solutions. *CNS Drugs, 27*(6), 457–468.

Turner, V. (1969). *The ritual process: Structure and anti-structure.* New York: Aldine de Gruyter.

VanDeCarr, P. (2013, March 10). Radical listening: An interview with Dr. Kaethe Weingarten. Inside Stories. Retrieved from http://www.insidestoriesonline.com/2013/03/radical-listening-interview-with-dr_10.html

van Gennep, A. (1960). *The rights of passage.* Chicago: University of Chicago Press.

Vygotsky, L. (1986). *Thought and language.* Cambridge, MA: MIT Press.

Vygotsky, L. (2004). Imagination and creativity in childhood. *Journal of Russian and East European Psychology, 42*(1), 7–97.

Wall, J. (2006). Childhood studies, hermeneutics, and theological ethics. *Journal of Religion, 86*(4), 523–548.

Walters, S., & Harrison, L. (2014). Not ready to make nice: Aberrant mothers in contemporary culture. *Feminist Media Studies, 14*(1), 38–55.

Watson, J. B. (1998). Against the threat of mother love. In H. Jenkins (Ed.), *The children's culture reader.* New York: New York University Press. (Original work published 1928)

Watters, E. (2010). *Crazy like us: The globalization of the human psyche.* New York: Free Press.

Watzlawick, P., Weakland, J., & Fisch, R. (1974). *Change.* New York: Norton.

Whitaker, R. (2010). *Anatomy of an epidemic: Magic bullets, psychiatric drugs, and the astonishing rise of mental illness in America.* New York: Broadway Paperbacks.

Whitaker, R., & Cosgrove, L. (2015). *Psychiatry under the influence: Institutional corruption, social injury, and prescriptions for reform.* New York: Palgrave Macmillon.

White, E. B. (1980). *Charlotte's web.* New York: HarperCollins. (Original work published 1952)

White, M. (1984). Pseudo-encopresis: From avalanche to victory, from vicious to virtuous cycles. *Family Systems Medicine, 2*(2), 150–160.

White, M. (1988). Saying hullo again: The incorporation of the lost relationship in the resolution of grief. *Dulwich Centre Newsletter,* Spring, 29–36.

White, M. (1988–1989). The externalizing of the problem and the re-authoring of lives and relationships. *Dulwich Centre Newsletter,* Summer, 3–20.

White, M. (1995). *Re-authoring lives: Interviews and essays.* Adelaide, Australia: Dulwich Centre.

White, M. (1997). *Narratives of therapist's lives.* Adelaide, Australia: Dulwich Centre.

White, M. (2000). *Reflections on narrative practice: Essays and interviews.* Adelaide, Australia: Dulwich Centre.

White, M. (2007). *Maps of narrative practice.* New York: Norton.

White, M. (2011). *Narrative practice: Continuing the conversation.* New York: Norton.

White, M., & Epston, D. (1990). *Narrative means to therapeutic ends.* New York: Norton.

White, M., & Morgan, A. (2006). *Narrative therapy with children and their families*. Adelaide, Australia: Dulwich Centre.

Winslade, J. (2009). Tracing lines of flight: Implications of the work of Gilles Deleuze for narrative practice. *Family Process, 48*(3), 332–346.

Winslade, J., & Monk, G. (2000). *Narrative mediation*. San Francisco: Jossey-Bass.

Winslade, J., & Monk, G. (2007). *Narrative counseling in schools: Powerful and brief.* Thousand Oaks, CA: Corwin.

Zimmerman, J., & Dickerson, V. (1996). *If problems talked: Narrative therapy in action*. New York: Guilford.

INDEX

Abbott Laboratories, 164
Adichie, Chimanda, 46
advertising, pharmaceuticals, 162–64
aggrieved entitlement, 232–33
Alice's Adventures in Wonderland (Carroll), *xv*
Anger, mother and daughter, 182–85
anthropology, *xviii*, *xix–xx*
architecture of man, 61
attachment theory, 177
attention deficit hyperactivity disorder (ADHD), *xv*, *xx*, 131, 157, 159, 161–62, 164–65
autism, 179

Bakhtin, Mikhail, 4
Barrymore, Drew, 186
bathroom
    inspiration in, 110–13
    toilet humor, 118–22
Baudelaires, Snicket characters, 97–98, 101–4, 109, 114, 116–18, 125–27
Bauman, Zigmunt, 130

Beating Sneaky Poo: Ideas for Faecal Soiling (Heins and Ritchie), 200
Bed Bug, 55–59
Bettelheim, Bruno, 179
Biederman, Joseph, 162
bipolar disorder, *xv*, 162
blame
    parent/mother, 64, 176–77
    psychotherapy's penchant for mother, 178–81
    responding to mother blame, 181–85
    responsibility, 65, 130
boys
    Captain Ordinary, 241–44
    Columbine violence, 232
    Gandhi and imagination, 234–40
    meeting Joel, 220–23
    payback and violence, 231–34
    revenge, 225–31
    specialness as birthright, 223–25
    story of American boyhood, 223–25
    violence, 219
    war story, 219–20

285

Bullock, Sandra, 185–86
bullying, 79–80, 239
   Diary of a Wimpy Kid, 223–31, 244
Burman, Erica, 178

capitalism, language of, 73–75
Caplan, Paula, 180
Capps, Linda, 12
Captain America, 227–28, 241–44
caregivers
   externalizing problems benefitting, 64
   wonderfulness interview guide, 40–41
Caro, Marc, 6
Carr, David, 18
Carroll, Lewis, *xv*
cases
   Alma and son Berto, 52–59
   Audrey and daughter Francine, 34–40
   Beverly and daughter Maureen, 5–6, 7–9, 10–11, 13–17, 22–24
   Brett and grandmother Peggy, 66–71
   Colin and family, 252–61
   Dalia and son Jonah, 188–92
   Danny and father Alex, 96–99, 101–4, 108–10, 114–18, 122–25
   fear and Harry, 79–80
   Harry and parents, 79–90
   Jira, 264
   Joel and mother June, 220–23, 226–31, 235–38
   Julie and Stealing, 136–38
   Kelly and parents, 99–108, 110–13, 118–21, 127
   Louise and children, 194–96
   Mary, son Joey and family abuse, 144–49
   Mia and aunt Vicki, 166–72
   Rafael and Trouble, 150–55
   Sarah and daughter Leah, 182–85
   tale of two friends, 131–35
   Tina and daughter Ginger, 176–77
The Cat in the Hat (Dr. Seuss), 78
characterization, narratives, 6–9
Charlotte's Web (White), 11, 17
children. *See* young people
The City of Lost Children (film), 6
Cloke, Paul, 4
Cloudy With a Chance of Meatballs (film), 225
Columbine shooting, 232
Combs, Gene, 268n.1
Comparison, dealing with, 51, 63
compassion, 47, 65, 173, 239, 244, 246, 249, 252, 255
conversation, imagination invigorating, 101–3
counterworlds, *xvi*, 80, 207, 244, 265
culture, narrative, 2–6

Dahl, Roald, 75
Depakote, 164
Diagnostic and Statistical Manual, 160–61
Diary of a Wimpy Kid (Kinney and Freudenthal), 223, 244

INDEX

Disney, 20, 209
Disrespect, 29, 64, 153, 258–59, 262
divorce, children dealing with, 50, 53–54
dream, Dr. King's, 38–40

ego, 61
Eli Lilly, 162
Embarrassment, 30, 139–44
entitlement, 232, 255, 260, 262
   aggrieved, 232–33
   privilege, 224–25
Epston, David, 96, 201, 267n2, 268n1
   Audrey and daughter Francine, 34–40
   "Growing Up Fairy Meets Sneaky Poo/Wee" approach, 203–9
   Kelly and parents, 99–108, 110–13, 118–21, 127
events sequence, narrative, 9–10
everyday life making mischief in, 75–78

Failure, 64
fairness, 36–40, 92
   full disclosure, 135–38
fairy dust, 95–96
fantasy literature, *xvi*
Fear, 80–90, 108
   Harry and "Harricanes," 84–86
   making appearance, 108, 126
Fear Fighters' Society, 89, 90, 268n1
feminist theory, *xix*, *xviii*
Food and Drug Administration (FDA), 162–64

forgiveness, 249–52, 254–55, 268n.1
Foucault, Michel, 31, 267n3
Frank, Arthur, 4, 7
Freedman, Jennifer, 268n1
Freud, Sigmund, 61, 178–79, 188
Frustration, 64, 96, 99, 201, 213, 246
Fuentes, Carlos, *xiv*
full disclosure, letter of, 135–38
fun
   bathroom as inspiration place, 110–13
   case of Kelly and, 100, 102–3, 105, 107–8, 110–13, 119–21
   Growing-Up Fairy, 209–11
   making mischief in everyday life, 75–78
   play, 73–75
   see also mischief

Gandhi, Mahatma, 234–40
genealogy
   reverse, 44–45
   wonderfulness, 106–8
Gergen, Kenneth, 157–58
Giggle Grower, 93
GlaxoSmithKline, 162–64
golden rule, 66, 68–70
Growing-Up Fairy (GUF), 268n1
   children being guided by, 203–9
   fun after planning, 209–11
Guilt, 64, 183–85

Hall-McCorquodale, Ian, 180
Hampkins, SueEllen, 268n1
Harris, Eric, 232
Hartzell, Mary, 177, 197

Heins, Terry, 200
heroism, 7, 18, 232, 240
Homework Helper, 93
Hoy, Mikita, 3
human brain, psychiatry, 157–59

id, 61
identity
 father and son, 139–44
 letter of full disclosure, 135–38
 mother appreciation, 144–49
 restoring mother and son, 144–49
 self-esteem, 129–31
 tale of two friends, 131–35
imagination, *xiii–xv*
 invigorating the conversation, 101–3
 know-how of, *xvii–xviii*
 making another attempt, 103–8
 one last imaginative charge, 125–26
 realm of life and death, 113–18
 from sorrowful silence to signs of life, 122–25
 therapist setting imaginative charge, 108–13
 toilet humor, 118–22
 young people, 95, 263–65
individualism, 130, 195, 230–31
individuation, 3
inspiration, *xviii*
 bathroom as unlikely place for, 110–13

Jeunet, Jean-Pierre, 6
Jobs, Steve, 77
Johnson and Johnson, 162, 164

Jones, Owain, 4
Joyce, James, 18

Katz, Jackson, 233
Killjoy, 105, 107–8, 111–13, 118, 121
Kimmel, Michael, 224, 232–33
King, Martin Luther, Jr., 38–40
Klebold, Dylan, 232

language
 of capitalism, 73–75
 externalizing, 59–62, 81
 narrative, 2–6
The Lego Movie (film), 225
letter
 fostering hope, 149–55
 full disclosure, 135–38
 pen pals, 131–35
 restoring a mother's place in her son's heart, 144–49
 solidarity between father and son, 139–44
Lewis, C. S., *xvi*
Lewis, E. B., 132
life and death, imagination in realm of, 113–18
Lindemann Nelson, Hilde, 12–13
lineage
 secret, 225
 suspect, 3
 wonderfulness, 43–44
Lobovits, Dean, 268*n*1
Lockwood, Flint, 225

McLeod, Kembrew, 77
Markham, Laurie
 Briana, 132–35

INDEX

"Joel" and male domination, 219–32, 234–44
Louise and children, 194–96
Mia and aunt Vicki, 166–72
Rafael, 149–55
Marsten, David, 96
   Alma and son Berto, 52–59
   Beverly and daughter, 5–6, 7–11, 13–17, 22–24
   Brett and grandmother Peggy, 66–71
   Colin and family, 252–61
   Dalia and son Jonah, 188–92
   Danny and father Alex, 96–99, 101–4, 108–10, 114–18, 122–25
   Harry and parents, 79–90
   Jira, 264
   Sarah and daughter Leah, 182–85
   Tina and daughter Ginger, 176–77
Matilda (Dahl), 75
Mattingly, Cheryl, 21
Meanness, 22
Miracle Mile Community Practice (MMCP), x, 82, 89
mischief, 94
   everyday life, 75–78
   outsmarting the problem, 90–94
   proposal for making, at problem's expense, 79–90
mistaken identity, 91–92, 120
mood disorders, 159, 164
moral agents, 65
moral character/virtue, 32, 40, 44, 45–46, 69, 71, 130, 267n2
moral code, 20, 234
moral commitments/intent, 21, 72, 94, 121, 183, 185, 187, 236, 249
moral identity, 58–59
moral reflections, 24
Morson, Gary Saul, 20
mothers
   benefits of mutuality, 193–94
   communal care, 194–97
   defense of, 175–78
   indebted, 185–87
   marginalized, 194–97
   psychology's penchant for blaming, 178–81
   reauthoring motherhood, 187–97
   responding to mother blame, 181–85
   restoring place in son's heart, 144–49

narrative, 1–2
   characterization, 6–9
   constraint, 17–19
   language and culture, 2–6
   linking events in sequence, 9–10
   persuasive, 13–17
   resonance, 20–24
   suspense, 19–20
   temporality, 10–13
narrative theory, $xvii$, xx, 2
narrative therapy
   illustrating wonderfulness interview, 34–40
   story development, 19
   underpinnings of, $xviii$–xx
   wonderfulness interview, 31–34
   wonderfulness interview guide, 40–45

Nervousness, 159, 262
neuroscience, 157, 197
Neverland, 95, 204, 263
The New Yorker Book of Cat Cartoons (New Yorker), 113
The New Yorker Book of Dog Cartoons (New Yorker), 113
Ninja Turtles, *xiii, xv*

O'Brien, Tim, 219
obsessive-compulsive disorder (OCD), *xv, xx*, 99, 158–59
Ochs, Eleanor, 12
O'Keefe, Deborah, *xvi*
oppositional-defiant disorder (ODD), *xx*, 157

Pan's Labyrinth (film), 7
parents
  protecting children, 4–6
  providing details to therapist, 29–31
  target of mischief, 77–78
  wonderfulness interview, 32–33
  wonderfulness interview guide, 40–42
passivity, 31, 32
payback, revenge, 225–31
performance of meaning, 116, 118
persuasion, powers of, 13, 25
persuasive narratives, 13–17
Peter Pan (Barrie), 49, 95–96, 263–64
Pfizer, 162
pharmaceutical industry, psychiatry, 160–65
play, fun, 73–75

Playful Approaches to Serious Problems: Narrative Therapy with Children and Their Families (Freeman, Epston, & Lobovits), 201
post-structuralism, *xvii, xx*
potty training. *See* Sneaky Poo and Sneaky Wee
powers of persuasion, 13, 25
privilege, 184, 188, 193, 224, 227, 255, 258–59, 262
problems
  benefit to caregivers, 64
  casting doubt on character of, 92–93
  exposing as clueless, 93
  externalizing, 59–61
  externalizing questions, 60–61
  externalizing rather than dividing, 61–64
  internalizing questions, 60
  jealousy of, 93–94
  letter of full disclosure, 135–38
  mistaken identity, 91–92
  outsmarting, by mischievous means, 90–94
  playing a joke on, 91
  proposal for making mischief at expense of, 79–90
  responsibility for, 65–72
  unfairness, 92
  young people's range, 52–59
progress, 245–51
  best-laid plans, 252–57
  case of Colin and family, 252–53
  case of Colin and father, 257–61

case of Colin and mother, 254–55
second time around, 257–61
psychiatry
human brain, 157–59
new faith, 159–60
pharmaceutical industry, 160–65
psychiatric hold, 166–69
psychology, 61, 64, 158, 177–82
psychotherapy, mother blame, 178–81
psychotic child, case of Mia, 166–72
Puppy Lover, 93

responsibility
intention, 65–66, 71, 79–80
for problems, 65–72
revenge
aggrieved entitlement, 233
boys and, 225–32
Gandhi, 236–37
mischief, 75
war and, 239
Revenge, 237
reverse genealogy, 44–45
Risperdal, 162, 164
risperidone, 162
Ritchie, Karen, 200

Sadness, 60, 62, 117–18, 122–25
Schmidt, Michael, 164
school shootings, 232, 244
self-reliance, 3
sequencing events, narrative, 9–10
Series of Unfortunate Events,

Book the Ninth: The Carnivorous Carnival (Snicket), 97
Sharp Mind, 256–58
Sheppard, Sherry, 185–86
Siegel, Daniel, 177, 197
Singer, Rhonda, 74
Sleep Thief, 158
Sneaky Poo and Sneaky Wee
Growing-Up Fairy (GUF), 203–9
story, 199–203
tricking, 211–16
Snicket, Lemony, 97, 126
social anxiety, 157
sociology, *xviii, xix*
Stealing, 136–38
Steve Rogers (Captain America), 227–28, 241–44
stories
backward-looking, 13
narrative, 1–2
problems of characters, 49
wonderfulness interview as, 45–46
see also narrative
superego, 61
suspense, narrative, 19–20

Tarpley, Natasha Anastasia, 132
TED talk, 46
Temper, 143, 145, 246–50, 252, 255, 258, 262
psychiatry, 159
resisting, 20–21
responsibility, 66–71
Temper Tamer's Club of America, 268n1
temporality, 10–13

Temptation, 17, 100, 153, 262
therapy
    imaginative charge by therapist, 108–13
    problems having first say, 29–31
    young people, 27–29, 50–52
Thomas, Katie, 164
Timimi, Sami, 161
toilet training. *See* Sneaky Poo and Sneaky Wee
Tooth Fairy, 204, 209
trichotillomania, 51
    hair, 52–57
trick-or-treating, problem, 91
Trouble, 150–55
Turner, Victor, *xvi*

Ulysses (Joyce), 18
Unfairness, 51, 63, 262

violence, payback in form of, 231–34
Voice, case of Mia, 166–72
Vygotsky, Lev, 21, 95

Wall, John, 28
Wall Street (film), 39
Watson, John B., 179
White, Michael, 2, 200, 267*n*3
The Wizard of Oz (film), 231
Wizzy (Worry and Dizzy), 50, 63
wonderfulness, 267*n*2
    genealogy, 106–8
    reverse genealogy, 44–45
    tracing lineage/genealogy of, 43–44
    tracing through time, 42–43
    wonderfulness interview, 31–34, 47
    case of Kelly, 102–3
    guide, 40–45
    illustrating, 34–40
    mothers and children, 181–82
    as story development, 45–46
    talents, 33–34
Wonderland, *xv–xvii*, 33
    Alice, 129, 204
    problems in, 49–52
work, play, 73–75
Worry
    engaging imagination, 50
    narrative style, 9–10
    toilet humor, 118–21
    trials with, 10–16, 19–20, 22, 25
Wozniak, Steve, 77

young people, 267*n*1
    Bed Bug bugging, 55–59
    bringing problems within range, 52–59
    dreaming up mischief, 75–78
    imagination, 95, 263–65
    knowing what matters to, 96–101
    pharmaceuticals, 160–65
    problems having first say, 29–31
    talents, 33–34
    therapy, 27–29
    therapy for dealing with problems, 50–52
    wonderfulness interview, 31–34